Janine Stephenson.

KU-243-208

ACTIONSRIPT
ZERO TO HERO

Jen deHaan
Glen Rhodes

friendsof

DESIGNER TO DESIGNER™

ACTIONSCRIPT: ZERO TO HERO

© 2002 friends of ED

All rights reserved. No part of this book may be reproduced, stored in a retrieval system or transmitted in any form or by any means, without the prior written permission of the publisher, except in the case of brief quotations embodied in critical articles or reviews.

The authors and publisher have made every effort in the preparation of this book to ensure the accuracy of the information. However, the information contained in this book is sold without warranty, either express or implied. Neither the authors, friends of ED nor its dealers or distributors will be held liable for any damages caused or alleged to be caused either directly or indirectly by this book.

First Printed November 2002

Trademark Acknowledgements
friends of ED has endeavored to provide trademark information about all the companies and products mentioned in this book by the appropriate use of capitals. However, friends of ED cannot guarantee the accuracy of this information.

Published by friends of ED
30 -32 Lincoln Road, Olton, Birmingham.
B27 6PA. UK.
Printed in USA

ISBN 1-904344-11-9

Credits

Authors	**Commissioning Editor**
Jen deHaan	Andy Corsham
Glen Rhodes	
	Technical Editor
Reviewers	Adam Juniper
Sham Bhangal	Caroline Robeson
Eng Wei Chua	
Leon Cych	**Author Agent**
Vicky Idiens	Gaynor Riopedre
Managing Editor	**Project Manager**
Sonia Mullineux	Jenni Harvey
Indexer	**Layout & cover design**
Simon Collins	Katy Freer
	Proof Reader
	Susan Nettleton

Jen deHaan

Jen is a fresh young Flash designer/developer in Canada. She has high ambitions, a die-hard mentality, a BFA in Art/Eduation and certification in New Media. She lives for compression, and loves Cleaner and After Effects about as much as coffee but not as much as Flash. She has enjoyed writing for and editing many books on Flash and ColdFusion with her husband Peter. Jen has two cats, and likes to think she is friendly.

Special thanks to Peter, my family, and the friends of ED team for all of their support

Her homes on the web are www.ejepo.com and www.flash-mx.com.

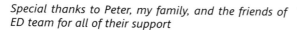

Glen Rhodes

Glen is a co-author on several books from friends of ED including Flash Games Studio, Flash Math Creativity, Flash MX Express and the Actionscript Designer's Reference. Glen splits his time between creating Flash games and other experimental Flash exploits, and writing music on his piano, which he has been playing since the age of four. Glen has created games professionally for console systems like the Sony Playstation, but now finds that Flash allows him an easy means for building his ideas. He shares his ideas at www.glenrhodes.com, and at his game company, Brain Jam Studios (www.brainjamstudios.com).

Contents

3 Parts Department   35

4 Quantitative Info   45

Contents

⭐5 Jimmy the body worker 69

⭐6 Steering and Operation 89

★ **7** **The Interactive Intelligent Dashboard** **113**

★ **8** **The Road: Driving Conditions and Logic** **133**

Contents

11 The truck of the future 199

12 Tuning and Customizing 215

Index 229

Zap! Pow! Kersplat!

From zero...

Zero to Hero is an exciting new series from friends of ED, and a whole new way of learning. These pages will take you from lowly beginner to ActionScript whizz – the same change from Zero to Hero that Clark Kent makes in a phone box, but without the risk of being arrested for public lewdness.

We know you're not stupid (or should that be 'a dummy'?), so we're not going to waste your time learning Flash from the ground up again, or wading through file types, operating systems and any number of other stuff that you know already. This book is designed to take Flash MX users, with a little experience of the basic interface, to the next level, and beyond.

If you're new to Flash, you'd be better off starting with Flash MX Express (ISBN: 1-903450-95-0) then coming back here when you're done!

...to hero

By the end of this book, not only will we have the basic principles of programming Flash ActionScript (and indeed many other languages) under our belts, but we'll be able to control videos, draw shapes and even create games, all in just a few lines of code.

Oh, and we won't stop there either; we said you'll be a hero and we meant it. In these pages you'll also find guides on creating real interactivity, and finally we round it of by showing you where you can go in the future. After all, ActionScript skills are pretty marketable...

Structure of this book

As we said, this book will get the basics out of the way with the minimum of fuss. That said, we're not going to get carried away here. Learning to write scripts isn't quite the same thing as learning a word processor, so we'll take it at just the right pace. By the same token, there may not be as many pictures as you might expect; sorry, but we thought writing the code out would be clearer than a lot of screenshots of the ActionScript pane all the time. Sorry about that!

In the first few chapters, we'll look at how ActionScripting relates to the real world, so you don't think of programming as a chore. Don't worry, there will be absolutely no math for math's sake here!

Once we're feeling at home, we'll work through the core elements of scripting in Flash MX; the library, variables and objects. From there, we'll look at the bits that really make ActionScript special; drawing and interacting with movie clips.

Towards the end of the book we'll take look at some of the bells and whistles on offer; sound, video, components and even server-side scripting.

Then, right at the end, when you're ready for it, we throw down the gauntlet. The last chapter shows you all the directions you can take your newfound knowledge, gives you some great web sites to visit and (we'll be honest) plugs a few of our higher-level books.

Code downloads

There a wealth of code, video and sound support files available for this book. They aren't essential to use this book to the full, as everything in the book can be built from scratch using your copy of Flash MX and your own mouse-clicking, ActionScripting fingers. But, if you'd like to see exactly what the authors have done, or use exactly the same clips as they have, then they are organized by chapter at www.friendsofED.com.

By the way, if you haven't yet got your dirty paws on Macromedia Flash MX you can download a fully-functional 30-day trial from www.macromedia.com.

Layout conventions

We want this book to be as clear and easy to use as possible, so we've introduced a number of layout styles that we've used throughout.

★ We'll use different styles to emphasize things that appear on the screen and also hyperlinks.

★ Keyboard shortcuts are written out like this: CTRL/⌘+S. PC users should press the Ctrl (Control) key and the S key at the same time, Mac users the ⌘ (Command) key and S key.

★ If we introduce a new **important term** then these will be in bold.

> If there's something you shouldn't miss, it will be highlighted like this! When you see the box, pay attention!

★ When we want you to click on a menu, and then through subsequent sub-menus we will indicate to like so: File > Import…. (see picture).

★ If there's something you might type in, or the name of a variable, then it'll be 'in single quotes'.

If there are any steps to follow:

1. Then the steps that you have to follow will be numbered.

2. Follow them through, checking the screenshots and diagrams for more hints.

   Further explanation of the steps may appear indented like so.

3. When you get to the end, you can stop.

Support – we're here to help

All books from friends of ED should be easy to follow and error-free. However, if you do run into problems, don't hesitate to get in touch – our support is fast, friendly and free.

You can reach us at support@friendsofED.com, quoting the last for digits of the ISBN in the subject of the e-mail (that's 4119), and even if our dedicated support team are unable to solve your problem immediately, your queries will be passed onto the people who put the book together, the editors and authors, to solve. All our authors help with the support on their books, and will either directly mail people with answers, or (more usually) send their response to an editor to pass on.

We'd love to hear from you, even if it's just to request future books, ask about friends of ED, or tell us how much you loved *ActionScript Zero to Hero!*

If your enquiry concerns an issue not directly concerned with book content, then the best place for these types of questions is our message board lists at http://www.friendsofed.com/forums. Here, you'll find a variety of designers talking about what they do, who should be able to provide some ideas and solutions.

For news, more books, sample chapters, downloads, author interviews and more, send your browser to www.friendsofED.com. To take a look at the brand new friends of ED Flash MX bookshelf from which this book comes, take a look at flashmxlibrary.com.

To tell us a bit about yourself and make comments about the book, why not fill out the reply card at the back and send it to us!

Welcome to the Garage

What's in this chapter:

★ ActionScript as a medium of communication

★ The power of the engine

★ The five Ws of ActionScript

   ★ What

   ★ Why

   ★ Who

   ★ When

   ★ Where

★ The lie of the land of the book

★ The cool destinations ahead

Mediums and communication

Pretty much every medium has a language of its own. For example, when we want someone to play our piano concerto, then we'll hand the pianist some sheet music. When we want someone to deliver the lines of our brand new screenplay, then a script must be presented. In a garage, the steps and procedures for work on most makes and models of vehicle are provided in detailed manuals and instruction books.

When we're talking about Flash, and computers in general, instructing them tends to require the knowledge of their language; how we talk to the computer, and convey what we would like it to do. With Flash MX, the language of its instruction is known as ActionScript, and in this language, the instruction is normally delivered in a form that is consistent with the medium.

However, Flash ActionScript would not look like this:

> *There was a young man in a clip,*
> *Who was trying to vertically flip,*
> *Being always the hero,*
> *He set _yscale to zero*
> *And now he's no more than a blip.*

Because that's not the way computers talk, or expect to be talked to; those are more like the instructions for a poetry reading, or a bad comedian. No, ActionScript expects things in a clearly defined, structured way. Like this:

```
youngMan._yscale = 0;
```

As we'll see throughout this book, the implementation of ActionScript in our Flash movies is a relatively easy task, but a few simple lines of ActionScript can yield powerful results. ActionScript is the engine and steering mechanism to our truck. If the graphics we have drawn are like the outer shell of the truck, then it is ActionScript that is required to make it go new places each time we run it. Sure, we can create animation using the traditional timeline animation of Flash, but the difficulty there is that it will be the same animation each time we run it. With ActionScript, we'll allow Flash to run a new course each time.

Flash without ActionScript:

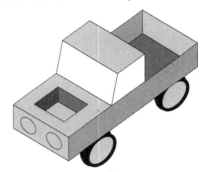

Flash With ActionScript:

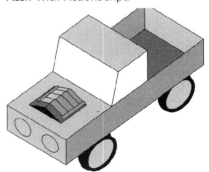

The five Ws of ActionScript

The easiest way to see and understand the practical uses of ActionScript is to break it down into What, Why, Who, When and Where.

What

Let's get technical for a minute here: what exactly is ActionScript?

Well, first of all, it's important to know that since computers were first invented, programmers have had various options for telling them what to do. Let's face it, if we don't tell a computer what to do, it will ultimately just sit there and hum (unless we're living in the future ruled by sentient machines).

Early computers did very little except the most basic math instructions, so their 'programming languages' were very small. Flip a few switches on a console, and you had 'programmed' the computer to do something like add a long list of numbers. At this point, programming was a hardware-based thing; switches would set the computer into a certain mode, and there it would stay. At this time, programs were communicated from programmer to programmer simply by word of mouth: "Hey Steve, set the switches like this: on, off, off, off, on, on, off".

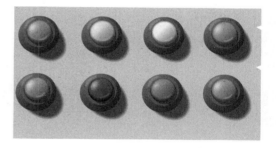

After a while, someone thought of the brilliant idea of putting the on/off codes on another medium that could be stored somewhere and then re-read into the computer at the desired time. So, punch cards and long reels of paper with holes were used. Much like the paper on a player piano, these could set the switches and internal controls of a computer. They could also be thought of as on/off controls, but conveyed through either 'solid' or 'hole'.

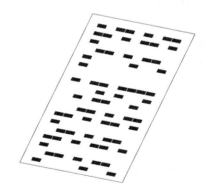

Finally, as switches got smaller (and became known as transistors) they were integrated on a single circuit board, their power and potential increased. Suddenly being able to set millions of tiny switches to one or zero meant that programming had to take a different approach. That's when the first languages appeared. These were readable sequences of instruction that could be typed into the computer, and then 'executed'. Languages started to become more widely accepted because of their accessibility and smaller learning curve; being able to 'read' the code decreased the learning curve.

In the years since, computers and their languages have become increasingly more powerful, allowing us to create applications, games, operating systems and more. When we look at Flash, we see that its programming language is known as ActionScript. ActionScript is the language required to code the instructions that will make Flash do what we want it to do. That language is read by Flash, which in turn talks to the computer itself, and our creations come to life. (This also means that our ActionScript doesn't talk to the computer directly; rather, Flash *interprets* what we've written, and then instructs the computer accordingly. This way, the same Flash movie can work on PC, Mac, Unix, Linux, and even handheld devices.)

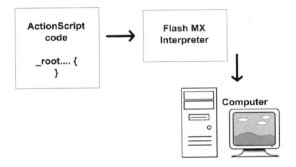

So, that said, we can look at ActionScript as a series of instructions. Much like the step-by-step guide in an auto-mechanic's manual, ActionScript tells Flash what to do in a sequential chain of 'sentences' or, lines of code. Let's imagine a Flash movie, which consists of a ball that follows the position of the mouse cursor on screen. The instructions for something like this might read:

```
Do this thirty times a second:
  Look at the mouse cursor on
  screen.
  Make a note of its position.
  Take the ball and Move it to that
noted position.
That's all for now.
```

Now, if *I* were a computer, I would know what that meant, and I'd respond accordingly! Of course, ActionScript isn't quite so... narrative. That code can purely be thought of as 'sort-of' code, or pseudo-code. See, in order to make valid code, we have specific things to follow.

> *Pseudo-code is actually a very important tool in the process of programming and development. It allows us to collect our thoughts into a clear logical fashion that is easy to read, before we dive into actually building it into ActionScript. Pseudo-code can be written in any manner; whatever's readable to the programmer – there are no hard rules. In general, if an idea or a design cannot be expressed in pseudo-code, it will probably be very difficult to program in general.*
>
> *Pseudo-code is also a great way of communication to non-technical clients just how something is going to work, and also helps them communicate to us how they want something to function.*

Code can be attached to events, like the progression from one frame to another frame known as the `onEnterFrame` event. When we have a movie in Flash MX that has a frame rate of 30 fps, then this code would be triggered thirty times per second.

Most on-screen objects that we want to move around are known in Flash as movie clips. When positioning these on screen, they must be referred to by their actual object names.

Ok, so, let's look at it more technically:

```
on EnterFrame
set horizontal position of ball to
horizontal position of mouse
set vertical position of ball to
vertical position of mouse
end of EnterFrame
```

Now, we can see that the code has been indented slightly in order to help us distinguish what's inside the EnterFrame event, and what's not. Also, the code refers to 'horizontal' and 'vertical' position. This is important because on screen, any object's position must be communicated to Flash using these two 'coordinates' (2-dimensional screen space), usually called x and y. In fact, let's get even more detailed:

```
onEnterFrame
  ball x = mouse x
  ball y = mouse y
end of EnterFrame
```

Wow! We're nearly there. That's almost ActionScript. There are just a few little things that ActionScript requires. First, blocks of code like events (onEnterFrame) and, as we'll see later on, functions, must be opened and closed with curly braces { and }. Secondly, all lines of ActionScript instructions must normally end with a semicolon ';'. Like this:

```
_root.onEnterFrame = function() {
    ball._x = _root._xmouse;
    ball._y = _root._ymouse;
}
```

In fact, that *will* work – that's ActionScript! Naturally, we would need to ensure that there indeed *was* a

movie clip named 'ball' on the stage, and the ball would follow the mouse.

This, however, is a start, and we'll be getting into movie clips later. For interest, this can be found in the file ballarrow.fla.

We can draw hundreds of things on the stage in Flash. We can use keyframes to animate them, using the traditional frame-by-frame animation of Flash. However, if we really want this to be original, then we'll have to use ActionScript to get more power out of Flash.

Why

Why we choose to use ActionScript is dependent upon our projects, and ultimately our goals. We may want to make a few menus move around the screen; if so, we'll want to learn about motion graphics in ActionScript. On the other hand, we may want to actually build a user interface that responds to user input and sends the results over the Internet to a database somewhere. In this case, we're interested in the application development aspect of ActionScript. Or, we may want to make a game in Flash, in which case we'll be interested in just about everything.

Why we would want to learn ActionScript is for the same reason that we would want to learn how to fully use a tool in a garage – so we can get the most use out of it, and create something cool and unique. In these days when users are demanding more and more out of their web experience, and in a time when the Web is becoming increasingly present in everyone's lives, we'll find it very useful to do everything we can with Flash.

How else can we make a web site that rearranges itself and repositions itself dynamically? How else can we apply a master volume control to the whole site? These are things that no timeline animator can bring about. ActionScript allows us to respond to changing conditions, and respond to user interactions, since each user will do different things at different times. ActionScript allows us to handle all of them.

Who

So, who in their right mind would want to learn ActionScript? You! And just about anyone else who ever wants to create something new, cool, functional, cutting-edge and memorable on the Web. At the most, ActionScript will be the very tool that you will use to create just about everything in Flash. At the least, ActionScript will be like knowing First Aid; something that could, one day, save us in an emergency.

Designers will benefit from ActionScript's 'easy-to-use and learn' syntax, and the extraordinarily short time in which things can be built. Also, designers will appreciate the close integration that ActionScript has with the visual aspects of a Flash movie via movie clips, buttons and drawing tools.

Web site designers and webmasters will enjoy ActionScript's similarity to JavaScript, and the ease with which powerful, dynamic web interfaces are built and integrated into existing web sites.

Programmers/developers will enjoy the breadth and depth of ActionScript. Anything can be created in Flash, and it only takes time to learn and do more. ActionScript follows programming standards and is therefore nearly instantly readable to most experienced programmers. Also, general programming methodologies can be brought from other languages and leveraged easily into ActionScript.

When

When is it time to whip out the ActionScript Reference and begin 'coding'? (Coding is the term used to describe the act of writing and typing any computer program). How do we know if our particular projects require ActionScript and not just frame-by-frame animation?

When we want to create a navigation system that relies upon user input. The simplest action of clicking on a button, and then jumping to a new frame in the movie requires at least two lines of ActionScript.

Any time we want user feedback, we need to create ActionScript to handle the results. Whether it is to simply print something on screen, or to send the results to the server, we'll need ActionScript to break down the data entered, validate it and then perform the desired task.

Whenever we want types of on-screen motion that are considered really 'cool' and dynamic. Most talented animators can create lifelike looking motion and physics, but to truly create dynamic, random and arbitrary motion, we need to use ActionScript to control the objects and their positions.

Whenever we want to create a movie that uses dynamic sound to produce sound effects or music tracks in response to actions; we'll need to use ActionScript to dynamically change the colors.

Whenever we really want to do *anything* above and beyond the simplest of intros or animations, we'll want to have ActionScript handy for those moments when the animated alternative simply doesn't cut it.

When we want our Flash sites to be dynamically controlled by an external source we must use ActionScript. Take, for example, a sports scores site. To truly make our site shine, we would 'pull in' the scores from an external data source over the Internet. Once that's done, we could easily use ActionScript to do anything from display the scores, to show an iconic replay of the game.

Where

As ActionScript can be placed in a number of places in a movie, we'll need to know where to best make use of it, and where it's actually better to stick to traditional frame animation.

Complex motions, like character animation, waves crashing, fire rising, etc., are usually best left to the skillful hands of an animator or designer. This is because ultimately, we cannot do much with ActionScript to accomplish this result. ActionScript is great at scaling, rotating and moving *finished* objects and animations around the screen, but the actual animations within those objects often need to be simply pre-drawn.

We can place ActionScript code both on actual frames, and in clips themselves, and based upon their location, their behavior (and interpretation by Flash) will differ slightly. This we'll get into later.

The lie of the land

What do we have on the road ahead of us? We're journeying into Flash, and into ActionScript, just as we're going to be journeying into the truck garage, and into the general operation, maintenance, creation and enhancement of trucks and machinery within this garage. We're going to be looking at Flash MX ActionScript in a metaphorical sense, comparing what we learn in ActionScript, with what we see in the garage, in an effort to make the whole thing more palatable.

We're going to be seeing the garage layout in **Chapter 2**: How the garage is put together, how that relates to the layout of a Flash MX movie, and where the ActionScript goes in that. We'll be looking at the general syntax (language rules) as well as the base parts that we use to make ActionScript.

In **Chapter 3**, we're going to look at how the concepts of the real-life garage are compared to ActionScript relationships and the movie clip/object approach.

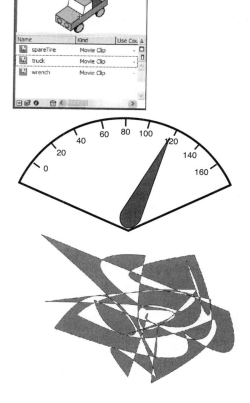

In **Chapter 4**, we're going to learn a lot about the core concepts like variables, and the really important concepts that are as 'programming-related' as they are 'ActionScript-related'.

In **Chapter 5**, we're going to take a look at the dynamic drawing engine of Flash MX, which is the body-worker, Jimmy, from the garage. This is responsible for creating cool graphics and images on the fly, using only ActionScript to guide the pen.

The steering and general vehicle operation will be looked at in **Chapter 6**. There, we're going to be looking at events, and how we can respond to different mouse and keyboard events and input, allowing us to control movement through ActionScript.

In **Chapter 7**, we're going to be building an interactive dashboard computer. Using ActionScript, we're going to learn about text fields, dates, and more.

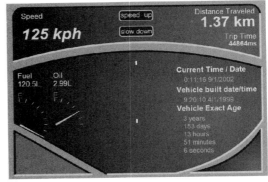

In **Chapter 8**, we'll see driving conditions and logic. We'll be looking at the math and logic behind the operation of the truck. We'll be building them all out of ActionScript.

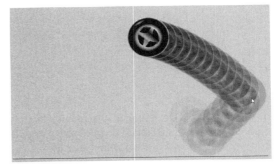

In **Chapter 9**, we'll be looking at sound and video, and many other cool multimedia vehicle enhancements.

In **Chapter 10**, we're going to learn how to make the truck behave in modular and intelligent ways. We're going to look at 'functions' and how to use them in ActionScript. We'll also look at using standard 'component' parts to enhance our truck, and our Flash movies.

Chapter 11 takes us out of the truck, into the real world for a look at network communication and image loading using ActionScript.

radio

Chapter 12 will take us to the next level, and where we can go from there.

At each step, we'll attempt to make it clear, and easy, with an intelligent progression through the topics.

The coolness of the destinations

In the end, it will be pretty clear that understanding and creating ActionScript is something that we almost already know how to do, because it has so many direct comparisons to real life. What we do in our vehicles can be directly rephrased in a way that we find ourselves understanding computer programming, with an ActionScript flavor.

Stick with us, enjoy the journey, and we'll be doing things that will give rise to new web sites, experiences and even entire careers. The world is becoming more and more connected each day, and as a result, the Web – the medium that connects us all – is becoming more and more important. The Internet has grown like an organism, and it's not stopping any time soon. Now is an exciting time to start learning one of the greatest and most distributed tools out there.

Flash ActionScript is only going to get more powerful as time goes by. As the average home computer increases in power, so too will the things we can do in ActionScript. Entire sites featuring interactive live video, sound and chat will soon become the norm, and getting to that level starts here, with ActionScript Zero to Hero. You will walk away from here knowing enough to get you going, and more than enough to move to the next level, and then soon to the status of Flash Superhero.

Garage Layout

What's in this chapter:

★ Knowing the garage layout

   ★ The timeline

★ The garage and your ActionScript

   ★ Frames, scenes, levels, layers and depth

★ Where to put all of that code

   ★ Frames, instances and the server

★ Structuring, and code syntax

   ★ What are scripts?

   ★ Where to write your code

★ Good coding practices

The ActionScripter's workshop

Before we start tinkering about under Flash's hood, we'd better have a look around our workplace. Otherwise things could get pretty frustrating when we're up to our elbows in grease and have forgotten where we put the wrenches! On the other hand, if we're confident about where everything is, getting Flash to sit up and beg for us should be a cinch.

Just like a mechanic, we know where to find things and have all the tools available to us. However, the end user viewing the movie has none of this, and just expects it to work. So it's all the more important that we have our ActionScript engine performing as well as possible, and integrated seamlessly with all the other parts of the car.

The timeline

One of the foundations of animation is the **timeline**. Timelines are used all the time in animation and video — and it's also a central part of many multimedia applications. Code and graphics can be represented in some way on one frame, or several frames, on a timeline. In the authoring environment, the timeline is a series of frames in sequence.

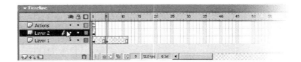

Your playhead will move along the timeline, like a car along a road. When graphics or code are encountered along the timeline, it will execute or be seen on the Stage. Your code is like the directions (signs) you see along the road, and the Flash vehicle responds to and follows these directions. Static graphics might be like the scenery you encounter.

Multiple timelines

Movie clips might be like other vehicles on parallel roadways, since they run on their own timelines. This can get somewhat complicated, but is extremely powerful when you need to create complex animations or effects. You can have other movies loaded on to different *levels*, which also run on their own timelines. Multiple timelines allow you to run animations or movies independently from one another, but all appearing together on the same Stage. This means you can start or stop an animation on one timeline, and keep one on another timeline still running.

Because there are multiple timelines, you will need to understand how to "talk" between the different timelines belonging to the movie clips and the main timeline of your movie. Although we said it works like the road signs, the advantage of ActionScript here is that it's virtual. Your Flash movie instantly leaps to any location you specify without spending hours in a traffic jam!

ActionScript

Flash is a tool that is commonly used for multimedia projects, since it integrates many different kinds of tools for communication. Having different data or media in different areas can help you create an efficient application, in the same way that you'd put your groceries in the trunk instead of scattered on and around the entire vehicle. Then, you would have all of your maps in the glove compartment under the dashboard. Everything inside the car can be neatly organized in a different place, and this will inevitably help you, the driver.

Frames

Many frames existing in a linear sequence create a timeline in Flash, each represented by rectangles in the Timeline panel. If you've ever driven over a 1960's concrete road, you'll have an idea of what the playhead is going through!

A keyframe is represented by a circle within a frame. If the circle is empty, then the frame in question does not have content. If the circle is filled, the frame has content (pictures, words, that sort of thing) in it.

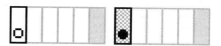

If you have code in your frame, an "a" will be seen in the frame. These are our road signs which, through code, tell the playhead to stop, start, or do any number of other things. This is where it gets interesting.

Frames are numbered from 1 – the start of your playhead's journey – to the last frame number in any given timeline. Movies do not have to have more than one frame though; many great Flash movies run everything on a single frame! You can also label frames, and give them a name. You can name a frame by giving it a 'frame label':

1. Select the frame (it must be a keyframe) you want to name by clicking on it.

2. Open the Properties inspector (CTRL/⌘+F3).

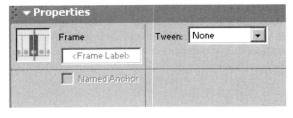

3. Enter your name into the `<Frame Label>` input field. This frame is going to be called 'Brian', but you could use a more sensible name!

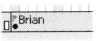

After it is named, a flag and the frame label name will appear on the timeline in question. Now, you can refer to this name in your ActionScript.

Frame labels are useful because you can move your content around the timeline, and then move the labels with the content. Just as temporary road signs are portable, frame labels can be dragged around if your movie's content changes. You do not have to change all of the frame numbers in your code if you move content in your movie.

It is good practice to have all of your labels on their own layer, called 'labels'.

Most of your code will probably go on frames. In Flash MX, it is possible to centralize all of your code in one place instead of placing code on object instances. We will look at places where you can put code later in the chapter.

Scenes

Scenes divide a Flash movie into separate areas in the authoring environment, in the same way that you might have more than one car in your garage (or, perhaps more obviously, in the same way as a play is divided into scenes).

Scene 1

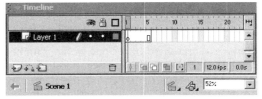

Scene 2

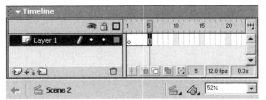

Scene 3

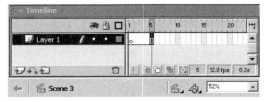

However, when the Flash movie is exported into a SWF file, the scenes are compressed into one timeline. The final SWF, were you able to take a peek inside, wouldn't have that clear boundary between each area of your movie and might look similar to this:

Single timeline at export

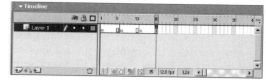

When you publish your movie, the SWF file denotes where the scene boundaries previously existed in the authoring environment with keyframes. Scenes progress from one to another in succession unless you specifically code the movie to do otherwise.

You can reference scenes using ActionScript. It is advisable if you do use scenes to use frame labels to navigate the timeline instead of frame numbers.

Its label should look like this, although this will be discussed further in **Chapter 4**:

```
gotoAndStop("sceneone","Brian");
```

You may find your movie will go to the incorrect frame if you reference using numbers. This is because the timeline is compressed into one single timeline when you export the movie.

Scenes are useful if you are creating animations, because they can divide up your work into separate, more manageable, areas. This is in some ways solved with the addition of **layer folders** in Flash MX.

Scenes only apply to the Main Timeline of a movie. You cannot create scenes within movie clips.

It is important to realize that scenes can sometimes be problematic when working with ActionScript. In addition to this, using scenes means your end user will have to download the entire series of scenes. A more elegant practice is to load individual SWFs using `loadMovie`, based on a user's request. If the user only wants to see one area (or "scene") then he or she will only have to download that one segment instead of the entire movie.

Layers

Layers are like a stack of graphics and instances, which are all within the same timeline in the authoring environment. They are necessary when you need to layer graphics, and/or separate different kinds of content on your site. The mentioned addition of layer folders means that you can organize similar kinds of things together, and collapse the folder when you are not using it – saving you some valuable screen real estate!

Layers are only available to you when authoring your Flash movie. Once the movie is exported, these layers are essentially flattened into a single visual presentation in the Flash player. You can also use layers when you need to organize your graphics so some lay on top of others. Layers can affect your ActionScript as well as your graphics. In some (but not many) cases, your code might work differently if one action is placed in a different layer than another. This is due to the loading order of the layers, and in what order the code loads and executes.

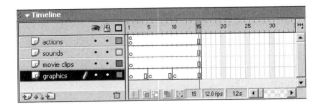

Layers load from bottom layer up or the top layer down. This depends on what order you choose in your Publish settings (File > Publish settings, then click on the Flash tab. By default it is set to bottom up). If you decide to have more than one layer containing ActionScript, you will want to make sure that there are no conflicts in the order these actions load into the movie. If there is conflict, you will want to try reversing the order, preloading content, or restructuring your code (possibly onto a single layer).

Take a look at the picture:

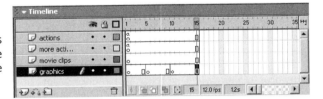

1. Open a new file, and create two layers as shown: actions, and more actions. On the actions layer, enter the following code into the Actions panel:

```
myword = "Bob";
```

2. and then on the more actions layer, enter

```
trace (myword);
```

3. Go to File > Publish Settings. Click on the Flash tab, and choose Bottom Up from the Load Order pull down menu.

4. Return to your movie, and press CTRL/⌘+ENTER to test it. In the Output window, you will see

```
Undefined.
```

This means that the variable *myword* has not been loaded yet, and so cannot be traced. We will learn more about variables in **Chapter 4**.

It is common (and good!) practice to have a separate 'actions' layer (at the top) designated to contain all of the ActionScript in your movie. Some more complex movies might have more than one layer for scripts: perhaps calling the layer by the kind of scripts in it, such as 'functions'. Organization is very important – just like it is with a tool chest that has compartments for each kind of nut or bolt.

However, if you have more than one layer containing ActionScript, just make sure you test your movie to make sure there are no conflicts between the layers.

Levels

Levels are like a stack of content (SWF files, JPG images or MP3s), which are all loaded on top of the `_level0` level (commonly the `_root`, but not always). The `_root` and `_level0` are not exactly the same thing. The `_root` is the base layer of the current timeline. Therefore, there is also a `_root` on `_level3`. The `_root` refers to the main timeline of each level, when you are referencing it in your code (as seen in the next example).

You might like to think of this like different management levels in a large company. A garage might have a manager for the office (its `_root`), a manager for the auto-body repair area, and then a manager for the gas bar. All of the workers report to their manager, but might also do jobs for and talk to workers in other areas. Each area is like a level. We will talk more about this in **Chapter 4**.

So, you can load movies (other SWF files, each with their own `_root`) into a Flash movie. You can either load the movie into a target (such as a placeholder movie clip, on an existing level), or you can load it onto a *new* level that you specify. The higher the level number is, the closer the image on the stage will appear to the viewer. If you load a movie onto the same level as other content, it will overwrite that content (effectively replacing it with the new content).

In the following figure, a new graphic is loaded into a level that already contains some content. The existing content is replaced with the new image.

wrench.fla

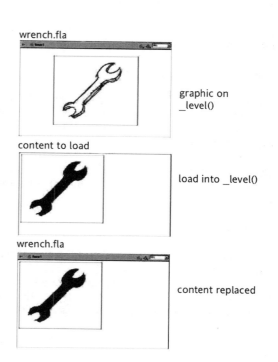

graphic on _level()

content to load

load into _level()

wrench.fla

content replaced

If you load the graphic onto a different level number, it will layer over the top (or underneath) the existing content. Also, the background will be transparent. Therefore, you will see the existing (old) content underneath the new image.

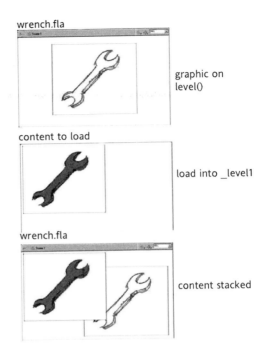

wrench.fla

graphic on level()

content to load

load into _level1

wrench.fla

content stacked

You can load content onto a layer using the `loadMovieNum` action:

```
loadMovieNum(URL, level);
```

You can specify the location of a SWF, JPG or MP3 file to load, and then the level you wish to load that content onto:

```
loadMovieNum("wrench.jpg", 3);
```

This code will load the `wrench.jpg` file onto `_level3`.

Locate `levels.fla` and `load_levels.swf` in the **Chapter 2** download files and copy them into the same directory on your hard drive. Open the file called `levels.fla`. In this file, you have a graphic on the main timeline. Let's load `load_levels.swf` into `levels.fla`, but on a new level.

Open the Actions panel and type the following code into frame 1 on the actions layer:

```
loadMovieNum("load_levels.swf",3);
```

Test your movie by pressing Ctrl/⌘+Enter. You will see another graphic on the stage, which is `load_levels.swf` loading into level 3. This is just like our example.

Now, go back to `levels.fla`, and open the Actions panel again. Change your code to look like the following:

```
loadMovieNum("load_levels.swf",0);
```

Test your movie again. What happened? Now we only have the graphic from `load_levels.swf`. As you can see, the original picture has disappeared. This is because we have bumped out `_level0` (in the `levels.fla` published movie), and replaced it with what is inside `load_levels.swf`.

Now open `levels2.fla`. This time, we are going to load the SWF file into a movie clip on the Stage. Go to the actions layer and enter the following code:

```
loadMovieNum("load_levels.swf",
"movie_clip");
```

Test the movie, and notice how the SWF file loads into our movie clip. This is the other way you can load content. What is different is our movie clip is in the movie when we load it initially, and the new level is created when we execute the `loadMovieNum` action.

Levels are typically used when you are loading content into a movie on demand. For example, when you load other SWFs into a movie based on user input. Each SWF file is similar to a "page" or "area" of an application or web site; instead of using scenes or content within the main movie a user would have to load it in all at once. This is not a user-friendly way of organizing a movie or web site. Using `loadMovie` means that content can be loaded by request. This can save on bandwidth and loading times for the end user.

Depth

Depth refers to how movie clips are stacked on any given timeline. Depth is not the same thing as levels. For example, many movie clips with varying degrees of depth would all appear below a movie (containing its own movie clips and depth levels) stacked over it on a higher level. Regardless of depth levels, the movie clips on a higher level will always appear above those on a lower level.

As you can see in this figure, you could have a movie clip with a depth of 5. This would appear behind one with a depth of 2 since it is on a lower level.

The depth level can be numbered from 1 up to 1048575. A movie clip with a lower depth number will be placed behind a movie clip with a higher depth number. As with levels, the higher the number is, the closer it will appear to a viewer. If a movie clip is loaded into a movie with the same depth, it will overwrite (replace) the existing movie clip.

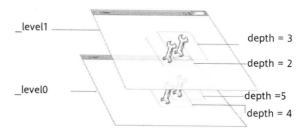

★ Two

You can specify depth when creating, attaching or duplicating movie clips. For example, when you duplicate a movie clip called circle, you specify a depth for the new movie clip. Let's look at a piece of code which includes depth:

```
duplicateMovieClip(target, name, depth);
```

When you duplicate a movie clip, you need to not only set its target (the instance it copies) and give it a name, but then also place it in a stacking order (depth). If you were to actually duplicate a movie clip instance called circle (located on the _root of the Flash movie), it might look like:

```
duplicateMovieClip(_root.circle,
"newcircle", 2);
```

In this code, _root.circle is the location of a movie clip with an instance name circle. newcircle is the name you are setting for the new movie clip. And finally, 2 is the depth being assigned to the new movie clip. In the following diagram, several circles are stacked in increasingly greater numbers of depth.

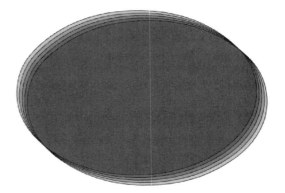

So then let's take a look at how the first two circles in this picture are created. First we need to make sure there is a movie clip in our movie to actually duplicate. We could either drag an instance to the Stage and give it an instance name, or we could attach it using ActionScript. You have to make sure that you have given it a Linkage name in the Library first. Then, add this code:

```
//attach a movie clip to the stage.
_root.attachMovie("myClip","myClip1",10
48575);
//duplicate the clip. depth mustn't be
greater than 16384
myClip1.duplicateMovieClip("myClip2",222);
//move the clip over so you can see
both clips
myClip2._x+=5;
myClip2._y+=5;
```

For a complete example of this, refer to duplicate_mc.fla.

Depth is used when you create, duplicate or attach movie clips to a particular timeline. This is useful for many animations, effects or even creating new code. You might create a new movie clip, and then write code to exist within it if you need the looping functionality of a movie clip. When you do this, you need to specify a depth level (and make sure it does not conflict with any existing movie level depths, unless you require this for a specific purpose of course!).

You can even create new movie clips (and put code in them) on the main timeline. This means you do not have to place code right on a button or movie clip instance in order to control it. As we explained earlier, this helps us organize our code all in the same place, which makes organizing and editing your movie easier.

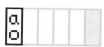

Where the code goes in the Garage

Let's take a look at where we can put ActionScript in relation to the many different parts of Flash. ActionScript can be placed in different places: frames, instances, and in some special cases, a server. However, changes in ActionScript for Flash MX allow you to put all of your code on a single frame and still control instances in your movie. You are able to control instances anywhere in your movie from the main timeline, no matter if the instance is on a different level, nested in a movie clip or dynamically loaded by user request.

Frame actions

ActionScript is commonly placed in a frame on the main timeline. All of your code can be placed here if you want to keep it together in one location. For example, you can stop your movie with the following line of code:

```
stop();
```

Or, you could ask your movie to go to frame number 5 and play, using:

```
gotoAndPlay(5);
```

You are also able to control movie clips, buttons, and other instances from a frame action. If you have a movie clip with an instance name "truck", you could move the timeline of the truck to frame 5 using:

```
truck.gotoAndPlay(5);
```

This is a lot like having everything that controls a vehicle in one central place: the on-board computer. This computer controls all of the pieces which make the vehicle operate: the wheels, engine, turn signals, radio and the like. If something doesn't work well, you will probably take a diagnostic of this computer first and see if the problem resides there. It is easy to do so, because most of the controlling actions/computations are in one place. Similarly, ActionScript is much easier to debug and control when written in one place

Actions placed on instances

You can also put code on individual object instances, such as movie clips and buttons. To make a movie go to frame 5 when a button is clicked on, you could write the following code right on the button. Meaning, you would select the instance on the stage, open the Actions panel, and write this code:

```
on (release){
   gotoAndPlay(5);
};
```

Handlers have traditionally been used on the instance itself to help control the movie. For example, code can be put on a button so that when it is pressed, something happens (like in our example, go to frame number 5). Movie clips can have code put on them too. Code can be put both *on* a movie clip instance, and within the movie clip on its own timeline. These actions can control either the movie clip itself, or the movie containing it.

Open a new movie, and draw a circle. Press F8 and turn it into a movie clip. Name it 'myClip1'.

Draw another circle, and turn it into a movie clip. Name the second movie clip instance 'myClip2'. Select the second movie clip and open the Properties inspector. In the Color drop down, select Alpha and decrease it to 50 or less. Then open the Actions panel. If you want to control the main timeline using code on a movie clip, you could write the following code on 'myClip1':

```
onClipEvent(enterFrame){
    _root.myClip2._alpha+=1;
}
```

This code will continually add alpha to a clip on the Stage called 'myClip2'. The second movie clip is controlling the first movie clip, and repeatedly! This is because movie clips loop, so the clip will enter frames continually (and cause the code to be executed over and over again).

Using instance actions might be useful to you for backward compatibility. If this is not a concern for you, you might want to consider putting your code on the main timeline (in a centralized location) to control your movie. We will discuss callback functions thoroughly in **Chapter 6**.

External code

Just to take things a little bit further, you can also have code residing on the server within .asr files using what is called Flash Remoting. This sort of thing is well beyond the scope of this book, but if you want to create what's called **dynamic content**, look out for other friends of ED titles coming soon, including *ASP.NET for Flash MX* (ISBN: 1-903454-08-9).

Syntax and Structure

In this section, we will take a look at what scripts are and where to write them in the Flash authoring environment.

What are scripts?

Scripts are what make the Flash car run. Scripts include all of the commands, actions, functions, objects, their methods and properties, and so on that you write help run the movie. You do not *need* any scripts to create a running SWF file. You could use tweening or frame-by-frame drawings to tell a story and not have one bit of code anywhere in the entire SWF file, but that'd be a bit like strapping our car onto rails.

ActionScript can dramatically enhance your movie, and change it from a moving graphic to a fully-fledged application or interactive interface. And learning how to write it is why you are here. The ActionScript language is used to build the scripts. The scripts define the path our movie will take, like the signs by the open road.

Where does the code go?

We know that scripts can go on frames, or on object instances themselves. But it is important to also know where to actually do all of that typing! ActionScript is usually written in the script pane, within the Actions panel (F9). The Actions panel looks like the following:

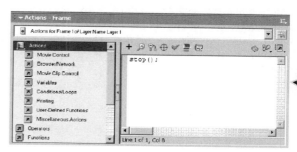

The Script pane and Expert mode

The script pane is the large white area where you can input text. Most of this book involves directly typing ActionScript into the Script pane, which means that you must be in **Expert mode**, as opposed to **Normal mode**.

Now the word 'expert' probably sounds a little frightening, but in reality it's a little more like the difference between driving a car and taking a bus. The bus is slower, and only stops at certain points. Not to mention, you should also know the route before you get on. If you want to learn how to drive, it won't help if you are sitting on a bus!

So how do you get into Expert mode? There are three ways: firstly, the Actions panel pop-up menu at the upper right hand side of the panel:

You can also press the View options button below the pop-up panel, and change editing modes here as well:

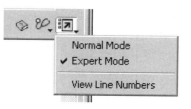

And of course, you can also use the keyboard shortcut: CTRL/⌘+SHIFT+E.

After changing your editing mode to Expert, you can select the Script pane, and enter ActionScript manually!

Color coding in the Actions panel

When you type code into the script pane, you will notice that some words turn blue, comments turn gray, and other words remain black (if you haven't changed the default settings). These colors help you notice ActionScript **keywords** in your code (which can help avoid problems if you use one as an instance name).

Color-coding can also help reduce typos, and makes scanning your code for bugs (checking for errors) much easier. You can change the default colors by selecting Edit > Preferences (CTRL/⌘+U) and then clicking the ActionScript Editor tab.

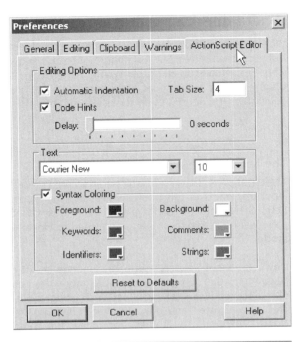

Checking your syntax and format

Another useful feature of the Actions panel is the Check Syntax and Auto Format buttons, which are found above the script pane.

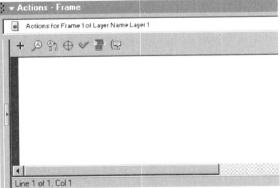

Before testing your movie, it is a good idea to press both of these buttons. The Check Syntax will alert you if there are any errors in your code, and provide feedback in the Output window. The output provided will tell you where the errors are in your code, so you can fix them before testing your movie. The Auto Format button will format your code correctly.

1. For example, type the following code:

   ```
   _root.gotoAndStop(5)
   ```

   What is wrong with this code?

2. Press the Auto Format button. Flash automatically adds a missing semi-colon!

   ```
   _root,gotoAndStop(5);
   ```

3. Now try entering the following code into the Script pane for frame 1 on the main timeline:

   ```
   on(release)
   _root.gotoAndStop(5)
   }
   ```

4. Press the Check Syntax button this time. Two errors! This should show you how useful this button can be: you now know that there is a syntax error (you have not opened your curly brace). Also, the Output window will tell you this event must be placed on a button instance. Refer to `actions_panel.fla` for the correct (and formatted) code.

Code hinting

Code hinting is a terrific way of speeding up the scripting process. You will notice that in certain parts of your code, a pop-up box will appear. You can scroll through this box (or use your arrow keys) and press ENTER to insert the word into your script.

Code hinting is another efficient way to work with your code. In order for code hinting to work with names that you give to objects (such as the XML object or text object), you will need to learn and use the proper suffixes:

String	_str
TextField	_txt
MovieClip	_mc
Sound	_sound
Date	_date
Color	_color
Array	_array
XML	_xml

When creating a new object, you need to add the appropriate suffix to the end of the object name. Let's create an XML object:

```
myXML_xml = new XML();
```

As you can see here, we have added _xml on to the end of the object name. This is like a special identifier plate, signifying *what* the object actually is. Now, whenever we intend to use the methods and properties of the XML object, we will get code hints in the script pane to help us out. This will make a lot more sense in the following chapters when we start to use these objects in our ActionScript.

You can also write ActionScript in external editors as well. Color coding and code hinting for ActionScript (as well as specific hinting for .asr and Flashcom versions of the language) can also be found in Dreamweaver MX. You might find it easier to use Dreamweaver when creating #include or .asr files. External editors can be much easier to read and edit with, or convenient if you want to edit your code directly on a server! You also get to skip the step of copying and pasting your code from the Actions panel.

Symbols and instances

As you may already know, there are many parts to a Flash movie. These parts are like the seats, rear-view mirrors, engine parts, or peripherals of a truck. You create these parts of the movie: maybe by using code, importing images or sounds, or by manually adding things directly on the Stage.

When something is in the Library, it is a symbol. Each symbol can have one or many instances placed on the Stage. Each of these instances can be given a different name – which means that you can control each instance in a different way using ActionScript. Instance **names** are used to target an instance on the Stage using ActionScript.

The symbols in your movie will commonly be movie clips and buttons, but will now probably also include the new video and component elements as well. In the movie, you can add names to these symbol instances after they are placed on the Stage. This is integral if you plan to control the instances using ActionScript. You can name an instance of an object by selecting it on the Stage, and then entering a name in the `<Instance name>` input field in the Properties inspector.

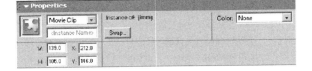

You can even take this further! You can have instances *within* other instances. This is called **nesting**. You can think of this like parts inside other parts of an engine, each having its own role in helping the truck perform its overall function. A piston has a different role, and works in a different way from a fan belt or a spark plug. But you might have several spark plugs which are copies of each other, but controlled separately from one another. However, they all work together to perform one overall task: your Flash application!

This is what happens when movie clips are nested within other movie clips. If you want to control several movie clips in the same way, you can give each one of them the same name. If you want to control each one separately, you need to give them different names. However, you cannot nest a symbol within itself.

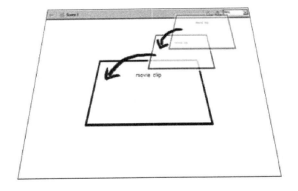

At this point, we should point out that some objects are very different in ActionScript from instances or symbols in the library. Objects in ActionScript are predetermined groups of the language. For example, the Sound object has its own methods and properties which you can use in your movie, to do with sound. Equally, the Math object has assorted calculation functions you can use. You will see many examples of these objects in the following chapters.

Using dot notation

Dot notation is used to target a particular part of the Flash movie. It is like a set of directions or **path** which leads the way to one instance inside the movie. When you are assigning methods or properties to a particular object or instance, you need to target it by telling Flash where to go to find it.

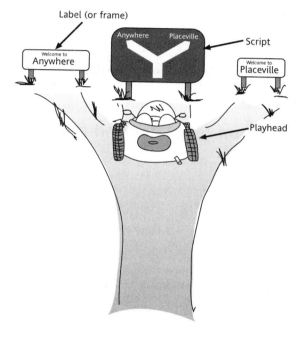

You can now reference your labeled frame using its name, and you can reference any frame using its number. In ActionScript the signposts are called **dot notation** or **dot syntax**. It's covered in **Chapter 4**, but just so you know, it looks like this:

```
_root.gotoAndStop("placeville");
```

This action will go to the frame labeled 'placeville', in the root timeline (or main road) and stop at this frame.

For example, you might want to target a particular part of the movie, which may lie inside many different layers. If you remember the points about movie clip instances existing inside other movie clip instances, you will need to target a nested part of the movie. Let's say you want to control the fuel injector of a truck in a certain manner. You would need to target it by providing directions to the Flash movie as to where it is. It might look like the following chain of directions:

```
_root.truck.fuel_injector;
```

Therefore, the frame labeled 'fuel_injector' is inside the 'truck', which is *inside* the '_root' timeline. You will use this kind of targeting when you have movie clips inside other movie clips

If you have trouble finding the proper way to target your instance, you can always use the Actions panel Insert target path button to help you determine the path. You need to have an instance selected on the Stage, and then press the Insert target path button.

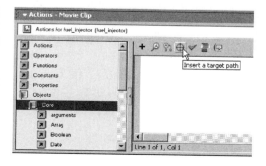

A dialog box will pop up, where you can select the instance you want entered into your code. If you selected the Insert target path button for the previous example, your path would look as follows:

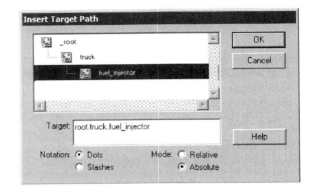

After pressing the OK button, the path will be entered into the script pane. If you were assigning a value to a property of the `fuel_injector` instance, it might look like the following:

```
_root.truck.engine.fuel_injector.workin
g = true;
```

This code sets the working status of the `fuel_injector` instance to the value of **true**.

Common practices and good habits

It is a good idea to practice sound ways of structuring your code and applications right from the beginning. This will save you from adopting bad habits, which might be hard to rectify. In this section we will take a look at a few of the common ActionScript practices coders use to simplify their lives.

Naming conventions in ActionScript

When you are writing instance names or choosing names in your code, it is a good idea to follow some standard practices which code writers typically use in Flash. If you are considering using two words together, they can be separated using a capital letter, as in:

```
myTruck
wheelSizeX
theMechanic
```

As you can see in these examples, they are descriptive words. Try to describe what you are talking about so that it is easy to remember when you come back to look at the code later.

You might want to use underscores to separate words, too. For example, you might have:

```
my_wrench
steel_pipe
```

We learned that, for code hinting to occur, we need to complete these names with particular suffixes. This is done using an underscore, so you might end up with:

```
myTruck_mc
```

This would be for a movie clip called 'myTruck_mc'. Typically, a mix of capitalization is used, followed by an underscore-suffix.

ActionScript has many keywords. These are certain words, such as predetermined object names, which should not be used as instance or variable names in your code. It is safe to say you should not use any word in the ActionScript language as an instance or variable name. If you do, in some cases you will find your movie will not work, or will run in unexpected ways.

You should also note that certain words in the ActionScript language are case-sensitive (such as `function`, `instanceof`, and `with`). If you use the wrong case, your code will not work. If you are encountering difficulties, you should make sure that you have the proper case (the same as the dictionary), and/or the word is color-coded. If the ActionScript word is color coded, you're ready to go.

Centralized code

Many Flash designers and developers put all of their code on one frame at the beginning of a movie (usually on frame 1 or 2, on a layer called *actions*). Centralizing code is much like organizing a garage into separate areas: supplies, tools, an office, and so on. Similarly, organizing a movie is much like having separate areas for all of the parts making up the end product. Therefore, it is a good idea to keep your actions, sounds, graphics and so on separate from each other on your timeline layers. And it is also a good idea to organize your Library in a similar way, which will also save you time and confusion.

Centralizing all of your code is a great practice to adopt for several reasons. First of all, it is much easier to locate within an application. If you are working with a team of designers and developers and transferring the FLA file between hands, it saves a lot of time to have all of the code in an easy-to-find location. This saves colleagues from having to search through different instances for code. If your file is being used as a tutorial file, it is much easier for those learning from your code to digest it as one block.

Having code in a single place also helps speed up the debugging process. All of your code is in one spot, so any conflicts are much easier to see. For example, if you created two movie clips on the same depth level, it is much easier to notice the conflict than if the code was in two completely different places.

Similarly, it is also much faster to search-and-replace words within the code. This is particularly useful if you are making major revisions to a site, or reusing blocks of code in a different application.

Commenting your code

Putting comments within your code is an excellent practice to adopt. Comments will help you every time you return to work on your Flash movie. Comments are like the notes a mechanic might put in the margin of a work order. Other mechanics might check up on these notes before making repairs to the vehicle. If the vehicle is brought back to the shop two months down the road, these notes will again help the mechanics when working on the vehicle.

You can comment your code by placing // in front of the line of comments:

```
//these are my comments
```

However, if you have longer comments, you might want to surround the block of comments in the following way:

```
/* the following application injects fuel
   sparks the ignition
   then makes the truck GO
   brings the truck to a stop at stop
   signs
*/
```

All of the above text will be commented, so the movie will not try to execute any of the contents when your movie is published. So as you can see, comments are simply directions we can give in our code, so we (or other people looking at the file) can remember what the code means while it is in the FLA file. Comments do not affect the SWF, they only exist in the authoring environment.

You will want to put comments in your code whenever there is a change in what the code is doing. You will also want to make points about any workarounds or problems encountered when writing the code. A good mechanic will note what he did, but also what he could not do. This will help if other programmers work on your Flash movie in the future.

Variables vs. hard-coding

Hard-coding means you are setting a definite value to something in your Flash application. For example, you might hard code

```
mechanic = "Jimmy";
```

somewhere in your movie, Jimmy being an unchanging value you assign to mechanic. This may work fine during the testing phase. However, you will be very limited in the "real world" when you have many mechanics at the site. Not all mechanics will be called Jimmy.

The solution to this is to use a variable instead of a hard coded value. Instead, you might have:

```
mechanic = username;
```

where username is a changing value based on user input. This would take a value entered by the user, perhaps into a login (input) text field given an instance name of username. Therefore, the value will be different depending on what is entered. We will thoroughly discuss variables in **Chapter 4**. However, what you can note here is that Jimmy cannot be changed in this example, because he is represented as a **string**. 'username' is not a definite number or name, because it does not have quotation marks around it. We can say 'username' can be different values, depending on what we need 'username' to be.

You want to use this practice as much as possible. Another example of this, seen earlier in this chapter, is when you used frame labels as opposed to frame numbers. Frame labels change, depending on where you move them to. Your code is therefore not hard-coded to a certain number, and you do not have to change your code if the number changes during an edit of the movie.

Using "pseudo-code"

And last, but not least, you will probably find it useful to "pseudo-code" your scripts. You might want to think of this step like drafting out a map before your road-trip. Pseudo-code is a literal, "English" rendition of a coding language. It resembles the way we speak, so it is very easy to understand.

Pseudo-code will be used heavily throughout this book to illustrate the way ActionScript works.

Pseudo-code is easy to create, because it is completely logical to just about everyone. For example, if you wanted to create a description of how to code an animation, you might write the following pseudo-code:

```
If the gas button is pressed
Play special animation movie clip
If the brake button is pressed
Stop the movie clip
If the horn button is pressed
Play the sound "beep!"
If nothing is pressed
Loop on main timeline
```

Since this pseudo-code is relatively easy to relate to ActionScript, it makes it easy for yourself and others to understand what needs to be accomplished. It is also a very literal explanation of the intent of an application, and a good way to start coding.

Summary

In this chapter, we discussed how to navigate a Flash movie. In particular, we:

★ Learned how to navigate a timeline, and multiple timelines in a movie.

★ Experienced the differences of levels, layers and depth, and learned how this will affect our movies in different ways.

★ Wrote code in a frame, and also on an instance.

★ Learned different ways of controlling a movie and instances within a movie.

★ Began using targets.

★ Learned about different coding practices which will help establish good habits when writing ActionScript.

Parts Department

What's in this chapter:

- ★ Things and objects
- ★ Movie clips
- ★ Parts department (library)
- ★ Logic
- ★ Trace Function

The Thing

When it comes to setting up our garage, we're going to see that everything has its place, and that in fact ActionScript can be found everywhere. In this chapter, we're going to start looking at our garage as something that is full of 'things'. We're going to see that everything is related to everything else, in a strange way.

What's a 'thing'?

Well, we have to think of this as a concept to which we apply our ActionScript concepts. For example, a person is a 'thing', a car is a 'thing'; a wrench is a 'thing'. These are all entities that exist in our garage, and have associated with them specific properties; descriptive words, pieces of information.

For example, a person, car and wrench all share these properties:

Height – Each has a specific height – 4 to 6 feet for a person or 5 to 10 inches for a wrench.

Width – Each has a specific width – 2 feet for a person or 1 or 2 inches for a wrench.

X, Y and Z position – Each is sitting somewhere in the garage, and therefore can be defined by their position.

Age – For a person, this will be years, and for a wrench or car, this will be the time from manufacture.

Now, these are not all of the common properties, but they're enough to demonstrate the point. In fact, we could say that these properties make up the base 'thing' that I mentioned above. The thing has a generic set of properties.

We can also take a 'thing' and make it into a specific type of object, by defining some more properties around it, so, for example, the wrench is no longer a 'thing' and is instead a 'wrench'.

Let's create a laundry list of rules to define, for example, a car.

Car is a 'thing'

So, we know that the car inherits all the properties of the generic 'thing' (width, height, x, y, z, age).

Extend the 'thing' car to have some specific properties:

★ Model

★ Make

★ Number of doors

★ Mileage

Now, 'thing' does not have the properties Model, Make, Number of doors or Mileage but 'car' does. We have *extended* 'thing' to include these new properties, and therefore create a new item all of its own, called 'car'.

Let's call each of these items an 'object', so 'thing' is an object, and 'car' is an object that extends thing. In fact, we could almost say that 'thing' is the 'base object' because it is not an extension of anything, it is, in itself, empty.

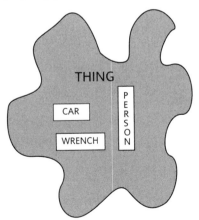

Making any sense? Why on earth are we breaking everything up in such a strange way? Well, remember, we're trying to learn Flash MX ActionScript here, and this is how Flash MX thinks, in terms of classes, and 'things'. In Flash, however, the common word for 'thing' is 'object', so we'll be calling them objects from now on.

Now, there's one more thing to note. When we're talking about 'objects', we're talking more about a blueprint, than an actual physical object. If we have a 'car' object sitting in a catalog somewhere, then yes, that's a car but, being on paper, it's not something we can drive away. In order to get to this object, we must create an 'instance' of it.

Or, we could say this. 'Person' is an object. Jimmy, Rufus and Charlene would all be called 'instances' of 'Person'.

Wax on, Wax off – what are we really learning?

In Flash MX ActionScript, our base 'thing' is called an 'object', and it's created with the simple ActionScript code:

```
myObject = new Object();
```

or, to use an item from our garage:

```
wrench = new Object();
```

Once this has been done, our new object exists, but it will have *no* properties whatsoever. If we want to begin adding properties, we do so using the dot notation illustrated in the previous chapter, like so:

```
myObject.weight = 76;
```

or

```
wrench.manufacturer = "SuperTools Inc.";
```

In the next chapter, we'll begin looking more in depth at how to add and work with properties in these objects.

You've probably heard the term 'movie clip' before. If not, let me put it to you this way; The movie clip is merely an object that has a few parameters associated with it from the beginning of its creation. As soon as we create a movie clip on the stage, it has several base parameters (width, height, x and y are among them), and we can extend the movie clip into anything we'd like, thereby turning it into anything we want (car, wrench and person included).

Keep all this in mind, because we're going to be exploring the detailed ActionScript of all this in the next few chapters.

Movie clips

You're probably already familiar with creating movie clips, but just in case you're not, creating a movie clip is a simple process, so let's try creating one now.

1. Open a blank movie in Flash (open Flash, or if it is already open, press CTRL/⌘ + N to start a new movie).

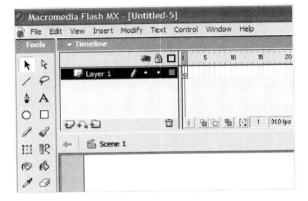

2. Using the drawing tools, draw a simple shape on the stage, like a circle or a square. (Technically, a movie clip can be any image, but for this demonstration, let's keep it simple).

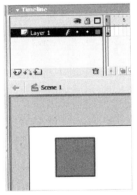

3. Using the selection tool ![selection tool] , select the entire graphic that you just drew (or press CTRL/⌘ + A).

4. Press F8 and the Convert to Symbol box will appear. Enter the name 'superShape' for the shape in the 'Name' box, and make sure that the movie clip behavior is selected.

5. Click OK.

We'll be left with an instance of the 'superShape' movie clip on the stage, which will be indicated by the blue bounding box, and the registration point with a small circle over it:

In order to perform any ActionScript commands on this movie clip later on, we must give it an 'instance name'. An 'instance name' is unique to each copy of a movie clip. Though we could have 50 copies of superShape on the stage, they must all have different instance names in order to be accessible with ActionScript.

6. To give the shape an instance name, select the movie clip, and make sure that the Properties panel is visible by opening it up, or pressing CTRL/⌘ + F3. The Properties panel looks like this:

7. The text field that says <Instance Name> is where we enter a unique instance name for our copy of the movie clip. Within this box, type 'shape1' and press ENTER.

Now we have a movie clip sitting on the stage, with the instance name 'shape1'. We can refer to it by that name now using any ActionScript. For example, placing this code on Frame 1 of a layer in the timeline:

```
shape1._rotation = 90;
```

will make the movie clip rotate 90 degrees to the right – its '_rotation' property will be set to 90, and therefore Flash will draw it rotated by 90 degrees. (There will be more on these properties next chapter.)

The Parts Department and Warehouse

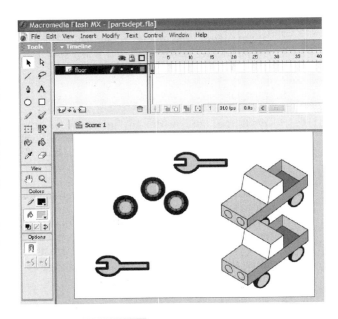

Within the garage, we have a wonderfully resourceful parts department that stocks a wide variety of items, tools, parts and yes, entire trucks! The parts department is quite powerful really. All our mechanics need to do is walk up to the window, reach in and then drag the required item onto the shop floor. Magically, the inventory will not be reduced from the warehouse itself, and our mechanics will always have an infinite supply of parts to choose from.

In Flash MX, we use something called the 'Library' to accomplish the same tasks. Let's take a look at Flash. Open the sample file, `partsdept.fla`.

We can see the Stage is strewn with movie clips. Specifically, we have three tires, two wrenches and two trucks. Since these are all movie clips, they're each going to be contained in the 'inventory' of the parts department warehouse. In Flash MX the 'Library' is accessed by pressing F11 or CTRL/⌘ + L from within Flash. When we create a new movie clip it is immediately entered into the library for us.

Alternatively, we can click on the 'plus' icon at the bottom left hand corner of the Library menu to jump to the NEW SYMBOL dialog box.

Moving a movie clip from the library to the stage is as simple as dragging and dropping it into place:

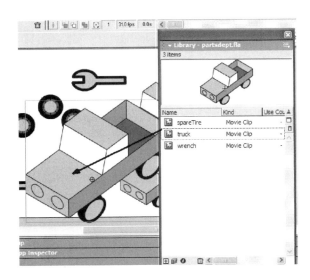

It is possible, of course, to bring a movie clip from the library onto the stage via ActionScript using a special command called `attachMovie`. Before we can use this, however, we must prepare the movie clips in our library for usage with this ActionScript. In the context of our garage, we must give the part a unique inventory serial number.

1. Open up `attachparts.fla`, and we'll see that there's nothing on the stage, but that the library contains the same three parts as the previous example:

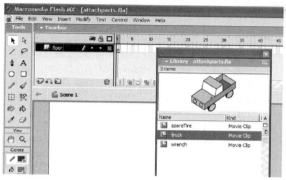

2. Now, right/CTRL-click on the truck in the library, and select 'Linkage'.

We will then see the Linkage Properties box for the movie clip. This is where we're going to give our inventory part its inventory serial number.

3. Notice that the "Export for ActionScript" check box is selected, and that the word 'truck' has been entered in the 'Identifier' text box. This is the identifier we'll be using with the `attachMovie` command.

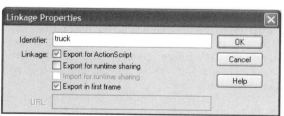

Once the linkage identifier is properly set up, we can use the `attachMovie` command, attached to frame 1 of any layer on the main timeline, like so:

```
attachMovie ("truck", "joesTruck", 0);
```

This function takes three parameters:

★ The first parameter is the linkage identifier of the movie clip that we want to attach from the library.

★ The second parameter is the unique instance name that we want to give this new instance of the movie clip, in this case, 'joesTruck'.

★ The third parameter is the depth level, or drawing order. The lowest number we can use here is 0, and the levels are drawn from lowest to highest. Only one movie clip instance is allowed per level (so, the next attachMovie must place its instance on a level other than 0).

If we run the demo (using the Test Movie command from the 'Control' menu, or by pressing CTRL/⌘ + ENTER), we'll see the following:

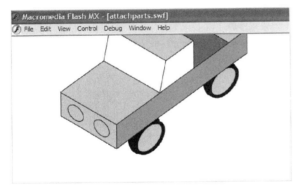

We've successfully used ActionScript code to bring in a truck from the 'warehouse'. This means that our Flash MX movies do not have to be rigid, and predefined at design time. Instead, we can dynamically add and remove any movie clips that we want, and at any time.

The logic of real life

As our garage is highly organized and efficient, all work follows a simple flow and set of procedures. Let's look at Rufus, the garage boss. He's responsible for getting the garage ready in the morning so everyone else can do their jobs. He has the responsibility of calling people and one-time contractors to work in the garage, as well as ordering all items and keeping the parts department stocked.

Before Rufus starts work, he follows a process:

He arrives in the morning at 9:00am and immediately begins by turning on all the lights, starting the coffee machine and plugging in the equipment.

Next, Rufus looks at the daily work board to see what jobs are on the slate for the garage today.

Depending upon what work must be performed today, at this point Rufus may call up Jimmy the auto-body painter, Charlene the tune-up girl, or Larry the mechanic.

Rufus will set his contractors and employees to work by giving them detailed instructions as to what must be done during the day.

The day goes on, and once several trucks have been built, repaired, painted or enhanced, the time will come for Rufus to shut down. He may then dismiss the workers and shut down the garage for the night.

In this garage, it's important to realize that everything mimics real life, and therefore has several rules that must always apply. For example, our garage suffers from the effects of gravity, and therefore everything falls to the ground. Gravity is something that is constant, and applies to the entire globe – in fact; you could say that it's a *global* value.

Sounds like a pretty strange garage, right? Well, what's supposed to be going on here is quite like ActionScript. Flash MX ActionScript follows a few clear and specific procedures as well.

First, when a movie is run, it will start at frame 1 and begin loading all the objects in that frame. Movie clips, graphics and the like will all be brought into existence. Essentially, this is where Rufus turns on the lights, coffee machine, and other machinery. In this moment, we're preparing all the assets that are going to be used in our movie.

Next, Flash MX begins executing the code on the frames that contain code starting at frame 1, from top to bottom. The ActionScript is executed in a linear fashion, from the top of the script to the bottom of the script.

The first few lines of code are generally considered to be the 'initialization' code, and tend to apply to the entire movie. This is the starting point where we set our variables and the properties that will be used by the rest of the movie, and this is when Rufus is looking at the daily work board.

After all the initialization is complete, we then create the objects and the functions that will be used in the functioning of the movie. Things like movie clips, buttons, text fields, color objects and sound objects to be used in the general operation of the movie. We'll be getting into these in more detail, later in the book.

What's Rufus doing here? He's calling up his staff, of course. He's employing all the people and machinery that will be working in the garage throughout the day.

Once our objects are created, we must then assign to them the various pieces of ActionScript (known as

functions) required to make them behave the way we need them to. For example, let's say we have a button with the instance name "startTirePump". We would set it to respond to a mouse click, like so:

```
startTirePump.onPress = function()
{
    tirePump.startUp();
}
```

We're using the onPress event of the 'startTirePump' button at which point we're running the startUp function of the tirePump object. That's some fun code, but it makes perfect sense if we read it carefully. As for what the 'startUp' function itself actually is, who knows? It doesn't really matter in the context of this example.

The act of assigning these functions to objects is, of course, the moment where Rufus is giving all his contractors their orders and instructions for the day.

Let's imagine first that we have a movie clip sitting on the stage with the instance name, 'truck'.

Now, let's say that we create a new Color object, known as 'JimmysBrush', and we want it to be applied to the truck movie clip. We do it something like this in ActionScript:

```
JimmysBrush = new Color(truck);
```

Then, we can use the setRGB function, which is specific to the Color object, to color the truck black:

```
JimmysBrush.setRGB(0);
```

The number 0 between the brackets corresponds to the color black.

As we can see, Jimmy has certainly done his job thoroughly; the 'truck' movie clip will now appear completely black. We've used object-specific code to perform the task that we're wishing to perform. In this case, the object is the Color object, and the object-specific code is the setRGB function, which happens to be built into Flash MX. We're not looking at specifics here but rather we're interested in understanding the relationships between objects, properties and their functions.

Trace

We have a truck in the repair bay because the engine light says that the temperature is in the red.

What are we supposed to do?

This is where we plug in our engine computer, and take a look at the values under the hood. We quickly find out that the temperature is fine and therefore the gauge itself is broken.

In ActionScript speak:

One of the most useful functions available to us in Flash MX ActionScript is the 'trace' command. Using the trace command, it's possible to display any text we want in the Flash MX output window. This is highly useful for determining what's going on beneath the hood when our movies and programs begin to act up in any way. We can use this to:

★ Make sure our program is reaching and executing a certain area of code.

★ View the values of properties and variables.

Let's look at an example. Look at trace.fla, and see the ActionScript that's attached to the first frame of the layer labeled 'actions' by opening up the Actions panel (F9):

```
trace ("I'm Here now");
age = 4;
trace (age);
trace ("Finally, I'm here");
```

We have four lines of code. Three of them are trace statements. The trace statement simply works by outputting to the output window whatever is in the brackets.

Let's try running this, and see what happens:

As we can see, the trace statements were outputted in the order that they were written in the ActionScript. Also, we created a 'variable' called 'age', and set it to the value '4'. Then when we did trace (age), the number 4 was displayed to the output window.

As the book progresses, we'll see the trace statement used in more helpful, necessary, unique and interesting ways. These will become more evident in coming chapters, as we make more contextual use of the trace statement. For now, it's just a good tool to be aware of, to understand and to recognize when the time comes.

In this chapter, we've learned some core concepts, and hopefully have an understanding of what an object is; especially when looking at all things in Flash MX as 'objects', and that they are merely extensions of the greater 'Object' of the whole. We'll see this in use soon.

Four

Quantitative Info

What's in this chapter:

- ★ Variables
    - ★ Simple variables
    - ★ Math
    - ★ Data types
        - ★ Strings
        - ★ Numbers
- ★ More about variable values
    - ★ Multiple variables
    - ★ Changing the value or data type
- ★ Local and global variables
- ★ Objects and variables
    - ★ Using properties
    - ★ Variables in objects
    - ★ Methods and parameters
- ★ Using variables with a method

Variables

In the last chapter, we finished off by seeing that the Trace window could 'read back to us' information in our ActionScript. Perhaps not very impressive in itself, but it gave us a glimpse of a very important part of creating scripts: **variables**. In short, variables are containers for data.

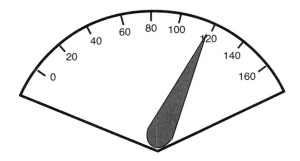

In a car, for example, there are a lot of variables of different types:

The speed on the speedometer, which can be any number between 0 and the car's top speed.

★ By the same token, the fuel gauge could be another numerical measurement, although this time it goes from 100% to 0 as the tank empties.

★ Other things can be described in terms of on and off, like the handbrake.

★ Some things in the car have a variety of possible settings. For instance, an automatic gearshift can be in Neutral, Park, Reverse, Second, or Drive.

★ Or a car could be "set" to something specific. The car might be called 'Brian'.

Simple variables

At its most basic level a variable is simply a piece of information that doesn't have to stay the same. The real advantages of variables lie in how you can use them in your ActionScript. A speedometer, after all, is not the same thing as the actual speed a car is traveling at. It gauges the speed (the variable) and displays it to the driver.

1. For now, we'll use trace to do that for us. Open a new FLA and type in this code (or use ch04example00.fla):

```
speed = 0;
trace(speed);
```

2. Test the movie using Control > Test Movie or CTRL/⌘ + ENTER.

3. The Output window should appear with a solitary 0 in it. The result of your trace.

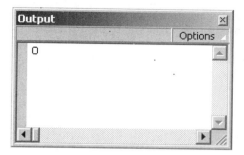

4. If we add two more lines below, we can change the value of the 'speed' variable like this.

```
speed = 0;
trace(speed);
speed = 20;
trace(speed);
```

5. Now when we run our test we should see the results of our second trace displayed too.

Math

All very clever, but for the moment this is quite a long-winded way of getting ActionScript to write out numbers. Where variables really come into their own is where they are changed to another value. In the long run we'll be attaching this to aspects of the user interface. For example, pressing an accelerator button on the Stage would increase the 'speed' variable.

This is sometimes called **evaluating** and it works like this:

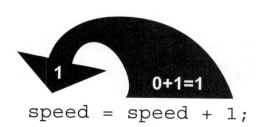

```
speed = speed + 1;
```

Here we are declaring the new speed value to be the old value plus 1. If speed started at 0, it would now be 1. It is important to note here that speed + 1 is evaluated before its output. Variables are always *first* evaluated on the right hand side of the equation.

1. To see for yourself, type out the following code into the first frame of a new FLA (or use `ch04example01.fla`):

```
speed = 0;
trace(speed);
speed = speed + 1;
trace(speed);
speed = speed + 1;
trace(speed);
```

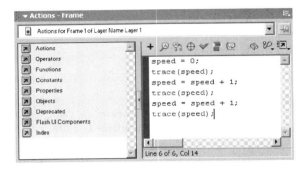

2. Test the movie using CTRL/⌘ + ENTER.

3. The Output window will report the value of the *speed* variable each time the trace action is made, like this:

Data types and the variable

Although variables are very useful as mathematical figures, they are by no means limited to them. To get an idea of the flexibility, consider Charlene's situation in our garage. You have taken your car into the garage for a tune-up and oil change. While she checks out your car, she needs to remember certain things about the state of your car when it comes in. For example, how much fuel is in the tank, so the garage doesn't waste money topping it up later!

She uses a ready-prepared sheet to make notes about your engine, mileage, and other things her cash-obsessed manager Rufus thought would be useful when he prepared the sheet.

Names and values

Variables are pieces of temporary data that you *store* in an application. These values can be deleted, changed, or just left alone. Variables are stored in the movie, and can be referenced at any time. The data can change or be deleted when it is necessary. A variable has a name, which is assigned (contains) a value. You might hear these referred to as name/value pairs. You should note that the name of a variable does not change, but the value can.

Therefore, when Charlene tests out your car, she'll make a few notes:

Charlene's notes here are a lot like setting variables. The total distance the car has traveled will always be called the mileage, but the value might change. In ActionScript we'd define this as a variable just as we did earlier. What about some of the other points that were made on the list? OK, fuel's easy – we can think of that as a number too because 0.5 is the same as a half.

mileage	*125000*
fuel	*half full*
tire brand	*Goodyear*
condition	*Not good*
tires flat	*no*

```
mileage = 125000;
fuel = 0.5;
```

But then we have 'tire brand' and 'condition'. They can be variables too, but there are a couple of problems. Firstly, we've used two words to write 'tire brand', which simply won't work because there is a space in between the two words. Variables should not contain any characters other than letters, numbers or underscores. Also, you cannot start a variable with a number.

You should not use the following variables:

```
Tire brand = goodyear;

4brand = goodyear;

_tires = goodyear;

*tires = goodyear;
```

Also, you cannot have any spaces in your variable. To simulate two words, it is common practice to alter the capitalization in a variable, or even use an underscore within the word: such as, `my_tire` or `myTire`. Usually programmers will alternate capitalization when naming variables, and underscores when using suffixes for code hinting (as discussed in **Chapter 2**). Try typing the following into your Actions panel:

```
myTire_mc = mc1;

myTire_xml = new XML();
```

After you type the _ and then the designated suffix, you will notice a code hint pop-up in the Script pane.

And finally, never use *keywords* as variable names. These are the words that make up ActionScript (pre-defined objects, constants, operators; essentially, anything that turns blue in the Script pane). You will probably run into problems if you use one of these words as a variable somewhere down the road.

In this case, we'll call our last two variables names that don't break the rules, even if Rufus didn't!

```
tireBrand = "Goodyear";
condition = not_good;
tireFlat = false;
```

Keen eyed readers will have spotted a couple more changes here (in the form of quotation marks and 'no' becoming 'false') which will become clear as you read about data types below.

It is good practice to give your variables descriptive names. For example, if you named a variable c, it might be difficult for you (or others working with your file) to remember that c represented a windshield wiper.

Data types

Variables, as well as storing numbers, are quite capable of storing special kinds of values or longer text (**strings**). These are different kinds of data, but perhaps the most common kinds of data stored in variables. Strings and number values which do not change when you use them in your movie are sometimes called *literals*.

Strings

Strings are the most flexible kind of variable, and can contain anything you want to put in between a set of quotation marks. In a variable with the name 'condition', we can store a whole sentence (although admittedly not a very eloquent one in this example).

```
condition = "Not Good";
```

We can also reference another string, if it is already defined in another variable. For example:

```
status = "Not Good";
condition = status;
```

The value of `condition` would then become the string `Not Good`, because it is written between quotation marks when `status` is defined.

Just to try it out, open a new movie and enter the following code into the Script pane of the Actions panel:

```
condition = "Not Good";
trace(condition);
```

After you have finished typing, test your movie by pressing CTRL/⌘ + ENTER. The Output window will open, and you will see:

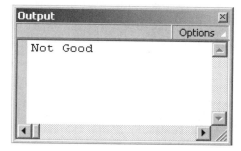

This means that the value of 'condition' variable is 'Not Good'. Notice how it does not have quotations around it – the quotes are part of the code that delimitates the string, not part of the string itself.

However, if you tried tracing the following code instead:

```
status = "Not Good";
condition = "status";
trace(condition);
```

The Output window would instead return:

```
status
```

As you can see, quotation marks make a lot of difference!

That means that if you try using double quotation marks (") within a string, it will think the first set you use is the end of the string

String

condition = "to call it "old" is too mild.",

Therefore, the rest of your text intended to be a string will **not** be treated as one. In the above figure, your string would start with 'to' and end with the space after 'it'. It is for this reason that you have to do one of four things:

★ Avoid using double quotation marks inside the string

★ Use single quotation marks inside the string

★ Escape the quotation marks

★ Use single quotation marks around the string and double quotation marks within it:

Try typing the following into the Script pane:

```
condition = 'to call it "old" is too mild.'
trace(condition);
```

Returns 'to call it "old" is too mild.'

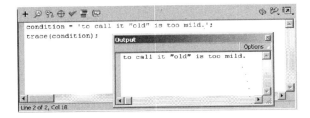

You could also *escape* the quotation marks. You would do this if you wanted to use double quotation marks. You would need to do the following:

```
myString = "it is a really \"old\"
truck";
```

Numbers

We have already seen numbers. Here is another pitfall to avoid though – remember not to put quotation marks around a numerical value, or it will become a string.

```
carWheels = "4";
spareWheels = 1;
totalWheels = carWheels + spareWheels;
trace(totalWheels);
```

In this code, the number '4' will be treated like a string. When we try and test it, the trace will simply stick the two figures together rather than add them.

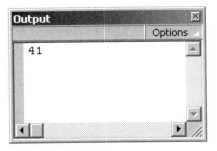

Why? Well, we already know that a string is treated as text. If you were to try and add a number to another written as text, it just wouldn't work. So, the most sensible thing to do is just to stick them together. ActionScript does just that, and it's called **concatenating** the strings.

Exactly the same thing happens if we try to stick any strings together:

```
myString = "old" + "bad" + "car";
trace (myString);
```

This returns 'oldbadcar' in the Output window.

If we wanted to get around the problem, we could use the global *Number* function, which is used to convert a non-numerical value into a number in the following form:

```
carWheels = "4";
spareWheels = 1;
totalWheels = Number(carWheels) +
spareWheels;
trace(totalWheels);
```

Now try testing your movie by pressing CTRL/⌘+ENTER. The Output window shows the number 5! The reason is that the `Number()` function takes the value between its brackets and converts it into a number data type. Of course, you can still fool it – it only works if the string is only made of numerical characters! Check out what happens:

Booleans, undefined, null and newline

Booleans, `undefined`, `null`, and `newline` have constant values – they do not change and are consistent across all instances. For example, in Math *pi* represents a specific value, or "thing". *pi* does not change in your equations – it is *always* one particular value every time it is used. Variables can have any one of these constants as their value.

Booleans are very common in ActionScript, as they only pass the value of either `true` or `false`. True and `false` are *keywords* because Flash recognizes them as particular values. Using a Boolean can be useful when a property can be one of two different things. For example, you might have a variable called `tireFlat`, indicating whether or not a tire is flat. There are only two possible choices: `true` (it is flat) or `false` (it is not). Therefore, you might use `true` or `false` to indicate the status of the tire.

Then, you can write your code which will work in a particular way based on this value:

```
if(tireFlat==true){
    gotoAndPlay("thegarage");
}
```

which could also be written as:

```
if (tireFlat){
    gotoAndPlay("thegarage");
}
```

This condition uses `true` to execute the `gotoAndPlay` action. As you can probably see, there are many situations where these values would be useful in our garage.

Another example of a constant is **newline**. Newline is used to break text into separate lines in a text field. This is commonly used when you are concatenating text (adding Strings together) in a text field, and need the Strings to start on a line below the previous one. `Newline` is another *keyword* Flash understands.

`Undefined` and `null` are also constants which can be used as values. These constants can also be used to check if a value has been assigned to a variable. If a variable does not have a value, `undefined` is returned.

Let's first take a look at `undefined`. You may have declared a variable, but no value has been assigned to it:

```
var tires;
trace (tires);
```

This would then return 'undefined', since there is no value given to the `tires` variable name.

Now let's take a look at the `newline` constant. In this example, we will break what would have been one line of text into two separate lines when it is returned.

1. Create a new movie, and enter the following ActionScript onto frame 1 on the main timeline:

```
myString = "The truck is broken" +
newline + "I need to take it to the
garage.";
```

2. Create a dynamic text field on the Stage, and in the Property inspector give it an instance name *myText*. Then in order to have this appear in a text field, you need to assign *myString* to a text field instance name: *myText.text*. This is done in a line of code following the above, also entered onto frame 1 of the main timeline:

```
myText.text = myString;
```

Test your movie. In the dynamic text field, your text will look similar to the following:

```
The truck is broken
I need to take it to the garage.
```

my TextField

Refer to the example file `textfield_04.fla` for a demonstration using `newline`.

Multiple variables sharing a value

Variables can also share a similar value. For instance, you might have several cars in a lot, which are different models but share the same color: blue. This could be expressed in the following line of code:

```
car1 = car2 = car3 = blue;
```

This is a shorthand way of assigning each variable its own value (which happens to be the same string or amount, and so on), which would have taken three separate lines. The values are not permanently linked, as you can see in this code (`ch04example02.fla`):

```
car1 = car2 = car3 = "blue";
trace("Car 1 is: " + car1 + ", Car 2
is: " + car2 + ", Car 3 is: " + car3);
car2 = "red";
trace("Car 1 is: " + car1 + ", Car 2
is: " + car2 + ", Car 3 is: " + car3);
```

The Output window (and note the use of concatenation to make the output easier to understand) will show this:

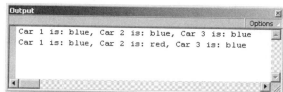
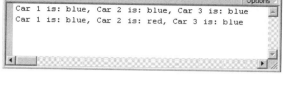

```
Car 1 is: blue, Car 2 is: blue, Car 3 is: blue
Car 1 is: blue, Car 2 is: red, Car 3 is: blue
```

Changing the value or data type of your variable

You can change the value of a variable by simply assigning a new value to it. For example, the mileage in your vehicle will change between tune-ups. The name 'mileage' does not need to change (nor can it!), but the value assigned to it needs to update. We can do this in ActionScript in the following way:

```
mileage = 10029;
mileage = 15899;
trace (mileage);
```

If you entered this code into the Actions panel, when you test the movie, you would have an output of:

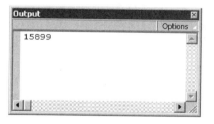

```
15899
```

This is because the variable mileage is assigned a new value. Therefore, when the variable is traced, the new value is returned.

ActionScript also allows you to update variables using a different data type. For example, you could change mileage into a boolean, array, object or string. You could type the following into the Script pane:

```
mileage = 10029;   //value is a number
mileage = "10029 KM";   //value is now a
string
trace (mileage);
```

Which would result in the following Output:

The data type has changed from a number into a string, "10029 KM". ActionScript automatically performs the conversion for you.

```
10029 KM
```

You can also write the same thing by adding a string to a numerical value. Type the following into the Script pane:

```
mileage = 10029 + " KM";
trace(mileage);
```

In the Output window, you should see the same text as in the previous screenshot:

```
10029 KM
```

Note how we have inserted a space before "KM". Had we not done this, the string would be "stuck" to the number next to it. This is a commonly used method for displaying variables and strings together within text fields.

Local and global variables

In **Chapter 2**, we learned about the different levels and timelines in a Flash movie. Movies loaded into different levels and movie clips have their own timelines. Variables, and how you use them, are affected by this structure. Where and how variables are created affect how you access them, or if they are accessible at all!

There are two other ways you can use variables apart from putting them on the timeline (timeline variables) as we have done so far. You can specifically have them as local variables, or global variables. These variables exist in your movie in a slightly different way than a timeline variable. This section will show you how.

Imagine Rufus's Garage, which is full of workers who perform varying shifts. There is always a manager on duty whenever the garage is open. Rufus the manager can get called in to perform his task in any area of the garage, at any time. This is like the global variable, which is accessible to every timeline (although, does not run on its own) and can be called in anywhere.

Then, you have the general part-time workers. They have their own schedules, and run for the duration of their shift performing their tasks when called for during their shift. These are like variables you might find along a particular timeline, called timeline variables. Lastly, you have employees who are only involved in specialized tasks. You have Jimmy, who only paints the racing stripes, and then leaves. This is like a local variable within a function: existing for the duration of the function and then deleted.

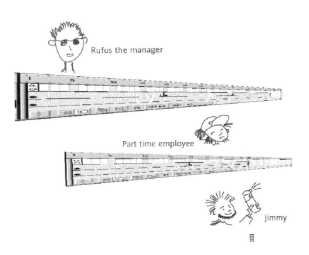

Rufus the manager

Part time employee

Jimmy

Global variables

Using global variables can be very helpful when you are programming your movies. These variables exist across all of the timelines in your Flash application (including different levels), just like a garage manager is in charge of the entire shop. Therefore, these variables can be accessed by all timelines in Flash anywhere in the movie.

You should also note that _global is *not a timeline* existing with your movie. _global is a repository of all the pre-determined objects, and your _global variables and objects which you call at any time during your movie, from any timeline. Pre-determined objects include the `MovieClip` and `Stage` objects. So just like objects such as these, you can access _global variables in all areas of your movie.

Global variables are simply prefixed with _global, as in the following:

```
_global.tires
```

As long as you have this prefix, the variable will be global. Therefore, the

```
_global.tires = 4;
```

variable will be accessible during the entire movie across any timeline, on any level, and on any frame after it downloads.

Global variables are used when you need to have one variable across an entire application, and only one copy of this information is required. A global variable might not be useful if you only need a variable once during a particular function. It shouldn't be used for loops within functions, which should be contained within the function while it is executing as opposed to continually on a timeline using up memory.

The _global level (accessible to all timelines) makes it a lot *easier* to reference. In **Chapter 2**, we spoke about dot notation and levels. You can probably remember how we had to target instances using _root, and a subsequent path to the instance specifically such as

```
_root.truck.engine.fuel_injector.
```

However, it is a lot easier when a variable is global! Instead of having to find it using a specific path using _root or _level0, you can simply have to reference _global.variableName. Such as:

```
_global.fuel_injector;
```

or just:

```
fuel_injector
```

> *You have to be very careful not to define two variables of the same name in your movie. For example, if you have set a variable* _global.fuel_injector=true; *on the main timeline, and then set it anywhere else (such as* fuel_injector=true; *in a movie clip) you will have trouble with your code since the variable has been set twice. It's a bit like a demarcation dispute between Larry the mechanic and Jimmy the painter.*
>
> *One idea is to adopt a naming scheme for your global variables, say by attaching a 'g' for global (or a different letter you will remember consistently) onto the variable name:*
>
> ```
> _global.gfuel_injector;
> ```

Local variables and _global variables with the same name will work alongside one another as long as you always reference _global.tires with _global included in your reference. However, it is not good practice to call global and local variables by the same name. For example:

```
_global.tires = none;
var tires = 2;
```

The 'global tires' can still be traced, using _global.tires, and Flash will output 'none'. If you trace tires, the output will still be 2.

It is recommended, and good coding practice, to take care to **name all of your variables differently.** Otherwise, it is very easy to get confused when calling a variable when multiple variables have the same name.

Local variables

Local variables are like our racing stripe guy, Jimmy, who only comes in for his very particular task. Local variables are only available to your Flash movie during the execution of the function (or script) they are located within. After the script has finished running, the variable is removed from memory.

In order to create a local variable, you must use the Flash keyword **var** before the variable name. Instead of:

```
myTire = 4;
```

you would type:

```
var myTire = 4;
```

If you need to access the local (or regular timeline) variable on a different level or timeline, you will need to target it using a path. For example, if `myTire` were in a movie clip called axle on the `_root`, you would target it as follows:

```
_root.axle.myTire
```

It is a good idea to use local variables whenever possible if you are concerned about excessive use of RAM or memory. Some people make a practice of using local variables in their code. Also, if a variable is only required for a function, it is best to use a local variable. When the function is finished, the variable will be deleted.

If a variable is set without a `var` preceding it, or a `_global` prefix, it is considered to be a *timeline variable*. Timeline variables are a lot like global variables in that they can be accessed across timelines. However, global variables can be accessed at any time during the application, even if a timeline ends (such as with a variable in a movie clip that is deleted).

When you call a variable in a timeline, you will want to make sure it has already been set (set in a previous frame along the timeline, or using the correct load order). If the variable has not been set when it is called from somewhere else, 'undefined' will be returned.

Try this out by creating a new movie (or using `ch04example03.fla`):

1. Create a layer called 'actions' and in frame 1 add the code:

   ```
   trace("Frame one trace: ");
   trace(myTire);
   trace("with dot notation: ");
   trace(_root.axel_mc.myTire);
   ```

2. Now copy this code for the next four frames on the timeline. Remember to change the text in the first line of the trace, so that it reads 'Frame **two** trace', 'Frame **three** trace' and so on.

3. Add a fifth frame with a stop action:

   ```
   stop();
   ```

4. Draw a small shape on the Stage and change it into a movie clip by pressing F8. Call the instance 'axle_mc'. In the first frame of that movie clip add the script:

   ```
   myTire = "Goodyear";
   ```

5. Now return to the root timeline by clicking on the 'Scene 1' button under the timeline.

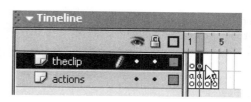

6. Add a new layer to the main timeline, above the actions layer. Add a keyframe in frame 2 of that layer by pressing F6, then F5 for a subsequent frame.

7. Press F11 to open the Library window and drag an instance of your axle movie clip into your newly created second frame. A small crosshair, or whatever shape you put in it, will represent the movie clip.

8. Name that instance of the movie clip 'axle_mc' using the properties dialog.

9. Your timeline should look like this...

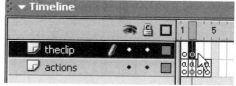

10. ...if it does, run our movie (CTRL/⌘ + ENTER). You should see that only one of your traces returns a value, frame 3 *with* dot notation.

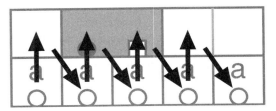

```
Output                                    ✕
                                    Options ▾
  Frame one trace:
  undefined
  with dot notation:
  undefined
  Frame two trace:
  undefined
  with dot notation:
  undefined
  Frame three trace:
  undefined
  with dot notation:
  Goodyear
  Frame four trace:
  undefined
  with dot notation:
  undefined
```

This depends on your Publish Settings, but by default Flash loads the frames from the bottom layer up. Our example above works like this:

So, in the first frame, there is no value in our 'myTire' variable as it's not been set. Also, in the second there is no value because Flash comes to the script in the lower layer first. In the third frame we get a value. By the fourth the movie clip is over in the timeline, so there is nothing again, nothing in the upper layer of that row and a stop action at the end.

1. Open a new movie, and create three layers: 'buttons', 'trace' and 'variables'. Make sure that 'buttons' is the bottom layer, 'variables' is the middle layer and 'trace' is the top layer. Then, make keyframes on frames 1, 5 and 10 on all three layers.

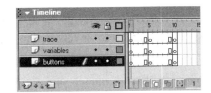

2. Select the 'buttons' layer. Open Window > Common Libraries > Buttons and drag an instance of a button onto the Stage at frames 1 and 5. We are going to place our code on the button, so it does not get confused with what we are doing in our traces for this exercise.

3. Select button1 on frame 1, open the Actions panel, and type the following code into the Script pane.

```
on (release) {
  gotoAndStop(5);
}
```

Then select the button on frame 5, open the Actions panel, and type the following code:

```
on (release){
  gotoAndStop(10);
}
```

As you know, this code will move our movie to each frame. The next step is that we want to create traces which will trace our movie as soon as the playhead reaches the frame. In order to achieve this, we want our traces to be on frame actions.

4. Select frame 1 of the variables layer, and enter the following code:

```
myVariable1 = "variable on frame 1";
```

Now go to frame 5 of this layer and enter:

```
myVariable2 = "variable on frame 5";
```

5. Select frame 1 of the trace layer, and enter the following code:

```
stop();
trace(myVariable1);
trace(myVariable2);
```

Now go to frames 5 and 10 and enter the same code for both frames. The stop action will stop our movie on each frame, and we will be tracing the variables we are setting:

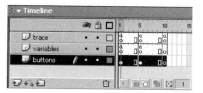

6. The final step is to make sure your Publish settings are set to the top-down load prder under the Flash tab.

7. Now test your movie. The first trace will output 'undefined' for each variable in the first set. Neither variables on frame 1 or frame 5 exist yet. Press the button, and you will notice that our variable set in frame 1. The final frame will reveal that both variables are traced in the final frame, as both have loaded.

8. Finally, switch the order of the variable and trace layers and note the changes it makes to your trace output. This is how the ordering of your layers makes a difference in your set variables!

Objects and variables

In **Chapter 3** you were introduced to objects. You learned to think of objects as things which contain certain variables. Objects are the things lying in and around our truck in the garage, and the variables describe these objects. Also, objects can contain other objects (which could be considered to be like a variable itself).

Objects can be predetermined, which means they are already written into Flash. These "pre-made" objects in Flash include Sound, Math, MovieClip, XML and so on. These objects are considered to be _global, and contain established sets of methods and properties. You probably have already heard of some of them, like MovieClip._visible, and MovieClip.gotoAndPlay(). We will consider properties and methods in relation to variables that we have explored earlier in this chapter.

Using object properties

An object contains certain elements that describe the various facets of that particular object. These are known as the *properties* of an object. Things usually have different ways to describe the various attributes that identify an object: such as size, color, speed and the like.

For example, you can create a new object:

```
myTire = new Object();
```

We have many variables which can be used to describe this car, such as color, size, make, and model. It is very easy to use a variable to describe one of these aspects of the car:

```
myTire.radius;
```

This is where myTire is an **object**, and 'radius' is a **property** of the object myTire. Then, you can add a value to this property:

```
myTire.radius = 15;
```

The property radius is assigned a **value**: 15. Therefore, we are using the familiar format of object.property = value.

Furthermore, these values can change. Type the following into the Script pane:

```
myTire = new Object();
myTire.radius = 15;
myTire.radius +=5;
trace(myTire.radius);
```

In the Output window you will see: 20.

The value assigned to a property can change during its existence on the timeline. Some of the predetermined objects have properties which assign values to _x and _y co-ordinates. These properties can continually change (or stay the same!) during their existence on a timeline. You might be familiar with instances that follow the mouse cursor. These rely on the _x and _y coordinates of the mouse object (which is *listening t*o the cursor placement). These properties change to a new value each frame. We will look more at the mouse object in **Chapter 6**.

Variables within objects

As we learned in an earlier exercise, we can use properties to describe various aspects of an object. However, an object not only contains different properties, but it can also contain other objects containing properties of their own.

Therefore, we have a car which has a make, model, color and so on. However, we also have many objects within this car as well, which include *engine*, *muffler*, and *gas tank*. These objects are like variables of the car, and each of these variable objects also contains variables of their own.

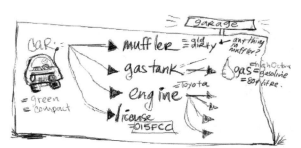

We can create a new object, and then within this object create a second. Type the following code into the Actions panel:

```
myCar = new Object();
//create a new object
myCar.engine = new Object();    //create
engine within myCar
myCar.engine.size = "V8";        //assign
value to property "size"
```

In this code, you are creating a new object inside of an existing one called 'myCar'. As you can see, we have to create a path to the new object we are creating, so it exists inside 'myCar'. This is why we create the path `myCar.engine` instead of just creating a new object with `engine = new Object();`

Now, try tracing the following:

```
trace("Engine = " + engine);
trace("myCar = " + myCar);
```

Press Ctrl/⌘+Enter to test your movie. The first trace, for 'engine', reveals nothing. However, try tracing 'myCar'. Now we can see that we have a 'myCar' object here, but not an engine.

Now try tracing inside the 'myCar' object:

```
trace("myCar.engine = " +
myCar.engine);
```

Test your movie again. Now you have found an object! It is inside the 'myCar' object instance. Refer to the example file `ch04example04.fla` for this example.

The engine object is within the 'myCar' object, and contains its own `size` variable. It is just a matter of using the correct path to assign properties and values. Remember that, in dot notation, the path will always go from general (the car object) to specific (the engine's size) just like in our diagram and example above.

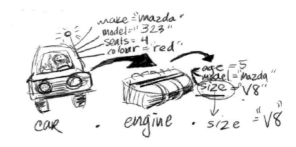

What are methods?

Methods are written in generally the same way as variables and properties. Because of this, we should take a quick look at what they are – just so we don't confuse them with the kind of code we have just gone through!

It is easiest to think of methods as something that makes the object and its properties perform a particular operation. For example, a property would describe what the color of the car is; whereas a method would be a set of instructions used for Jimmy to apply the racing stripes to the outside of the vehicle.

We write methods pretty much the same way as we write variables and properties. You might be familiar with some of the basic predetermined methods available to Flash. `gotoAndStop();` ,and `gotoAndPlay();` are two very common methods used all the time by programmers. These are instructions about where to move the playhead.

We can apply a method to an object by using the following formula:

```
object.method();
```

Therefore, our 'myCar' could have `go` or `stop` methods applied to it in the following way:

```
myCar.go();
```

or:

```
myCar.stop();
```

As above, methods have double parentheses (braces) following the method name. With information in between these parentheses, you can tell 'myCar' where you want it to 'go' to. In the next section we will look at parameters, which can sometimes be inserted within the set of parentheses.

1. Open a new movie and create a keyframe on frames 1, 5 and 10. Enter static text numbers on each frame indicating what frame number the frame is at. Call this layer *graphics*:

2. Go to Window > Common Libraries > Buttons, and drag a button instance onto the stage at frame 1. Give this button an instance name of *button1*. Drag a button instance onto frame 5 and give it an instance name *button2*.

3. Create a new layer, and call it actions. Select frame 1 of this layer, and enter the following action into the Script pane of the Actions panel:

```
stop();
_root.button1.onRelease = function()
{
    _root.gotoAndStop(5);
};
```

Then go to frame 5, and enter the following code onto the actions layer:

```
stop();
_root.button2.onRelease = function()
{
    _root.gotoAndStop(10);
};
```

Finally, go to frame 10 and enter the following action:

```
stop();
```

4. Test your movie. Try pressing the buttons. These `gotoAndStop()` and `gotoAndPlay()` methods are controlling the playhead on the main time-line. Then on frame 10 we have the `stop()` method stopping our movie. Refer to `ch04example05.fla` for the entire example file.

What are parameters?

Parameters are a certain value you put in between the parentheses of a method. Not every method will accept a parameter, and if it does it must be understandable to the method itself. So you have to know the kinds of value (for example, string, Boolean, number, or even object) that can go between the parentheses.

This is much like a gas pedal used to accelerate the car. When the gas pedal is pressed, it is pressed a certain amount, depending on how fast the user wishes to accelerate. The amount the user presses must be passed to the gas pedal in a certain amount (a numerical value). It could be represented as follows:

```
myCar.pressPedal(5);
```

A parameter is therefore a value that the method will use to perform its function. The method (or function) will be coded so it will understand the kind of values it has been passed. You should also be aware that certain methods will accept more than one kind of value.

Let's look at a very simple, and well-known, method:

```
myCar.gotoAndStop("lastFrame");
```

We are passing a string, 'lastFrame', to the `gotoAndStop()` method. This method will take the frame label `"lastFrame"` as the directions of where to take the playhead in a Flash movie. You could also pass a numerical value (a frame number) to this method as well:

```
myCar.gotoAndStop(15);
```

Not only this, but you can also form this method in a different way. If you worked with scenes, you would separate two strings using a comma delimiter.

1. Create a new movie, and go to Insert > Scene. You will now have a new scene in your movie. Go to Window > Scene to open the panel which will show you the two scenes. Double-click on each scene to rename them scene_one and scene_two.

2. On the first frame of each scene, place a simple graphic (perhaps a number 1 on scene 1, and the number 2 on scene 2). This is so you can tell which scene you are on.

3. On scene 1 place a button from Window > Common Libraries > Buttons. Give this button an instance name 'myButton'.

4. Create a new layer, and call it 'actions'. Enter the following code:

```
stop();
_root.myButton.onRelease = function(){
  gotoAndStop("scene_two","frame_one");
};
```

5. Go to the clapperboard on the timeline panel, and navigate to scene 2.

Select frame 1 on the main timeline, and go to the Property inspector. Give this frame a frame label name *frame_one*.

Test your movie by pressing CTRL/⌘+ENTER. Now, the playhead will move to a scene called 'scene_two' to the frame labeled 'frame_one'. Refer to `ch04example06.fla` for a full example.

Using variables with methods or functions

Variables play an important role in how functions, methods and objects work. Functions execute some code in your Flash movie. However, functions are reusable. You give a function a name, and when you call that name it will execute from its central location. You can pass variables into functions so they can use the data while they execute. Sometimes the function needs to know *what* to do, or what information to work with. This is why variables are used: to provide the function with this data.

Since functions are discussed in depth in **Chapter 10**, we will simply cover how to use variables with a method of the String object at this point. We will use a very simple example which should already look familiar to you.

For this example, you can either open the sample FLA called `string_04.fla`, or type the code into a new movie on frame 1 of the main timeline.

We will create a variable with a value which is a String:

```
myString = "this is A STRING";
```

Next, we will pass the value of 'myString' into the new `stringObj` object.

```
stringObj = new String(myString);
```

Finally, we will trace the method `toLowerCase` to see how all text in the 'myString' string has been changed to lower case characters:

```
trace(stringObj.toLowerCase());
```

This method is a method belonging to the pre-defined String object. You may notice that we actually have an extra line of code here. If you comment out the second line of code (where we create a new String object) the trace will still work properly if you change the third line to:

```
trace(myString.toLowerCase());
```

This is because the string initially created is already recognized as a String. As long as you are dealing with strings only, you should not require the second line of ActionScript.

For a working example of this code, refer to `string_04.fla`.

Summary

In this chapter we learned:

★ What variables are in relation to a Flash movie.

★ How to create variables for use in a Flash timeline.

★ How to determine what kinds of data types we can use for a value.

★ How to use local and global variables in a Flash movie.

★ How to target variables on different timelines.

★ How to work with parameters, properties, methods and functions.

Jimmy the body worker

What's in this chapter:

★ Introducing Jimmy.

★ Drawing dynamic graphics.

★ Understanding color mixing.

★ Using the Color object to solidly fill.

★ Using the Color object and transform to tint and shade.

★ Using the Color object to fill and shade components of movie clips.

★ The Paint-O-Rama 3000.

★ Drawing shapes dynamically.

★ Understanding the methods of the drawing API.

★ Understanding `curveTo`.

Introducing Jimmy

There was a man named Jimmy. He dreamt of one day becoming a great painter, roaming the banks of the Seine, creating great masterpieces as he went. Then, one day, someone reminded him that it was 2002, not 1802, and that the days of the classic painter were all but gone.

So Jimmy headed off in search of a new, contemporary means of expression. It was then that he came across Rufus, the owner of a state-of-the-art automotive garage. Rufus was sitting on a wooden box outside his garage, looking sad and dejected. Jimmy, being a concerned individual, asked Rufus what was wrong. Rufus explained that his recent auto-body artist had been tragically crushed under a stack of 10,000 duplicate wrenches.

Feeling sad, while at the same time recognizing a terrific opportunity, Jimmy explained that he knew a thing or two about art, and could most definitely perform the duties of an auto-body artist.

Encouraged, Rufus said, "Really? Step into my garage and show me what you can do!"

Dynamic graphics

In Flash MX, we can draw and create simple and complex images using the draw tools and the color palette. However, what happens if we want to create images, shapes and colors 'on the fly', with ActionScript, instead of pre-drawing them?

That's where Jimmy comes in.

Jimmy is the master of all things dynamically drawn and colored. Before we get into the specifics of the code, we must first make sure we understand how 'paint' is mixed in this garage.

Color mixing

Every color, shade, scale and tint of paint used in this garage is derived by mixing exact amounts of the three 'primary' paint colors; red, green and blue.

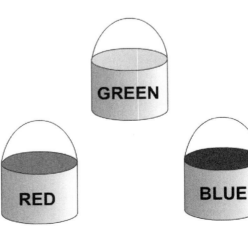

Most artists know that the primary colors of paint are red, yellow and blue, but in this garage, things are a little different. Because the garage exists in the Flash MX digital world, our colors are based on the mixing colors of light, not paint.

When it's time for Jimmy to order up a color from the paint machine, he must specify what color he wants by specifying the mix of the primary red, green and blue. All the colors in the visible spectrum are available to him using this means. Each primary color ranges from 0 to 255, meaning there are 256 possible values for each primary color. This means that, when they're combined, there is a palette of 16,777,216 possible colors (256 x 256 x 256)

Now, there's one catch: colors must be specified as a neatly combined number, which is the result of the red, green, and blue amounts combined. Something like this:

    0xRRGGBB

What's that? Well, Jimmy walks up to the paint machine, and keys in the eight-digit paint code, starting with "0x" and then followed by the double-digit amounts of R, G and B.

So, if each primary color goes from 0 to 255, then how come there are only two digits specified for each color? Well, that's because our colors must be specified in the 16-based 'hexadecimal' numbering system, where numbers are counted not from 0 to 9 but from 0 to F. This means that where our largest 10-based double-digit number is 99, our largest double-digit hexadecimal number is FF.

Counting from 00 to FF takes some understanding of hexadecimal, and that can take some time to get your head around. Just remember that when counting up from 0, do it like this:

    00, 01, 02, 03, 04, 05, 06, 07, 08, 09,
    0A, 0B, 0C, 0D, 0E, 0F

Then, we have:

    10, 11, 12, 13, 14, 15, 16, 17, 18, 19,
    1A, 1B, 1C, 1D, 1E, 1F

This pattern will repeat until the last 16, which are:

    F0, F1, F2, F3, F4, F5, F6, F7, F8, F9,
    FA, FB, FC, FD, FE, FF

So, in the end, Jimmy will have the following for black:

    0x000000

for white:

    0xFFFFFF

for red:

    0xFF0000

for green:

    0x00FF00

for blue:

    0x0000FF

for yellow:

    0xFFFF00

for cyan (light blue):

    0x00FFFF

for magenta (purple):

    0xFF00FF

Every other color is an intricate combination of hexadecimal values. For example, a medium olive green is:

```
0x72AA24
```

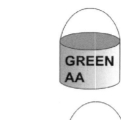

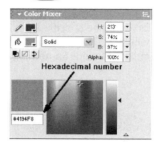

The best way to figure out these colors is to use the color mixer in the Flash MX design environment to pick your color, and then write down the hexadecimal number that appears in the lower-left hand corner of the window.

Flash will display it with a '#' at the beginning of it, but in ActionScript we must ignore the '#' and instead tack on a '0x' to the beginning. The difference between these two is simple: The '0x' prefix has been used for years in programming languages and is a programmers way of indicating a hexadecimal number, while the # has been used by web designers in HTML to indicate hexidecimally formatted colors. So, for us, the '0x' prefix tells Flash that the number immediately following is to be treated as a hexadecimal number, and not just a normal decimal number. For example, the following ActionScript:

```
a = 42;
trace (a);
```

will produce the following output:

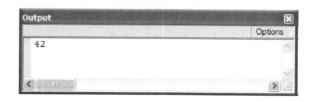

However, the following ActionScript:

```
a = 0x42;
trace (a);
```

will produce the following output:

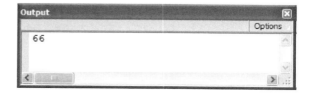

Notice that Flash traces out the decimal equivalent of the hexadecimal number, '0x42'. As mentioned before, using this combination there are 16,777,216 possible colors using 2-digit hexadecimal numbers. To prove this, look at the output of this code:

```
a = 0xFFFFFF;
trace (a);
```

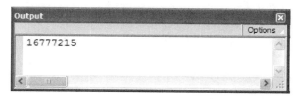

The highest color, white, corresponds to 0xFFFFFF or 16777215 in decimal. (The number is not 16777216, because that is the *total* number of colors, but they *span* from 0 to 16777215, which totals 16777216).

Jimmy's brushes

We've talked about the paint; we've talked about Jimmy, what's in between? The brushes, of course. Whenever Jimmy wants to paint something, he needs a brush. If Jimmy plans on painting more than one object, he needs more than one brush, because once a brush is dedicated to a particular object, it may not be reused.

What are we talking about here? We're talking about the Color object in Flash MX. The Color object is used to change the RGB values of any movie clip. The Color object is used by first "constructing" it, during which time you specify the movie clip to which it will apply.

Creating or constructing a Color object works with the following ActionScript code:

```
myColor = new Color(myMovieClip);
```

In this code, 'myColor' will be the name of the color object itself, and 'myMovieClip' would be the name of the movie clip to which color effects, changes and transformations will be applied. It could be thought of like this:

```
sixInchBrush1 = new Color(theHood);
```

where we're creating a new brush, and defining its application to be 'painting the hood of the car'. In Flash MX, we can also specify a 'timeline', instead of a movie clip. For example, we could say:

```
myColor = new Color(_level5);
```

or:

```
myColor = new Color(_root);
```

which would cause Flash to color all objects (graphics, buttons, movie clips) within a particular timeline.

Ok, let's give Jimmy some work - let's see this in action.

Dummy paint

It's Jimmy's first day, so his methods are somewhat crude as he learns the machinery and brushes. Consequently his paint job is a bit ... solid. What do we mean by that? Well, take a look at dumbpaint.fla.

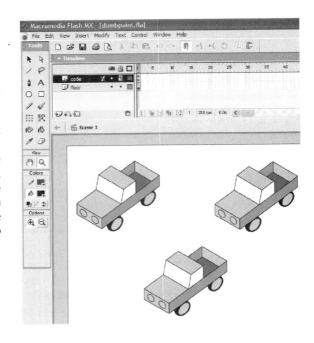

We have three trucks on the shop floor. Jimmy has been given the task of painting one black, one red, and the last one yellow. The trucks have the instance names truck1, truck2 and truck3. (As a reminder, the instance name of any movie clip is set in the Property inspector, which is activated by clicking on the movie clip, and pressing CTRL/⌘+F3.) Here's the code by which Jimmy will do his work (attached to frame 1 of the code layer):

```
c1 = new Color(truck1);
c2 = new Color(truck2);
c3 = new Color(truck3);

c1.setRGB(0x000000);
c2.setRGB(0xFF0000);
c3.setRGB(0xFFFF00);
```

First, we're creating three brushes, c1, c2 and c3. Notice that each brush is being attached to its own consecutive truck. Once these brushes are created, c1 will be used to paint truck1, c2 will be used to paint truck2 and c3 will be used to paint truck3.

Next, we use the setRGB method of the Color object. The setRGB method does one simple thing: it turns all solid areas in a movie clip into the color specified by setRGB. The effect? Let's put Jimmy to work by pressing CTRL/⌘+ENTER:

Those are some well-painted vehicles. One is solid black, the other is solid red, and the last one is solid yellow. However, the art of auto-body painting requires a greater attention to detail. And, we want our trucks to look a little less like solid cutout shapes, and more like painted trucks.

Smarty paints

Let's look at `smartypaint.fla`. From the outset, `smartypaint.fla` looks like `dumbpaint.fla`; three trucks on the stage, with actions on frame 1 of the code layer.

However, this time the actions are substantially different. Rather than use the `setRGB` method of the `Color` object, we're going to be using the `setTransform` method. The difference between `setRGB` and `setTransform` is simple: `setRGB` completely changes all solid areas to a specific color, while `setTransform` *modifies* the color of all solid areas. Essentially, `setTransform` will take a movie clip and increase or decrease its RGB values so that we're still able to see its details and lines, but on the whole it will change color.

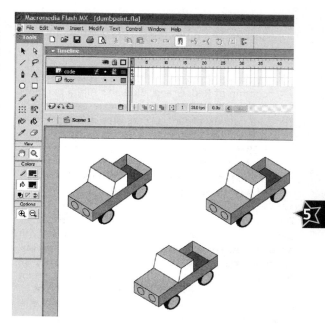

The `setTransform` method works like this:

```
myColor.setTransform(transformObject);
```

Notice the 'transformObject'? That's not a color. That's an object, which contains several values that will be used to modify, or "transform" the colors of a movie clip. The transform object is created like so:

```
transObj = new Object();

transObj.ra = 100;
transObj.ga = 100;
transObj.ba = 100;
transObj.aa = 100;
```

What's that? Those are percentage values – percentages of each color to maintain in the transformed movie clip.

1. Before we go on, let's try something. Click on a movie clip (any one of them will do) and open up the properties panel with CTRL/⌘+F3. At the far right portion of the panel, there's a drop-down menu next to the word 'Color'. From this menu, select Advanced, like so:

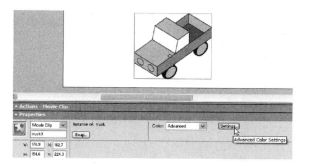

2. A button that is labeled 'Settings...' will appear. Click on this button now. We will then be presented with the 'Advanced Effect' box:

3. In the left column, we can see that there is a column of Red, Green, Blue and Alpha percentages. In the right column, we can see that there is a column of Red, Green, Blue and Alpha offsets. The percentages work by scaling the RGB/A values of any movie clip by a certain percentage, while the offsets work by merely *adding to* or *subtracting from* the RGB/A values of any movie clip.

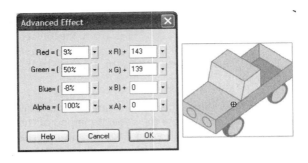

This dialog box has exactly the same effect as `setTransform`, only `setTransform` does it with ActionScript. For example, if `ra` was set to 100, but `ga` and `ba` were set to 0, then we'd be saying 'keep all red values in the movie clip while discarding green and blue'. Since every color is made up of a combination of red, green and blue, the effect this would have would be to tint the entire movie clip into nice shades of red. It is also possible to set any of these values to a number greater than 100, which will have the effect of brightening up a particular R, G or B component of the colors. This is just like our left column of the Advanced Effect box.

The 'aa' value is to specify the amount of alpha to maintain. The alpha value refers to the semitransparency of the movie clip. Look at this:

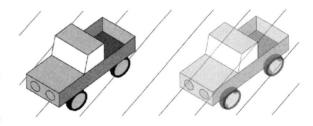

The left truck has an alpha value of 100%, while the right truck has an alpha value of 50%.

Lets look at the code attached to frame 1 of the code layer:

```
c1 = new Color(truck1);
c1obj = new Object();
c1obj.ra = 30;
c1obj.ga = 30;
c1obj.ba = 30;
c1.setTransform(c1obj);

c2 = new Color(truck2);
c2obj = new Object();
c2obj.ra = 100;
c2obj.ga = 0;
c2obj.ba = 0;
c2.setTransform(c2obj);
```

```
c3 = new Color(truck3);
c3obj = new Object();
c3obj.ra = 100;
c3obj.ga = 100;
c3obj.ba = 0;
c3.setTransform(c3obj);
```

We're creating three Color objects, each of which are attached to a truck. However, since we're using the `setTransform` method, this time we're creating three generic objects: `c1obj`, `c2obj` and `c3obj`.

In the first example, we're setting the `ra`, `rg` and `rb` values of the transform to 30, 30 and 30. This will be our 'black' paint. We're equally setting all red, green and blue values to 30%. The second transform is using 100 for `ra`, but 0 and 0 for `ga` and `ba`. This will cause all green and blue to be removed from our truck, and only shades of red will remain. The third transform retains 100% of the red and green components but discards the blue component. The effect is coloring the image yellow.

Since the original truck movie clip is grayscale, coloring it will make the truck become evenly painted using the transform object. Think of this as like a light spray paint, rather than the thick solid color applied by something like `setRGB`. Let's try running this movie with CTRL/⌘+ENTER:

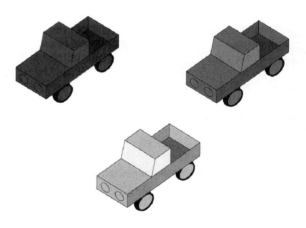

Now that looks a bit nicer! Those trucks have been painted with the artistic skill of Cézanne himself.

Now, though we're not going to use it here, we can also use the color offset value (the right hand column in the advanced color box) in the `setTransform` function. The only difference is in our object, we specify `rb`, `gb`, `bb` and `ab`, like so:

```
c1 = new Color(truck1);
c1obj = new Object();
c1obj.rb = -40;
c1obj.gb = 20;
c1obj.bb = 0;
c1obj.ab = 0;
c1.setTransform(c1obj);
```

In this example, the value 40 would be subtracted from any red component of the colors in the movie clip, and the value 20 would be added to any green component. Blue would be unaffected, because since bb is 0 then nothing is being added to or subtracted from the blue value. Alpha would also be unaffected.

From now on however, we're going to stick to using the percentages (ra, ga, ba, aa) with setTransform because they have the clearest and most intuitive affect on the colors. The offsets can get a bit "strange" looking at times, and consequently, can become confusing.

Now, there's one more level we can take this to. Let's ask Jimmy to paint the entire vehicle in an assorted array of colors.

Component paint

Let's look at our truck as something broken down into these eight basic component movie clips:

bedfloor – The floor of the bed of the truck.

bedinside – The inside walls of the bed of the truck.

grill – The front grill of the truck.

hood – The hood.

lights – The headlights of the truck.

rims – The rims of the wheels.

roof – The roof above the cab.

side – The side running the length of the truck.

Since we must create one Color object per area colored, we must create eight Color objects. There are two ways to approach this. First, we could use the setRGB method to solidly paint each of the truck's components, and create something like this:

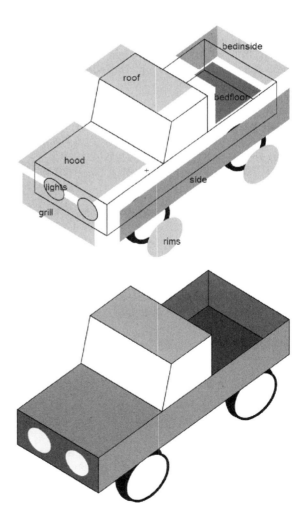

The bodywork of this particular truck was ordered specially by a circus. This is found in the movie `componentpaint-a.fla`. When loading this, look at the Library:

Now, loading the movie up, we can see the stage looks like this:

There's one truck on the shop floor, and it has an instance name of simply, 'truck'. All of the other components are contained within it, so that they would be referred to as `truck.hood`, `truck.roof`, `truck.rims`, etc. In the case of our multicolored truck, the code attached to frame 1 of the code layer looks like this:

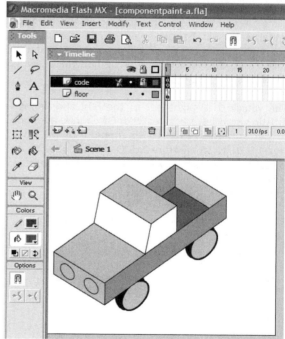

```
cbedfloor = new Color(truck.bedfloor);
cbedinside = new
Color(truck.bedinside);
cgrill = new Color(truck.grill);
chood = new Color(truck.hood);
clights = new Color(truck.lights);
crims = new Color(truck.rims);
croof = new Color(truck.roof);
cside = new Color(truck.side);

cbedfloor.setRGB(0x4F2700);
cbedinside.setRGB(0x944901);
cgrill.setRGB(0x0033FF);
chood.setRGB(0xFF3300);
clights.setRGB(0xFFFF33);
crims.setRGB(0xFFFFFF);
croof.setRGB(0x00CC00);
cside.setRGB(0xFF6600);
```

We're creating eight Color objects, one for each component, and we're pointing them at their respective truck body part. Then, we're simply using the setRGB method of each Color object and coloring each body part individually. The colors chosen are deliberately disparate to illustrate the effect.

Now, the second method we can use to color our truck is to use the setTransform method. Look at the movie componentpaint-b.fla. Notice that our truck has some more detail now:

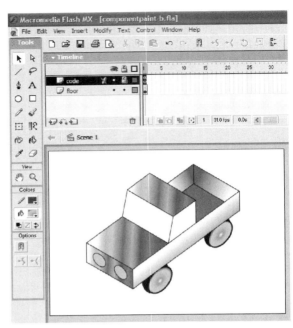

Each of the components has been painted to include the use of gradients. This is where the advantage of setTransform becomes apparent. We're going to let Jimmy paint each part of the truck, but because we're using setTransform, the shading of the gradient underneath will be preserved. While setRGB will completely paint our truck in a strange sort of lifeless solid color, the setTransform method will allow us to do this:

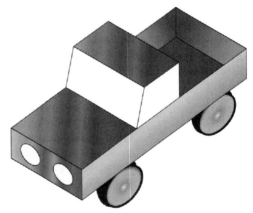

The vehicle is straight out of the 60s, and Jimmy's artistic vision has been realized. Of course, the code to perform this (attached to frame 1 of the code layer) is quite straightforward. Our Color objects are created in the same way as the previous example. However, rather than use setRGB, we use the setTransform methods, like so:

```
cbedfloort = new Object();
cbedfloort.ra = 100;
cbedfloort.ga = 0;
cbedfloort.ba = 0;
cbedfloor.setTransform(cbedfloort);

cbedinsidet = new Object();
cbedinsidet.ra = 100;
cbedinsidet.ga = 0;
cbedinsidet.ba = 50;
cbedinside.setTransform(cbedinsidet);

cgrillt = new Object();
cgrillt.ra = 100;
cgrillt.ga = 60;
cgrillt.ba = 150;
cgrill.setTransform(cgrillt);
```

```
choodt = new Object();
choodt.ra = 100;
choodt.ga = 0;
choodt.ba = 100;
chood.setTransform(choodt);

clightst = new Object();
clightst.ra = 200;
clightst.ga = 200;
clightst.ba = 100;
clights.setTransform(clightst);

crimst = new Object();
crimst.ra = 10;
crimst.ga = 100;
crimst.ba = 0;
crims.setTransform(crimst);

crooft = new Object();
crooft.ra = 100;
crooft.ga = 0;
crooft.ba = 60;
croof.setTransform(crooft);

csidet = new Object();
csidet.ra = 20;
csidet.ga = 90;
csidet.ba = 30;
cside.setTransform(csidet);
```

Each body part has its own Color and transform object, and they are being applied to it using the setTransform method.

Armed with these powerful paint tools, Jimmy is able to create some truly stunning and somewhat rare color combinations on the trucks in the garage.

Dynamic drawing

At his disposal, Jimmy has the new state of the art Paint-O-Rama 3000. It's an amazing new auto-body tool that allows him to paint perfect logos and images on the bodies of his cars. At its core, the Paint-O-Rama 3000 has the ability to draw lines, and to draw solid filled areas.

Let's imagine that the surface of the hood of the car is a grid. Upon this grid, Jimmy would like to paint his new logo, the Jimmy "J", like so:

Jimmy still has a thing or two to learn about logo design, but alas, it will have to suffice. The first thing to do is look at our grid, and imagine how we must draw upon it.

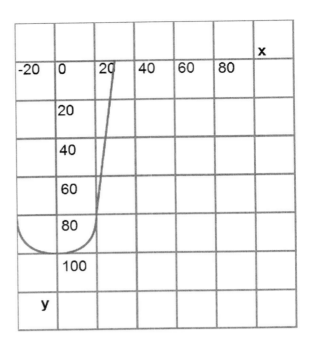

Here we can see the J mapped on the grid surface. The grid is made up of x (horizontal) and y (vertical) coordinates, where x goes from left to right, and y goes from top to bottom. The top-left corner of the J logo starts at x=0 and y=0, or simply "(0,0)". In fact, the drawing instructions that Jimmy would give to the Paint-O-Rama 3000 for this image, are like so:

1. Begin at (0, 0)
2. Draw a line out to (30, 0) - The top of the J.
3. Draw a straight line down and left to (20, 80) – the diagonal
4. right edge.
5. Draw a curve down and left to (0, 100), with the point at (20, 100) being where the curve will 'pull' towards.
6. Draw a curve up and left to (-20, 80), with the point at (-20, 100) being where the curve will 'pull' towards.
7. Draw a straight line right to (0, 80).
8. Draw a straight line back up to (0, 0).
9. Fill in the enclosed J.

Once these instructions have been fed into the Paint-O-Rama 3000, it will get to work drawing the lines and then filling in the shape to produce a perfect Jimmy "J" every time.

In ActionScript we have our own version of the Paint-O-Rama 3000, but it is known by the slightly less catchy name 'Drawing API (Application Program Interface)'. Our Paint-O-Rama 3000 uses the stage as its canvas, rather than the hood of a car. The stage is typically (by default) 550 pixels wide by 400 pixels high, and position (0,0) is in the upper left hand corner. Here is the typical stage:

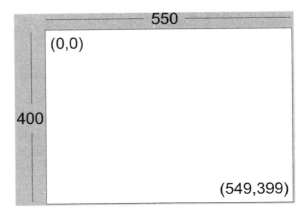

The drawing API has several important functions that we can make use of:

★ moveTo(x, y) – This moves the 'drawing pen' to a specific location on the stage.

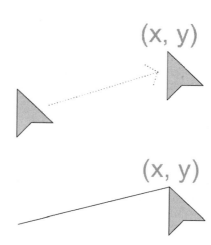

★ lineTo(x, y) – This draws a line from the pen's current position, to the position (x, y), using the current line style.

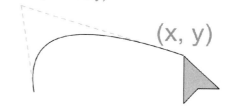

★ curveTo(controlx, controly, x, y) – This draws a curved line from the previous pen position to (x, y), while using the point at (controlx, controly) to influence the path of the curve.

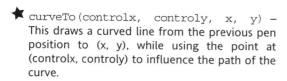

★ lineStyle(thickness, color, alpha) – This sets the line style of the current drawing pen. In this method we specify the thickness, color and alpha (transparency) value of the line. The thickness is the same as we would specify in the Flash design environment when drawing lines by hand. If we specify a thickness of 0, then Flash will make the line into a hairline thickness. If we want no line at all, then we must specify 'undefined' for the thickness.

★ beginFill(color, alpha) – This is used to tell the drawing API that any subsequent lines will be used to define an area that we'd like to use to define a solid, filled area.

★ endFill() – This is used to tell the drawing API to fill in the area we have just defined.

How

These are the basic drawing functions. To draw a solid, 1 point black line from (0, 0) to (100, 100) we would do this:

```
_root.lineStyle (1, 0);
_root.moveTo(0, 0);
_root.lineTo (100, 100);
```

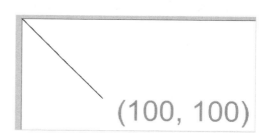

This line is being drawing straight on the _root timeline. Generally, we would want to create an empty 'container' movie clip to contain our drawing API creations. We do this using the `createEmptyMovieClip` method. It works something like this:

```
source.createEmptyMovieClip
(instanceName, depthLevel);
```

Once we've created an empty movie clip, we can then move it around the screen freely using its _x and _y properties. To create the simple line using a dynamically created movie clip, we would do this:

```
_root.createEmptyMovieClip ("myLine", 0);
myLine.lineStyle (1, 0);
myLine.moveTo(0, 0);
myLine.lineTo (100, 100);
```

Now, if we wanted to, we could move the whole line movie clip to a new location:

```
myLine._x = 50;
myLine._y = 50;
```

...and then the line would, on screen, extend from (50, 50) to (150, 150), because it is still 100 x 100, but it now begins at (50, 50) on screen.

Let's say that we wanted to program the drawing API to create a simple solid shape, like a triangle. Open up `triangle.fla`, and look at the output when it's run (CTRL/⌘+ENTER):

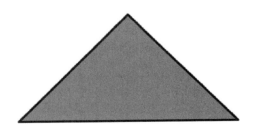

There is nothing in this movie except for some code on frame 1 of the code layer. Let's look at that code here:

```
_root.createEmptyMovieClip("triangle", 0);

triangle.lineStyle(1, 0);
```

```
triangle.beginFill(0xFF0000);
triangle.moveTo(50, 0);
triangle.lineTo(100, 50);
triangle.lineTo(0, 50);
triangle.lineTo(50,0);
triangle.endFill();

triangle._x = 100;
triangle._y = 100;
```

It's as if we're looking at Jimmy's own handwriting! First, we're creating a nice empty movie clip, with the instance name 'triangle', on depth level 0. Then, within it, we're using the drawing API to set the line to solid black, 1 point, and then beginning a fill of solid red (0xFF0000). Finally, we're drawing a triangle that has it's top point at (50, 0) and then its two lower points at (100, 50) and (0, 50). This triangle is 100 wide, and 50 high.

Once all the lines are drawn, we're telling the drawing API to fill in the shape with `endFill()`. Finally, we're moving the triangle movie clip to position (100, 100). Remember, the positions of the drawn lines within the triangle movie clip are relative to the internal coordinate system of the triangle movie clip itself. So, if the tip of the triangle is at (50, 0), but the entire triangle is moved to (100, 100), the tip will physically be sitting at (150, 100), but internally, it will still be at (50, 0).

Think of it like this; if Jimmy paints a 100 x 50 centimeter triangle on the hood of a car, at position (100, 100) it will be fixed on the hood of the car permanently in that location. Jimmy can, however, pick up the hood and move it elsewhere in the garage. The painted image will move with the hood, meaning that its location relative to the hood does not change, but relative to the shop floor the triangle is moving around.

The Logo

Now, let's take a look at `jimmyslogo.fla`. When this movie is loaded up, we'll see that it's empty – there's nothing on the stage. That's because everything is being created and drawn dynamically when the program is "run", or "at run-time" The only thing to be seen in this movie is the code layer.

Think back to Jimmy's logo, and the way the Paint-O-Rama 3000 was told what to do. The drawing API code is quite similar:

```
_root.createEmptyMovieClip ("jimmysLogo", 1);

jimmysLogo.lineStyle(2, 0xFF0000);
jimmysLogo.beginFill(0x330000);
jimmysLogo.moveTo(0, 0);
jimmysLogo.lineTo(30, 0);
jimmysLogo.lineTo(20, 80);
jimmysLogo.curveTo(20, 100, 0, 100);
jimmysLogo.curveTo(-20, 100, -20, 80);
jimmysLogo.lineTo(0, 80);
jimmysLogo.lineTo(0,0);
jimmysLogo.endFill();

jimmysLogo._x = 110;
jimmysLogo._y = 110;
```

We're creating a movie clip with the instance name 'jimmyslogo', on depth level 1. After this, we're using the drawing API to set the line to 2 point, bright red, and the fill to `0x330000`, which is a dark red color. Then, we're drawing our outline, by following the same list of instructions given to the Paint-O-Rama 3000. Once the logo is drawn, we're using the `endFill` method to fill the logo in, and then moving the whole position of the logo movie clip to (110, 110).

The `curveTo` method calls for some brief explanation. Basically, `curveTo` uses a method known as a 'bezier' curve, which creates curves based on the tangent line between the control point and the end points; a very complex series of calculations. Don't worry!! Luckily for us, the drawing API does all the work, and we simply need to specify two points: the control point and the destination point.

The control point acts by 'influencing' or 'pulling' the curve towards it. The farther out the control point is, the larger the curve will be. In these images, the control point is the small dot, and its influence is shown on the curve.

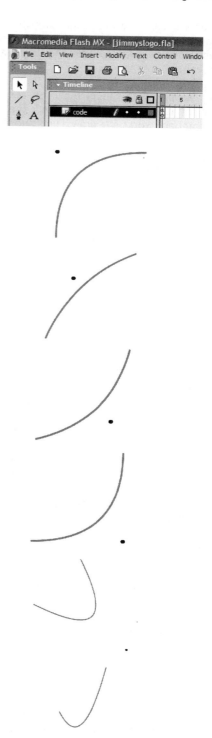

As we can see, choosing the position for the control point involves a bit of trial and error, but it can be done with practice. Take some time to have a go and get the feel of it.

We can also play with this in the Flash MX design environment itself because this is how the curve-drawing interface works: We draw a line, and then we pull it into curves. Flash keeps track of an invisible control point that we cannot see. Here, we can see a curve being manually drawn in Flash MX:

Summary

Once Jimmy masters the use of the paintbrush, and the Paint-O-Rama 3000, the sky is the limit. Sure he may never be painting the ceiling of the Sistine Chapel, but as chrome is his canvas, he'll be creating the artwork that we see every day on the road (and on the Web). To finish it all off, here's a neat little program that Jimmy wrote for the Paint-O-Rama 3000, for the days when he's feeling lazy, and looking for a neat design. This is found in `randompaint.fla`.

This code is attached to frame 1 of the Actions layer (the only layer).

```
_root.createEmptyMovieClip("painting", 1);

painting.lineStyle(0, 0);
painting.beginFill(0x000099, 50);
for (i = 0; i < 20; i++)
{
  controlx = Math.random() * 550;
  controly = Math.random() * 400;

  pointx = Math.random() * 550;
  pointy = Math.random() * 400;
```

```
  painting.curveTo(controlx, controly,
➥ pointx, pointy);
}
painting.endFill();
```

Any guesses as to what this does? Here's some examples:

That's right – never the same image twice. The `Math.random` function is being used to come up with four random numbers; one each for 'controlx', 'controly', 'pointx' and 'pointy'. For more on `Math.random`, see **Chapter 8**.

The power is endless. Remove the lines `beginFill` and `endFill`, and we can get some random celebrity's autograph every time (from `randomautograph.fla`).

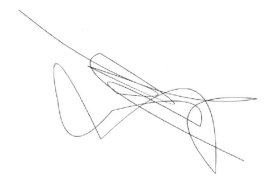

List of Decimal numbers from 0 to 255 with their
hexadecimal equivalents (0 to FF).

Dec	Hex		Dec	Hex		Dec	Hex		Dec	Hex
0	0		47	2F		94	5E		141	8D
1	1		48	30		95	5F		142	8E
2	2		49	31		96	60		143	8F
3	3		50	32		97	61		144	90
4	4		51	33		98	62		145	91
5	5		52	34		99	63		146	92
6	6		53	35		100	64		147	93
7	7		54	36		101	65		148	94
8	8		55	37		102	66		149	95
9	9		56	38		103	67		150	96
10	A		57	39		104	68		151	97
11	B		58	3A		105	69		152	98
12	C		59	3B		106	6A		153	99
13	D		60	3C		107	6B		154	9A
14	E		61	3D		108	6C		155	9B
15	F		62	3E		109	6D		156	9C
16	10		63	3F		110	6E		157	9D
17	11		64	40		111	6F		158	9E
18	12		65	41		112	70		159	9F
19	13		66	42		113	71		160	A0
20	14		67	43		114	72		161	A1
21	15		68	44		115	73		162	A2
22	16		69	45		116	74		163	A3
23	17		70	46		117	75		164	A4
24	18		71	47		118	76		165	A5
25	19		72	48		119	77		166	A6
26	1A		73	49		120	78		167	A7
27	1B		74	4A		121	79		168	A8
28	1C		75	4B		122	7A		169	A9
29	1D		76	4C		123	7B		170	AA
30	1E		77	4D		124	7C		171	AB
31	1F		78	4E		125	7D		172	AC
32	20		79	4F		126	7E		173	AD
33	21		80	50		127	7F		174	AE
34	22		81	51		128	80		175	AF
35	23		82	52		129	81		176	B0
36	24		83	53		130	82		177	B1
37	25		84	54		131	83		178	B2
38	26		85	55		132	84		179	B3
39	27		86	56		133	85		180	B4
40	28		87	57		134	86		181	B5
41	29		88	58		135	87		182	B6
42	2A		89	59		136	88		183	B7
43	2B		90	5A		137	89		184	B8
44	2C		91	5B		138	8A		185	B9
45	2D		92	5C		139	8B		186	BA
46	2E		93	5D		140	8C		187	BB

Dec	Hex		Dec	Hex
			238	EE
188	BC		239	EF
189	BD		240	F0
190	BE		241	F1
191	BF		242	F2
192	C0		243	F3
193	C1		244	F4
194	C2		245	F5
195	C3		246	F6
196	C4		247	F7
197	C5		248	F8
198	C6		249	F9
199	C7		250	FA
200	C8		251	FB
201	C9		252	FC
202	CA		253	FD
203	CB		254	FE
204	CC		255	FF
205	CD			
206	CE			
207	CF			
208	D0			
209	D1			
210	D2			
211	D3			
212	D4			
213	D5			
214	D6			
215	D7			
216	D8			
217	D9			
218	DA			
219	DB			
220	DC			
221	DD			
222	DE			
223	DF			
224	E0			
225	E1			
226	E2			
227	E3			
228	E4			
229	E5			
230	E6			
231	E7			
232	E8			
233	E9			
234	EA			
235	EB			
236	EC			
237	ED			

Steering and Operation

What's in this chapter:

★ Events and the car
 ★ The event model
 ★ Handling handlers
 ★ Using this
★ Using scripts with buttons and movie clips
★ Introduction to functions
 ★ Writing functions
 ★ Writing inline functions
★ Buttons
 ★ Button events
 ★ ActionScript and the button
★ Movie clips
 ★ Movie clip events
 ★ ActionScript and movie clips
★ Listeners and objects
 ★ How do they work
 ★ Callback functions
★ Mouse listeners
★ Key listeners

Controlling Frank's car

In this chapter we will look at the driver having control over his vehicle. Frank is a new driver, excited about learning all about his new set of wheels. However, there are many new things to learn about both the car and driving on the road. There are numerous things within the car (steering wheel, accelerator, air conditioning, etc.) and outside the car (roads, barriers, cats, etc.), which can cause things to happen to it.

It is also true that when Frank is driving his car, he wants complete control of it. He wants to be able to press a button, and for something to happen as a result. Frank also wants to be able to have programmed reactions to things happening in his car. If the inside of the car reached a certain temperature, it would be nice for the heater or air conditioning to come on. Or, if there was a strong impact, then the air bags should deploy. Also, he wants his car to constantly be checking the amount of gas in the gas tank, so when it reaches a certain point, a light will turn on telling him it is low. Frank hates to be stranded.

Functions and event handlers will help us do all of these things in our Flash movie. Events help control the playback of the movie, and aid interactivity, animation and effects. Functions based on events execute script based on certain occurrences during playback. Understanding functions and event handlers is extremely important if you want to take control of the ActionScript language in Flash MX. They are used very heavily now with new additions and some restructuring to the ActionScript language.

Using ActionScript with button and movie clip instances

In this chapter we will be looking at the scripts involved with buttons and movie clip instances. We will see how code can be put in two different places when it comes to these instances. Planning the structure of a movie is important.

Let's remember how a well-organized garage is very easy to work in. When the part-time employees arrive for their shift, they don't need to search for all the tools and car parts to get the job done. They know where they are, because they are trained to use a certain system. Keeping all the tools together in one place makes inventory a breeze, as opposed to trying to count the wrenches when they are scattered all over the place.

Organizing code should be like this, as we briefly discussed in **Chapter 2**. Nowhere is this more important than when dealing with instances and code. Keeping code on the timeline means a couple of things: it keeps things all in one place. Secondly, you won't repeat code anywhere near as much. As you will discover, if you have to put the same ActionScript on three different instances directly as opposed to on the main timeline, that's a lot more typing than having one function on the main timeline and having it called three times! Remember these points as you are dissecting the examples in this chapter and starting to build your own creations.

How are Buttons and Movie clips different?

Buttons and movie clips are actually quite similar to one another. This is because buttons are objects and can have many different methods, properties and events applied to them. Buttons can also have an instance name. This means they can be targeted with ActionScript from the main timeline.

There are some very obvious differences – when you open up a button and then open a movie clip you will see that buttons have four states, and movie clips have a timeline. Buttons will behave like they have a timeline in special circumstances, but you still cannot do certain animations or put code inside a button on a timeline like you can inside movie clips.

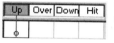 

It is possible to create movie clip buttons. It is a good idea to use a button when you only need its simple functionality and not the added power that a movie clip timeline can provide. Therefore, if you are creating a complex button or are using a complex set of actions to interact with a button you will probably want to use a movie clip. You can easily make movie clips behave just like a button, which we will do later in this chapter.

Events in and around the car

Luckily, Frank in his car can respond to events in real time. This means that the car can do a certain action when something is pressed, turned, or occurs. Let's consider some pseudo-code:

```
When there is an impact
Deploy air bags
Stop engine
End.
```

Therefore, if Frank hits a tree then the air bags will deploy. This is good. If something didn't happen in response to this event, tragedy would ensue. Fortunately, Flash can recognize things happening in and around the movie. Read on!

event

something happens

impact occured
execute reaction

When you press on a gas pedal, a car will move. When you spin a steering wheel, the car turns. Both of these are examples of *events*, which cause things to happen in a Flash movie. Events can trigger scripts which execute once a particular thing happens.

Therefore, you can think of events like a trigger and response: something (a key press, mouse click or the like) will need to occur before the response action can execute. When Frank presses the gas pedal of his car, it triggers a chain of reactions that make the car move. This is why if you place a script on a button, it must also include an event to trigger it. You must specify the press or release of the mouse (like the press of a gas pedal), for example, as the trigger of a resulting action. If you don't, Flash will really have no clue *when* to execute your 'gotoAndPlay("mymovie")' action, for example.

But events don't only occur using buttons or movie clips. You can also consider keyframes as events. Once the playhead reaches a keyframe, something occurs. Therefore, it too is an event.

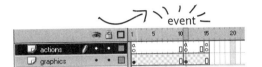

However, events do not have to execute script at all – many events happen all the time without any resulting action. Every mouse click, movement of the cursor, and keypresses on the keyboard cause an event in the Flash movie. As you know, a reaction does not occur each time.

The fun part is that you get to define the executed code when an event occurs! Anything that can be registered by the car can trigger a "response" action. And the good news for Frank is that he gets to fully customize what his car does when certain things happen to it.

There are two different ways you can deal with events. You can use the backward compatible `on` or `onClipEvent` events, which are attached to button and movie clip instances. These are two different ways events can be handled, and are sometimes called *attached scripts*. An example of such a script is:

```
onClipEvent(enterFrame) {
  _root.myCar._alpha += 10;
}
```

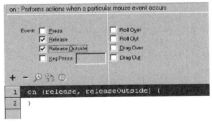

This script, when attached to the *myCar* movie clip instance with alpha set lower than 90, will increase the alpha to 100. `enterFrame` is the event: when the playhead enters the frame (which happens continually at the current frame rate). There are many different events we can listen to in buttons and movie clips.

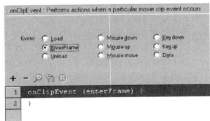

These windows show you all of your options. If you want to check them out, they can be found if you switch to Normal mode (CTRL/⌘+SHIFT+N) and in the scripts library select Movie control > on or Movie clip control > onEnterFrame. Remember to switch back to Expert mode after you are finished (CTRL/⌘ +SHIFT+E).

You can also write an inline function to control a button.

1. Drag a button instance onto the stage from Window > Common Libraries > Buttons. Double-click the button instance, and take a look at the Timeline panel. As you can expect, there are four states on the timeline: up, over, down and hit. Return to the Stage by clicking 'Scene 1' below the Timeline panel.

2. Select the button and open the Property inspector. Call the button instance 'myButton'.

3. Create a new layer called actions, then open the Actions panel. Select frame 1, and then enter the following code into the Script pane:

```
_root.myButton.onRelease = function() {
    trace("Button has been clicked!");
};
```

4. Test your movie by pressing CTRL/⌘+ENTER. Now we have created a script on the main timeline which will listen to the event of this button being clicked on. The Output window will open and show the text:

You use events when you need to execute some script based on a particular occurrence. This script can do any number of things. For example, it could cause an animation to take place. The script might trigger a different script in your movie to do something. Your script could even call for certain information (input values, for example) and then process that information in a certain way. For more information on this and an example, refer to the **Listeners** section later on in the chapter.

Using the event model in your movies

The new event model is an easy way to handle Flash events. We have already used it in the last section, when we clicked a button and the Output window popped up. The event model allows you to have a lot of control over the movie. What kind of events can you control? Let's take a look:

- ★ The mouse

- ★ The keyboard

- ★ Movie clips

- ★ Text fields

- ★ Tab ordering

- ★ Selection

- ★ Server interaction and data

This gives you a lot of control over what happens in your movie. More control means more stuff you can do in your ActionScript!

You will find that events will start with 'on'. Let's look at a comparison of the movie clip events (on the left), and the newer event methods (on the right) It is possible to use any of these in your movies. Remember that the code on the left in the following two tables is used in *attached scripts*.

onClipEvent(enterFrame);	onEnterFrame
onClipEvent(unload);	onUnload
onClipEvent(load);	onLoad
onClipEvent(mouseDown);	onMouseDown
onClipEvent(mouseUp);	onMouseUp
onClipEvent(mouseMove);	onMouseMove
onClipEvent(data);	onData
onClipEvent(keyUp);	onKeyUp
onClipEvent(keyDown);	onKeyDown

And in this comparison, button events are on the left and new button event methods are found on the right side of the following table:

on (release);	onRelease
on (releaseOutside);	onReleaseOutside
on (press);	onPress
on (drag);	onDrag
on (dragOut);	onDragOut
on (rollOver);	onRollOver
on (rollOut);	onRollOut
on (keyUp);	onKeyUp
on (keyDown);	onKeyDown

There are additional event methods which you can find in the ActionScript Reference guide. You might also find that these actions are referred to as *event handlers*.

To begin, we will start with the simplest of code, first with an attached event, and then using the new event model.

1. Open the example file called eventmodel_06.fla, which has a few things set up already for you. Save it as eventmodel_06_100.fla. In this file, we have a couple of stop(); frame actions on the main timeline. The main timeline also has a frame label called 'movie'. You will also notice a button instance on the stage, and the text 'movie' on frame 5.

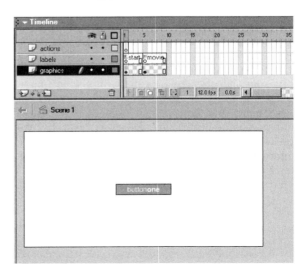

2. To add a script to an instance, first open the Actions panel. Then, select the button instance on the Stage you want to add the ActionScript event to.

3. In order to execute a script after a button is pressed then released; you need to add the following script into the script pane:

```
on (release){
   //run some code
   //example being:
   gotoAndStop("movie");
}
```

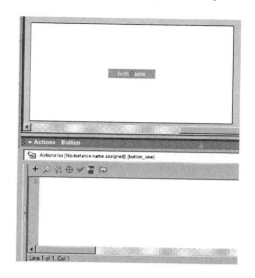

Test your movie by pressing CTRL/⌘+ENTER, and click on the button instance.

This is typical of an event placed on an instance in Flash. As you can see from our previous section, the script we run based on the event happens in between two curly braces { }. You will probably notice that the code within the { } is completely valid on its own. If you put that code on a frame of the main timeline, it will execute as soon as the playhead reaches it. In our case though, the code will only execute when the button is pressed.

You can do the same event-based script for a movie clip using the onClipEvent event. It listens to various events around a movie clip like we saw above. We could write the same sort of code as we did for a button, but this time it is for a movie clip instance:

```
onClipEvent (mouseDown){
   //run some code
   _root.gotoAndPlay("movie");
}
```

One of the most important things to remember is every parenthesis, bracket or brace in your code must be closed. If they aren't, your code will not work properly. Carefully check your code for brackets – which is easy to do when you allow Flash to control your indentation (default in the Actions panel). If your first line of code is indented at the same place as your final bracket, your code is probably fine. If not, go back and check each bracket that is opened, is closed later in your ActionScript.

In our car, the code that makes the gas pedal work would go on the gas pedal, and the window wipers code would go on the window wiper toggle, and so on. Now, say you want to rearrange all of the commands in the car, because you are upgrading. You would have to go to each control spot, and restructure your instructions to each part of the car. Imagine a central control for all the parts of your car: that is what you can do with the MX style of event handling.

Now we will try writing our code, but in a different way. This time we won't attach the code to the instance.

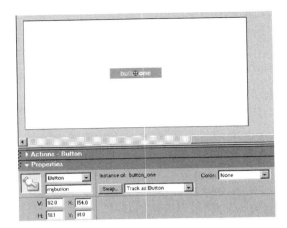

1. Open `eventmodel_06.fla` again, but this time rename the file `eventmodel_06_200.fla`. The first thing to do is give our button an instance name. Select the button, and open the Property inspector (CTRL/⌘+F3). In the `<Instance name>` field, enter `mybutton`.

2. Now, select frame 1 of the actions layer, and open the Actions panel (F9). In the script pane, add the following code:

```
stop();
mybutton.onRelease = function(){
    //run some code
    _root.gotoAndPlay("movie");
}
```

3. Test the movie (CTRL+ENTER). If you press the button on the Stage, notice how it goes to the movie frame, just as it did with the earlier example.

4. Open your Library (F11), and drag another instance of the button onto the Stage. Go to the Property inspector and give it the same instance name: `mybutton`. Test your movie again, and try each button to see what happens.

We will discuss functions later on in this chapter. What you need to notice here is how the code looks quite different from what was necessary in Flash 5. Although it looks a bit longer, be assured that it will make your life much easier in the long run!

There are a few good reasons to put your code in the main timeline, like in this particular example. Imagine if, at Rufus's Garage, he made all of his important managerial notes on Post-its, and stuck them all around the garage. Imagine the craze and confusion of all the workers trying to follow these directions. It could very well end up being mayhem, and this could be like you or your buddy trying to update, edit or debug your code.

However, if Rufus put all his notes on one single white-board for his staff, things would be a lot more organized. All of your code to control the instances running in the garage (the fork lift, the garage door opener, the coffee machine) can be run off of code on the white board. This is thanks to functions and event handlers, which we will look at next.

Introducing functions

Let's go back to the garage. Rufus, the owner, enjoys making money (much of which he spends on sunglasses). Therefore, he runs an efficient garage and reuses and recycles parts and equipment when he can. For example, it would be foolish to use a brand new wrench every time a wrench is needed – the same one can be used over and over again.

Functions are commonly used in Flash because they can save you writing a bunch of the same code in numerous places. Functions can be written on any given timeline: within a movie clip, or on the main timeline.

There are a few different ways you can write, and use, functions. First of all, a function can be written in one place, but called in another place to execute. Therefore, you have two steps: writing it, and then calling it to execute.

Secondly, you can have an inline function (as we used above with the event handlers). An inline function does not have a name. They are generally used for event handlers or listeners (callback functions), which we will take a look at later in this chapter.

And lastly, you could have functions built right into Flash. This kind of function is the easiest kind of function to use: all you need to do is call it. Examples of this kind of function are `String()` or `Number()` (as we used in **Chapter 4**). The function is called by simply calling the name of the function followed by the parentheses.

```function clickme() { trace("button1 clicked"); }```	We are creating a function which is called *clickme*. You write the function and then call it from another place in your code.
```_root.button1.onRelease = function() { clickme(); };```	This inline (or anonymous) function calls the `clickme()` function we made above. This function is not named like the function we wrote above.
```myNum = Number("55"); trace(5+myNum);```	The Output window will show 60. This example uses the `Number()` function which is built into Flash.

Methods and functions are practically the same thing: both perform some sort of operation. They are also similar because methods and functions are both followed by a set of parentheses. This means that, like methods, in some cases a parameter can be set between them. You will learn more about functions and parameters in **Chapter 10**.

> Functions attached to the event handlers are sometimes referred to as **callback functions**.

Writing functions

The most basic way of writing a function is as follows:

```
function myFunction(){
    //stuff to execute goes here
}
```

Pretty easy! In this code, we are defining a function called myFunction. When we call *myFunction* to be executed, it will look like the following:

```
myFunction();
```

You will just need to remember not to use another ActionScript word as your function name. You should also remember that the word 'function' is case sensitive. Therefore, if you use a capital F it will color-code itself dark blue, but even so, your code will not work.

Just like most of the targeting we have done before, calling a function will require you to target it depending on where it is. Therefore, if you call a function from a movie clip, you will need to target it like this:

```
_root.myFunction();
```

Where *myFunction* is the name of the function.

Random numbers

In the garage, the staff is often asked to estimate how long a car will be out of action, or how long a part will take to arrive. Although they know roughly, sometimes they need help generating a random (but reasonable!) number to tell the customer off the top of their heads. Not to mention that customers are probably more inclined to believe the mechanic if he or she has checked a computer first.

The `Math` object can automatically generate a random number between 0 and 1, but we want a function that can take a couple of inputs and pick a random number between them. This can then be reused any time staff are required to give an estimate.

1. Before we get carried away, the first step is always to think out what we want to achieve in pseudo-code:

   Get minimum and maximum possible numbers
   Work out range by taking maximum from minimum
   Multiply this by the random number (between 0 & 1)
   Add to original minimum to get answer
   Round the number so it is an integer

2. Open a new movie, and save it as `func-tion_06.fla`. Create a dynamic text field anywhere on the stage, and call it 'thenumber'. Call the layer you have placed the field on *graphics*. Feel free to add any static text or graphics to this layer, as we have below. Then, create a new layer, and call it *actions*.

3. On frame 1 of the actions layer, enter the following code into the script pane:

   ```
   function RandRange(from, to) {
   ```

   Our function, called `RandRange`, will generate a random integer between "X" and "Y". These are represented by the parameters *from* and *to*. These numbers will be determined when we call the function to return numbers in step 4. Remember that we are still *writing* (not executing) the function at this point.

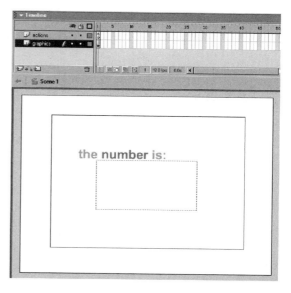

4. The next step is to grab a random number (decimal) between 0 and 1, which we do with the built in `Math.random()` method. This number is then multiplied by the difference between the `from` and `to` variables. Then, we add this value to the lower of the two numbers, and finally round the number off so it is a full integer. Enter this code onto frame 1 of the actions layer:

```
var myNum = Math.round((Math.random()*(to-from))+from);
return (myNum);
}
```

5. Finally, the text is returned in a text field. We are asking the function RandRange to return a random number between 6 and 16.

```
function RandRange(from, to) {
  var myNum = Math.round
  ➥ ((Math.random()*(to-from))+from);
  return (myNum);
}
_root.thenumber.text = RandRange(6, 16);
```

the **number** is:

7

Open function_finished_06.fla for a full example, which includes some additional commented ActionScript which performs data validation.

```
// make sure that the supplied
// parameters are numeric. if not
// assigndefaults.
if (isNaN(from)) {
  from = 0;
}
if (isNaN(to)) {
  to = 1;
}

// create a temporary variable with the
// value of the lower number.
var temp = from;

// make sure that the "from" is less
// than the "to", if not then swap the
// two values.
from = Math.min(from, to);

// grab the higher of the "temp" and
// "to" variables. we're using "temp"
// because we've changed the value of
// "from" already.
to = Math.max(temp, to);
```

You can also find more information on the Math object in **Chapter 10**.

Functions should be used whenever you might otherwise need to duplicate your code. You can call a function any number of times, and it will execute that same block of code which means you don't have to keep typing it out. Therefore, if you find yourself reusing the same code, creating a function is a smart way to go.

Inline (or anonymous) functions

The basic set up of an inline function for movie clips and buttons is as follows:

```
instance.myEvent = function(){
    //stuff to execute goes here
}
```

This is where 'instance' is the name of either a button or movie clip instance. 'myEvent' would be an event handler, such as `onPress` or `onEnterFrame`. This kind of function is typically used for writing code to control buttons and movie clips. We will write many inline functions in the following pages.

Pressing buttons

As we have seen earlier, there are many events which can trigger the code applied to a button, just like there are many different kinds of things that can happen to a car. Mouse events are perhaps the most common triggers for button code. However, the Key events can be very useful too. We will look at key events later in this chapter.

Buttons can have graphics, which usually serve as a **hit area**. This is the active area where the button is pressed, sometimes known as a hot spot. Just like a car has a specific area set where you can press the car's horn, you can create an area where your button is active. Buttons can be used in many different and interesting ways though. You can have invisible buttons, which perhaps activate when people roll over the active area. They can serve as a quite powerful tool, allowing you to create QTVR-like environments, or 3D-like games.

In this example, we will have a few different buttons on the stage. We will control the buttons in several different ways, and make the instances control other instances on the Stage. We will manipulate the instance of the button visually. We will control another button with an event, and the third button will be invisible.

1. Open the file called `buttons_06.fla`. The file has been prepared with three buttons ready on the Stage, and one movie clip. You will notice that the invisible button is a bright blue square on the stage, representing the hit area only. It is invisible if you test the movie. We have placed an empty box around the area, so you can tell where the button is.

2. Let's make the button on the far left control the middle button. The first thing we want to do is give our buttons instance names. Open the Property inspector, and give the button on the left the name 'button1'. Then name the middle button instance 'button2', the last instance 'button3', and the movie clip 'myClip'.

3. Select frame 1 of main timeline, and open the Actions panel. Add the following code to the script pane:

```
button1.onRollOver = function() {
  _root.button2._xscale = 175;
  _root.button2._yscale = 175;
};
button1.onRollOut = function() {
  _root.button2._xscale = 100;
  _root.button2._yscale = 100;
};
```

What we are doing here is controlling some of the properties of the 'button2' object instance by changing their scale. However, let's take it a bit further, and involve a movie clip too.

4. A piece of code we haven't looked at yet is the createEmptyMovieClip method. All you need to be concerned with at this point is that it creates a new movie clip! We will be creating an empty movie clip, and then designating an instance name and a depth. After we finish this, we can enter code into the instance we have just created. The basic format we use is:

```
createEmptyMovieClip("instanceName",
➡ depth);
```

When button1 is pressed, the function will create a new movie clip, and then we will use the onEnterFrame event to fade out the button2 instance. onEnterFrame is typically used when you need to loop a particular piece of code. A very simplistic way of fading out an instance is as follows:

```
button1.onRelease = function() {
  _root.createEmptyMovieClip
  ➡ ("fadeout",222);
  fadeout.onEnterFrame = function() {
    if (_root.button2._alpha>0) {
```

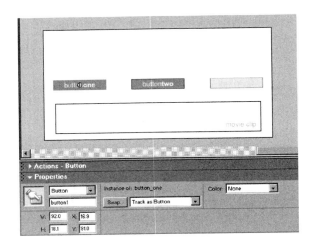

```
    _root.button2._alpha -= 5;
    } else {
      removeMovieClip(_root.fadeout);
    }
  };
};
```

Add this code to frame 1 of the main timeline, following the code in step 3. In this ActionScript we are creating the new instance fadeout on the _root timeline (which, essentially, is a clip itself!). `fadeout` will fade 'button2' to a zero value of `_alpha` as long as it is greater than zero. Meaning, when you press 'button1', 'button2' will fade out. It does this because when you press a button, you create a new movie clip. This movie clip will sit invisible on the Stage, and into this clip you can put some code. We are going to put an `onEnterFrame` function into this clip, which means it will continually loop through the code. On each loop we are asking the clip to decrease the alpha of our button by 5. When it's done, we delete the clip. For more information on conditions like the if/else statement, refer to **Chapter 10**.

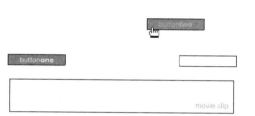

5. For the `button2` instance, we will use a new event to us: the `onDragOut` event. This means that if a user presses the button then, while holding their Mouse button down pulls, away from the button, it will execute code. Let's look at the functions now:

```
_root.button2.onDragOut = function() {
  _root.button2._y=_ymouse;
  _root.button2._x=_xmouse;
};
_root.button2.onRelease = function() {
  _root.button2._x=_xmouse;
  _root.button2._y=_ymouse;
};
```

Now add this code following what you wrote in step 4. Here we have two different events, `onDragOut` and `onRelease`. We are using the `_y` and `_x` properties to point to a particular spot on the Stage. The `_ymouse` and `_xmouse` properties are the current `_x` and `_y` positions of the mouse. In this function, we have the position of the button on the stage equaling the position of the mouse: and therefore following it.

Try testing your movie, and dragging the 'button2' instance. 'button2' will follow your mouse as long as you have the button depressed. It is a little 'clunky', but this shows you a different mouse event, and a few button properties we haven't yet worked with. In this step you used a couple properties to change the x and y position of your button, which you see in the `button2._x` and `button2._y` lines. Then, you made this position of the button match that of the mouse positions: `_xmouse` and `_ymouse`. These properties can be used with movie clips too.

Using this can certainly save a few lines of ActionScript in your movie. This can also be useful if you want to create the same effects for each button for a particular state. For instance, you could have a function which is called when all the buttons listed are clicked on:

```
myClick = function () {
   trace("you clicked me!");
};
_root.button1.onRelease =
_root.button2.onRelease=_root.button3
➥ .onRelease= myClick;
```

You could use this for rollover effects or anything you want to be universal across several instances.

6. The final button we are going to look at in this example is the invisible button. Our invisible button is going to do two things. First of all, we don't want the hand cursor to appear. This is useful: it makes our button truly invisible (if only we didn't have that box behind it to show you where it is). Secondly, we will have the button control a movie clip (called *myclip*) – so when you roll over the hit area, something happens. We'll make it a simple `gotoAndStop()` action.

```
button3.onRollOver = function() {
   this.useHandCursor = false;
   _root.myclip.gotoAndStop
   ➥ ("theframe");
};
button3.onRollOut = function() {
   _root.myclip.gotoAndStop
   ➥ ("frameone");
};
```

You can set multiple buttons to the same property all at once. You might have an event, such as `onRelease`, *where you want two buttons to have* `_visible` *set to 'false'. The following code could do this:*

```
myButton.onRelease = function(){
myButton2._visible =
➥ myButton3._visible = false;
}
```

So now we have controlled a few buttons in different ways: using movie clips, controlling movie clips, and changing button properties. Now we are more than ready to move on to movie clips!

Movie clips

Movie clips behave in similar ways to buttons. Like two different pedals in a car, they each serve their own purpose and work in slightly different ways. Movie clips and buttons both have *some* of the same properties as one another. This can be useful for many things, like using a movie clip as a button. However, it can be easy to accidentally confuse the two instances. You might try a certain property exclusive to a movie clip, on a button. It's like putting square wheels on a car: it won't get you anywhere. And the biggest problem is that you won't get any errors from Flash, since it won't recognize the problem.

It might help you to be consistent in the way you build your movies: stick with buttons, or movie clips, if you are repeating instances. For example, if you are using buttons for your navigation, use either all buttons or all movie clips.

A movie clip is great as an animation, as designers are probably well aware. But if you want to add more life to your movie clip, perhaps by controlling the clip itself as well, ActionScript is needed. Movie clip buttons also allow you to store information on the local timeline. A great advantage to the designer is how you can animate your buttons in intricate and interesting ways using a movie clip button. For example, we faded out the button in the earlier exercise. You can fade out a certain state of your button right on the timeline. You will find out how in the next exercise.

In this section, we will exclusively be putting code on the main timeline. This is by no means your only option. Functions can also go within the movie clip on its own timeline, or events can be placed on the instance if you so choose.

Making a movie clip button

Making one thing behave like another can be useful, depending on your needs. You might like a car to act like a truck, so you may modify the engine to give it more power. This gives you the compact size of a car, but the power of a truck. You are customizing your vehicle!

This is similar to how you can make movie clips behave like buttons, one very useful aspect of the event model allowing you to assign the same events to movie clips as you do to buttons. Therefore, you can have the timeline of a clip, but the functionality of a button. This gives you more flexibility when programming because there are many more ways you can control a movie clip. You also have more freedom in the number of *button states* available to you. In the following example, we will replicate a button with a movie clip, which will make it plainly obvious how you can extend a button's functionality.

1. Open `mc_button_06.fla`, which has been started for you with a movie clip, and a couple of layers on the main timeline.

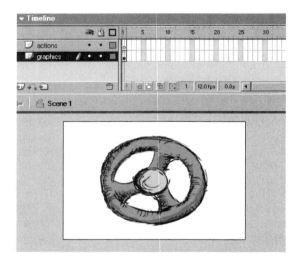

2. Double-click the movie clip `clipButton` on the Stage so we can work with the movie clip timeline. The movie clip has graphics to represent each basic state change on a timeline layer called 'graphics'. These will be used to represent *Up*, *Down*, and *Over*. Since we are creating these states manually, it means that you could create many additional states than these three. For simplicity though, we will stick to these three. What you now need to do is create a few new layers: 'actions', 'labels', and 'hit_area'.

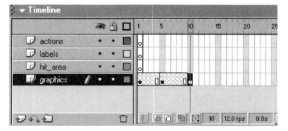

3. The next step is to make some labels. Go to the labels layer, and create enter keyframes on frames 1, 5 and 10. Because this is where the graphics change on the graphics layer, we need labels so the playhead can progress to each area. Open the Property inspector and create a label on frame 1 called '_up', the label on frame 5 '_over' and the label on frame 10 '_down'. Add a `stop()` action on frame 1 of the 'actions' layer.

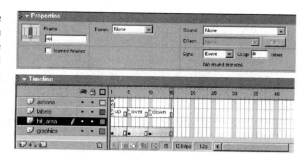

4. Now we will need to create a hit area for the button, because this hasn't been done yet. The hit area is the hot spot where the button can be pressed. A new movie clip property called `hitArea` allows you to set a certain graphic as this hot spot. So in frame 1 of the *hit_area* layer, draw a solid shape around the graphic where you want the active area to be.

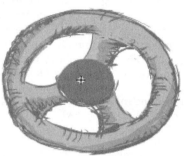

Sometimes it helps to make this area somewhat transparent, particularly if you are dealing with an odd shape. Go to the Color Mixer and change the Alpha level if necessary.

5. After you are finished, change the graphic into a movie clip, by selecting it and pressing F8. Then, name the instance *hit_area*.

After you have done this, move the play head to frame 5 and then 10. You might need to create a new keyframe, and then resize or reshape the instance, depending on the animation. Since the movie clip does not move or tween, you do not need to worry about this. However, if you are working with a button which does move or animate, you will want to move the graphic in order to fully cover the art on our graphics layer.

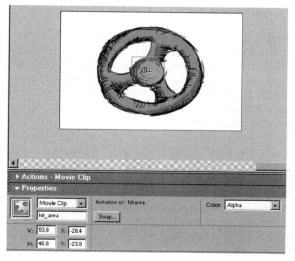

One final step and we are finished! Now we need to add the ActionScript to make our button work. Before we leave the movie clip, we need to add one small piece of code. Make sure you are on the *steering_wheel* timeline, and select frame 1 of the actions layer. Add a stop action: `stop();`

Now we need to add the rest of the ActionScript onto the main timeline. You can, however, add code within your movie clip, which will slightly shorten your code. You can check out the example file, `mc_button_finished_06.fla`, which includes commented out code on frame 1 of the `mybutton` movie clip instance. This is simply a different way of organizing your code, and is entirely up to you. Both pieces of code will accomplish the same thing.

6. Return to the main timeline by clicking Scene 1 or the Back button (arrow).

7. Then, select frame 1 of the *actions* layer, open the Actions panel, and enter the following functions into the script pane:

```
_root.mybutton.hitArea =
➥ _root.myButton.myhit_area;
_root.mybutton.myhit_area._visible =
➥ false;
```

8. Then, we should add the code which will cause the movie clip to execute an action when it is clicked:

```
_root.mybutton.onRelease = function() {
  getURL("http://www.flash-mx.com",
  ➥ _blank);
};
```

Now press CTRL/⌘+ENTER to test your movie. When you move your mouse over the button, you will notice the movie clip changes states. This is because Flash recognizes our *_up*, *_over* and *_down* states as button states and animates the button for you! If you click the button, a new browser window will open with our target web site.

That is the basic way of creating and adding script for a movie clip button. The button we have created isn't overly exciting, because it resembles most typical buttons. You can certainly make it more interesting by adding an extra state or two and some animation. However, the process is exactly the same as we have covered in this exercise!

Button and movie clip events can also be removed or deleted. This can be done in a few different ways:

```
_root.removeMovieClip(myClip);
```
or:
```
delete myClip.onPress;
```
or:
```
myClip.onPress = null;
```
or:
```
myClip.onPress = undefined;
```

Looking at listeners

Listeners can be a very powerful tool for controlling interactive environments in a Flash movie. Let's go back to the garage for a minute. Jimmy the racing stripe boy has a couple of co-op students, who want to learn how to paint the stripes. The co-ops follow Jimmy around wherever he goes, watching everything he does. Jimmy programmed all his young co-ops to do so. And during his shift, Jimmy can keep giving his co-ops new things to do and watch for when following him around. Like good students, the co-ops start performing these things immediately, while following Jimmy around. Then, at the end of Jimmy's shift, he removes the co-ops from his side.

In this section, we are going to turn it up a notch, now that you are comfortable with the functions we have learned in the previous sections.

Listeners are similar to Jimmy and his young interns, and the event handlers we have already discussed. However, they offer you some additional functionality you cannot achieve using callback functions. Listeners are attached to global objects, of which there is only one. There is only one mouse cursor, one Stage (that can be resized), and one keyboard. Listeners will "listen" to input from the user, and one or more parts of your movie can listen to these inputs. Several different instances can listen to the one single continuous event (such as the mouse). Callback functions can be executed based on a response to the events of these global objects.

We will look at how to construct listeners in the next two sections. But for now let's consider how they are built. A listener uses a *constructor* to create a new object. Then, you must add at least one event, and then register the listener (addListener).

The events for the following listeners are:

* ★ Mouse object: onMouseMove, and onMouseDown

* ★ Key object: onKeyDown and onKeyUp

* ★ Stage object: onResize

* ★ Selection object: onSetFocus

* ★ TextField object: onScroller, and onChanged

Using Mouse listeners

In this exercise, we will listen to the movement of the Mouse object, using the onMouseMove event. We will also capture the current X and Y position of the mouse cursor, to demonstrate how the listener constantly updates its reading. We will be using this to replace the mouse cursor with a new custom one we have made and record the mouse coordinates in a text field.

1. Open mouse_listener_06.fla. There is a dynamic text field on the Stage. Select the field and call it *mousecoord*. You should notice two instances on the stage, which will follow the cursor. Call the larger of these instances *mouseCursor*.

2. The next step is to hide the mouse cursor, which is accomplished using the Mouse.hide method. Following this, we need to create a new object, called someListener. Open the Actions panel, and add the following frame action to frame 1 of the actions layer:

```
Mouse.hide();
someListener = new Object();
```

3. Next, we need to add an onMouseMove event. Essentially, this will make the mouseCursor instance listen to the position of the mouse (which are the _xmouse and _ymouse properties). The following property places the X and Y coordinates into the mousecoord text field. This is using the parseInt function, which is used to convert a string to an integer. Add the following code to frame 1 of the actions layer:

```
someListener.onMouseMove = function() {
  _root.mouseCursor._x =
_root._xmouse;
  _root.mouseCursor._y =
_root._ymouse;
  _root.mousecoord.htmlText =
"X:"+parseInt(_root._xmouse)+",
Y:"+parseInt(_root._ymouse);
};
updateAfterEvent();
```

4. And lastly, we need to register the someListener object as a listener:

```
Mouse.addListener(someListener);
```

To see this movie in action, refer to `mouse_listener_finished_06.fla`.

Using Key listeners

Key listeners listen to which keys are being pressed on the keyboard. You can get key codes by tracing them using `Key.getCode`. Every key on the keyboard has a code that represents that key. This is what you can use when you need to listen for a keypress in particular.

1. Open the FLA file called `key_listener.fla`. You will notice a movie clip instance on the Stage, which is called 'myCircle'. As you can see, the circle has been enhanced somewhat, just to make it a little more interesting! There is also a background, and a layer for actions. First we need to create a new Listener object. In frame 1 of the 'actions' layer, enter the following ActionScript:

```
myListener = new Object();
myListener.onKeyDown = function() {
```

This code creates a new Listener object called myListener. Following this, we create a callback function assigned to the `onKeyDown` event.

2. Now we will check what keys are pressed. If a key press matches the one we are looking for, then properties of the object instance 'myCircle' will be altered. `Key.getCode` retrieves the key code of any given key pressed. Add the following code after what you typed in step 1 into frame 1 of the actions layer:

What are key codes? Key codes are the numeric number given to a key press on the keyboard. For example, T is represented by 84, and the Space bar is represented by 32 or by SPACE. Some keys have more than one way in which they can be represented. You can find ASCII key codes in your Flash Help. Press F1 and search for ASCII. You will find the numbers listed in:

Keyboard Keys and Key Code Values > Letters A to Z and standard numbers 0 to 9

```
        // check which key was pressed.
        switch (Key.getCode()) {
        case Key.UP :
          // if the UP key was pressed then move the circle up.
          if (_root.myCircle._y>0) {
            _root.myCircle._y -= 2;
          }
          break;
        case Key.DOWN :
          // if the DOWN key was pressed, then move the circle down.
          if (_root.myCircle._y<Stage.height) {
          _root.myCircle._y += 2;
      }
      break;
    case Key.LEFT :
      // if the LEFT key was pressed, then move the circle left.
      if (_root.myCircle._x>0) {
        _root.myCircle._x -= 2;
      }
      break;
    case Key.RIGHT :
      // if the RIGHT key was pressed then move the circle right.
      if (_root.myCircle._x<Stage.width) {
        _root.myCircle._x += 2;
      }
      break;
    case 187 :
      // if the + (PLUS) key was pressed, then increase the size of the circle.
      if (_root.myCircle._xscale<300) {
        _root.myCircle._xscale = _root.myCircle._yscale += 2;
      }
      break;
    case 189 :
      // if the - (MINUS) key was pressed, then decrease the size of the circle.
      if (_root.myCircle._xscale>10) {
        _root.myCircle._xscale = _root.myCircle._yscale -= 2;
      }
      break;
    default :
      //trace(Key.getCode());
      break;
    }
    updateAfterEvent();
};
Key.addListener(myListener);
```

3. Then, the 'myListener' object is registered as a listener to the Key object.

```
Key.addListener(myListener);
```

> *The Switch Statement: The* `switch` *statement is sometimes useful in simplifying* `if/else` *statements. It can sometimes be a quicker or more graceful way of writing code. In the code above, the* `switch` *statement creates a case for each key press possibility. It checks which key was pressed and then modifies the properties of the circle on the stage. For more information on statements in general, refer to* **Chapter 8**.

Test the movie and you should be able to make kitty move around and get bigger or smaller. You can find the example file under the name of `key_listener_finished_06.fla`

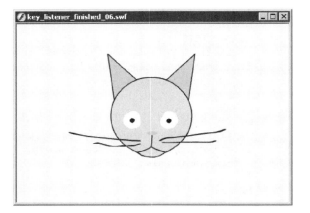

Summary

In this chapter we covered many of the basics of learning how to use ActionScript with buttons and movie clips. Now you know how to:

★ Work with the event model, and write inline (anonymous) functions for buttons and movie clips.

★ Write ActionScript to control a button, or control other instances using a button.

★ Create a movie clip button.

★ Use key listeners and mouse listeners in your movies.

The Interactive Intelligent Dashboard

What's in this chapter

★ The dashboard

★ Text fields

★ Static text fields

★ Dynamic text fields

★ Input text fields

★ Moving the vehicle

★ Changing the variables

★ Rotating movie clips

★ Moving movie clips

★ Buttons controlling variables

★ The Date and Time object

★ Changing the frame rate

The interactive intelligent dashboard

Every truck that is produced in this garage is fitted with the latest on-board interactive dashboard computer. This computer gives the driver instant feedback on engine conditions, temperature, oil, mileage, time, age of the truck and the efficiency at which it is operating. It's all displayed in one convenient, self-contained visual system.

Let's look at the dashboard display:

This is for the ultimate truck driver, in the ultimate of futuristic handling and convenience. Notice that we have the following items neatly displayed in front of us:

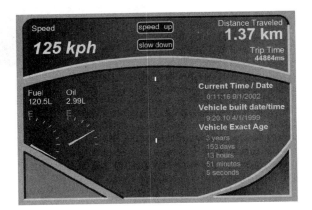

★ Speed. Measured in kilometers per hour (this is the future, and metric is easier to compute with).

★ Speed up / Slow down buttons. That's right, acceleration in this new truck is controlled not with the archaic foot pedal, but with the press of two friendly buttons.

★ Distance Traveled. The total distance that we have traveled since starting up the truck. This is ultra accurate.

★ Trip time. The total time elapsed (in milliseconds) since the truck was started up.

★ Fuel gauge. The amount of fuel remaining in the fuel tank, measured in liters. The needle below also visually indicates the fuel level.

★ Oil gauge. The amount of oil remaining in the system, measured in liters.

★ Current date / time.

★ Build date / time. This is the exact second that the truck rolled off the assembly line.

★ Vehicle exact age. Using the current date and the build date, here we are shown the exact age of the vehicle, to the second.

To ensure that we don't even have to look at the road in this advanced truck, we have simulated road lines zooming past, down the middle of the dashboard. These zoom past at a rate that accurately reflects the speed of the vehicle.

Isn't it convenient then, that this dashboard interface was built in Flash? Yes, that's right, the engineers at the truck's manufacturing plant decided that the best way to present all this information, and perform all the necessary calculations, was to use Flash MX, and then create a Flash player for the dashboard computer.

We've been given privileged, top-secret access to the headquarters of the truck manufacturer, where we've been given access to this Flash application, and now we're going to look at it!

The Flash application

Let's start by loading up `dashboard.fla`, and looking at the stage, without the application running.

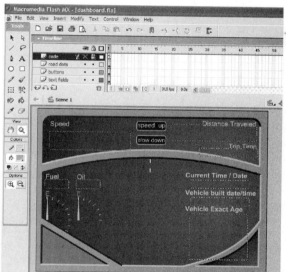

Upon closer examination, we can see that the interface is made up of several elements:

The graphical background:

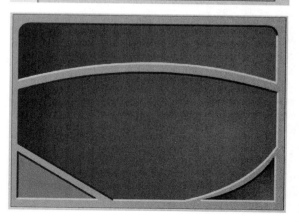

This is merely the base upon which everything else is presented.

The Text Fields.

All of the text that is displayed on the dashboard is contained in Flash elements known as 'text fields'. These are boxes within which any text can be placed and displayed. In the FLA, we can see that there are two types of text field: Static and Dynamic.

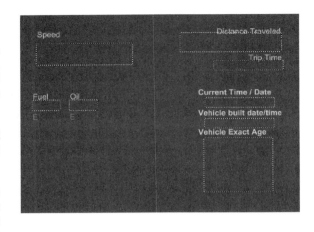

The static text fields are the titles, which do not change ('Speed', 'Fuel', 'Trip Time'), and will remain that way from design time to run-time.

The dynamic text fields, on the other hand, are the areas of text illustrated by dotted line boxes in the above screen image. These contain no text at design time, but rather they're filled in when the application is running.

More on text fields in a few moments.

The needle movie clips.

On the stage there are two instances of a movie clip called 'needle'. The instances are called 'fuelNeedle' and 'oilNeedle'. As we'll see later, the level of oil and fuel is reflected in these needles by the simple act of rotating them.

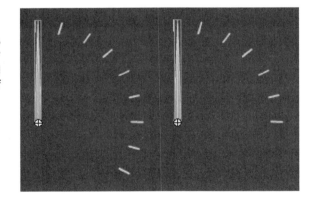

The Road Dots

We also have two other movie clips on the stage, both an instance of the 'roadDot' movie clip. They're called 'roadDot' and 'roadDot2', and their positions are determined based upon the speed of the vehicle.

The Speed Buttons

In the instance of modernization, speed control has been moved from the more traditional 'foot pedal' to the on-screen Flash buttons, freeing up the driver's feet for other things, like making use of the (optional) built-in foot massager. These two buttons trigger two button functions (as discussed in the last chapter), one for speeding up by 5kph, and the other slowing down by 5kph.

That's it. Those five components make up the entire dashboard interface for our truck. Let's now look at them in detail, and see just how these things are done.

Text fields

In Flash MX, we have the ability to display text to a user in a very easy and straightforward method using the text field. The text field is created using the Text tool from the Tools panel from within the Flash MX design environment.

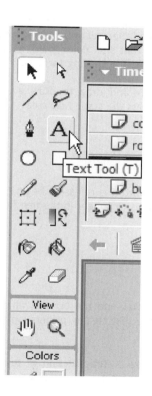

Text fields come in three distinct flavors:

★ Static Text Fields: These are text fields that simply display text, and do not change once the Flash movie is running. They are like labels on a wall; once they're placed, they do not change.

★ Dynamic Text Fields: These are text fields that display text, but they also have associated with them an instance name, which gives us the ability to change their contents at run-time, using ActionScript.

★ Input Text Fields: These are text fields that display text but also allow the user to input their own text. We use this type of text field to receive text-based input or feedback from the user, and then store or manipulate that text in any way we want. These are like fields in a form.

Static text fields

Let's quickly look at how we create a static text field in Flash MX.

1. First we must open up a new movie with CTRL/⌘+N.

2. Click on the Text tool in the Tools panel, or press "T" to activate the text tool.

3. Open the Properties panel by clicking on it at the bottom of the screen, or pressing CTRL/⌘+F3.

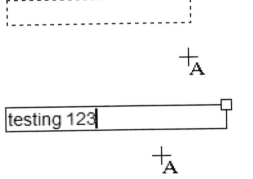

4. Ensure that the text type drop-down box says 'Static Text' in it, and then set your text settings as you wish (font, font size, color, bold, italics, paragraph alignment and spacing format).

5. On the stage, click and drag to draw a box which will encompass the static text area:

6. Once the mouse button is released, begin typing in the text that is to appear in the text field.

7. Click outside the box, and the border will disappear, leaving the text cleanly printed on the stage.

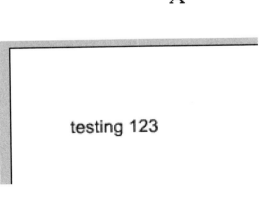

And that's it. That is how a static section of text is drawn on the stage. At run-time, there is not much we can do with it, other than look at it; Flash sees this text as nothing more than a graphic image when our movie is running. Notice that this type of text field does not have an 'instance name' associated with it, which we will see in a moment is a critical part of making text dynamic. If we want to start doing cool things with the text field and Actionscript, we must use the Dynamic Text field.

Dynamic text fields

The initial steps in drawing a dynamic text field are very similar to drawing a static text field. In a new, blank movie select the text tool, and then look at the Properties panel. This time, however, the properties will be set a little bit differently.

1. Ensure that "Dynamic Text" is selected from the Properties panel.

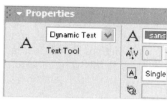

2. On the stage, press the mouse button and drag to draw a text field box.

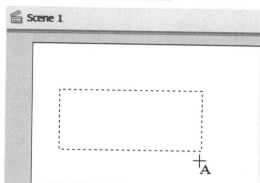

3. Once the text field has been drawn, the Properties panel will change slightly. The newly drawn text field will have a new property, beneath the "Dynamic Text" text type: The Instance Name panel.

   The Instance Name box is initially filled in with the text '<Instance Name>', but we must put our own name in there if we wish to fill in the contents of this text field using ActionScript at run-time.

Note: We can change the type of any text field, at any time, just by changing the value in the Text Type drop-down menu, in the Properties panel.

4. Within the instance name box of our newly created dynamic text field, enter the word 'myTextField':

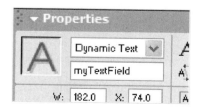

5. Now we can place any text we want into this text field at run-time, with a few simple lines of ActionScript. Let's try this. Create a new layer, and give it the name 'code'.

6. Click on the first frame of the code layer, and press F9 to bring up the actions panel. In the actions window, enter the following line of code:

```
myTextField.text = "Hello, this is
dynamic";
```

Now run the movie by pressing CTRL/⌘+ENTER, and we should see the following:

Hello, this is dynamic

We're using the '.text' property of the dynamic text field object to tell Flash to place text within the text field. This sample can be found in `dynamictext.fla`.

Input text fields

The third type of text field is the Input text field. This has all the same properties as a dynamic text field, except that the user is able to type arbitrary text within the text field as well.

1. Load up `inputtext.fla`.

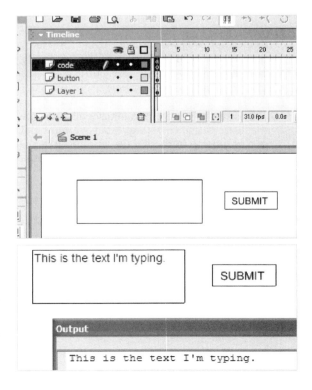

Notice that we have one text field on the stage and one button, which is labeled 'SUBMIT'. This is a small sample application, which works by simply allowing the user to type anything in the text field, and when 'SUBMIT' is pressed, that text will be traced out using the trace command.

2. Select the text field, and look at the Properties panel:

Notice that it still has the instance name, 'myTextField' but it is now an 'Input Text' box. Also, notice that the text field has a black box automatically drawn around it. This is because we have selected the 'Show Border Around Text' option.

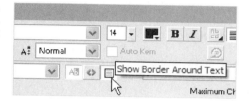

This can sometimes make it easier for input text fields to be seen and recognized. This will make it easier for the user to know where to click when entering information, and means that a border around an input text field is necessary in order to convey maximum usability.

Look at the code that's attached to frame 1 of the code layer:

```
submitButton.onRelease = function()
{
  inputTextVar = myTextField.text;
  trace (inputTextVar);
}
```

The button on our stage has the instance name 'submitButton'. We have one function here, and it's attached to the onRelease action of the 'submitButton'. First, we're assigning the value of the text in our input text field (myTextField) to a variable called 'inputTextVar'. Then, we're using the trace command to display the value of 'inputTextVar' in the output window.

Why are we using a variable intermediary, instead of tracing 'myTextField.text' directly? Well, that's to illustrate the point that the value of any input text field can be assigned to a variable, and then we can do anything we want with that variable, including submit it with forms to a server (as we'll see in **Chapter 11**).

The dashboard in action

Now that we understand how text fields work, let's go back to the dashboard application. The dashboard is highly intelligent, and it takes into consideration the current speed of the vehicle and the elapsed trip time, and from that is able to compute the distance traveled and the fuel and oil consumed.

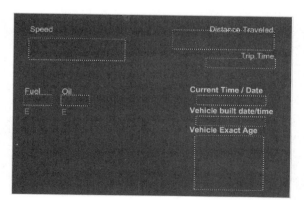

★ Seven

We have the following dynamic text fields on the interactive dashboard:

- ★ Speed (instance name 'speedText')

- ★ Distance Traveled ('distText')

- ★ Trip Time ('elapsedText')

- ★ Fuel ('fuelText')

- ★ Oil ('oilText')

- ★ Current Time / Date ('currentDateText')

- ★ Date built ('buildDateText')

- ★ Vehicle age ('ageDateText')

Now, it's important to understand how the dashboard computer keeps track of the information about the car. The dashboard keeps track of four main variables: 'mySpeed', 'myDist', 'myFuel' and 'myOil'. These are all initially set on frame 1 of the code layer, like so:

```
mySpeed = 0;
myDist = 0;
myFuel = 121;
myOil = 3;
```

This means that the truck starts at 0 kph, with a mileage reading of 0 km. It also begins with 121 liters of fuel, and 3 liters of oil. It is from these four simple variables that the dashboard constructs itself. In order to display these values in their respective text fields, this ActionScript is used:

```
speedText.text = mySpeed + " kph";
distText.text = (Math.floor(myDist *
100) / 100) + " km";
fuelText.text = (Math.floor(myFuel *
10) / 10) + "L";
oilText.text = (Math.floor(myOil * 100)
/ 100) + "L";
```

So, in the 'speedText' dynamic text field, the initial value will be '0 kph'. We're setting the value of the text field to be the value of 'mySpeed' followed by ' kph' (note that kph has a space at the beginning of it).

'distText', 'fuelText' and 'oilText' are all very similar, except for one slight difference. They're using the special `Math.floor` command to format and round the number display so that:

```
3.443212144
```

would be displayed as

```
3.44
```

The formula works like so:

> ROUNDED = (Math.floor(OLDNUMBER * 100) / 100);

This would round the number to the closest 2-digit decimal (1.33, 6.22, 855.64, etc). If we change the '100' to a '10', then it will instead round the number to the nearest 1-digit decimal (2.5, 6.3, 7.7). To make a 3-digit number, then the number used must be 1000, like so:

> ROUNDED = (Math.floor(OLDNUMBER * 1000) / 1000);

And this continues, up to as many decimals as we would like. Once the 'distText', 'fuelText' and 'oilText' have been displayed, then ' km' is added to the end of 'distText.text' and 'L' is added to the end of the other two.

Moving the vehicle

Every time the vehicle's display is updated, we must update the variables depending upon how much time has passed between now and the last time the display was updated (normally only a few milliseconds). What this means is that we have to do some very simple math, and use another special function called 'getTimer()'.

Like the trip odometer in a truck, Flash MX has the ability to determine exactly how long it as been since a movie started running. The `getTimer` function returns this number in milliseconds. Every time our dashboard display is updated (once per frame), we perform this simple piece of code:

```
g = getTimer();
```

In fact, it is this value that we display in the dynamic text field, 'elapsedText'. We use the following ActionScript to do so:

```
elapsedText.text = g add "ms";
```

Just like that, we have a trip time display on our dashboard that is rapidly increasing at a perfectly timed rate. This rate is fixed to the powerful clock inside the computer itself, and as a result, is highly accurate.

In fact, if we wanted to find out how much time had elapsed in seconds, rather than milliseconds, then we just have to divide g by 1000, because there are 1000 milliseconds per second. So:

```
elapsedText.text = (g / 1000) add " sec";
```

... would display the time in seconds rather than milliseconds.

What we must do with this value is determine how much time has passed since the last update. We do so with the following ActionScript:

```
/* How much time has passed since last
update */
tPassed = (g - last) / 3600000;
```

We have this variable called 'tPassed', and we construct it by taking the current elapsed time (in g), and subtracting from it the elapsed time of the previous update (last). Then once that has been done, we will be left with a value in milliseconds (usually around 20 or 30). We must then divide that by 3600000, to convert this time interval into *hours*. Since all the speed measurements are in kilometers per *hour*, then it's not useful to know the elapsed time in milliseconds.

Now that we have the critical elapsed time measurement, we can perform the next great task of determining the distance traveled since the last update. This will simply be the speed multiplied by the passed time, or 'mySpeed * tPassed'. This is how far the truck moved since the previous frame. We increase the 'myDist' trip odometer like so:

```
/* change the things that need to be
changed */
myDist += (mySpeed * tPassed);
```

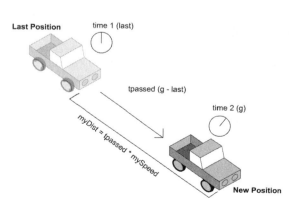

The '+=' operator is responsible for increasing the value of a variable by a specific amount. Like so:

```
Variable += Amount;
```

We'll be looking more at that later, but we also have another similar, but opposite operator, '-='. This is responsible for decreasing a variable by a specific amount:

```
Variable -= Amount;
```

Next we can remove some fuel and oil. The fuel and oil consumption in this truck is generally dependent upon the speed being traveled. The faster we drive the truck, the faster the truck will use up fuel.

```
myFuel -= mySpeed / 700000;
myOil -= mySpeed / 500000000;
```

'myFuel' and 'myOil' are decreased by a scaled-down version of 'mySpeed', which has been scaled by 700,000 or 500,000,000, according to typical vehicle fuel and oil use. These numbers are essentially arbitrary and they have very little actual meaning. They are numbers used to make the vehicle run out of fuel or oil in an average amount of time for a typical truck. At this rate, fuel will be empty after about 600 kilometers. The oil will last much longer, 20,000 km or more before it will be empty.

Remember, because this is a simulation that is based in real-time, we must compute our new values based on the values we had in the previous frame. So, the fuel we have now will be a number slightly less than the last frame. The distance we have now will be slightly greater than the previous frame.

The needles

Earlier we saw that there were two instances of the needle movie clip on the stage: 'oilNeedle' and 'fuelNeedle'. Being movie clips, we can use their _rotation property, and cause the needle to rotate based upon the amount of fuel remaining. At its core, the needle movie clip looks like this:

The center point / registration point of the needle is at its base, and its resting position (where _rotation is 0) is pointing straight up. This means that if we use 'myFuel' to decide the _rotation of the 'fuelNeedle', then it will be pointing straight up when 'myFuel' is 0, or empty.

Because we have markings on the fuel meter that indicate straight up to be 'E', or 'empty', we can safely say that straight up does represent 0 for 'myFuel'. The same applies for the 'oilNeedle' and the 'myOil' level.

What this ultimately means is that setting the _rotation of the 'fuelNeedle' is as simple as:

```
fuelNeedle._rotation = myFuel;
```

When the fuel level starts off at full ('myFuel' = 121), then the needle will be rotated 121 degrees, and will appear to sit at full:

As 'myFuel' decreases over time, the needle will automatically rotate counterclockwise back to empty. Setting the oilNeedle's _rotation is almost the same:

```
oilNeedle._rotation = myOil * 20;
```

Except this time we're multiplying it by 20, because the oil level is much lower than fuel (only 3 liters of oil, as opposed to 121 liters of fuel), but we still want the needle to appear to be more than only 3 degrees rotated. So, we multiply it by 20, which will make the full 3 liters place the needle at 3 * 20, or 60 degrees.

The road dots

The road dots position themselves based upon the distance traveled, and so the faster we drive, the faster the dots will move down the screen. There are two dots. One is named 'roadDot', and the other is named 'roadDot2'.

We're setting the '_y' position (vertical position) of the dots, like so:

```
roadDot._y = 120 + (myDist * 10000) % 250;
roadDot2._y = 120 + ((myDist * 10000) +
125) % 250;
```

This may seem a bit strange, but all we're doing is making each dot move down the screen starting at 120 pixels down, and moving down 250 pixels (to pixel 370). Once it reaches this point, it will loop back around to the top of the screen, and repeat.

The '% 250' achieves this by preventing the number calculated exceeding 250. When the number exceeds 250, it will automatically be 'looped' back around to 0. We must multiply 'myDist' by 10000 if we want the dots to move at anything faster than a snail's pace. The second dot sits exactly 125 pixels below the first dot, so that the two dots are perfectly, evenly spaced.

When the vehicle is running, as 'myDist' is increasing, so will the '_y' position of the dots. They will continue to scroll down, and loop back to the top as the vehicle motors along.

The speed buttons

The speed of this vehicle is controlled using the state of the art 'slow down' and 'speed up' buttons. These buttons are sitting on the dashboard, and they have the instance names 'slowDownButton' and 'speedUpButton'.

Attached to frame 1 of the code layer, is the following ActionScript:

```
speedUpButton.onRelease = function() {
  mySpeed += 5;
};
slowDownButton.onRelease = function() {
  mySpeed -= 5;
};
```

When the speed up button is pressed, then the variable 'mySpeed' is increased by 5. This will cause the vehicle to go 5kph faster. When the slow down button is pressed, 'mySpeed' will decrease by 5, and the vehicle will then go 5kph slower.

This is all that's required to make the entire dashboard display correctly, as the dashboard intelligently computes its status based on the 'mySpeed' variable. The dashboard makes no disallowances for speed limit, engine limitations, etc. This means that we could hit the speed up button many, many times:

...and then we'd be at the wheel of the world's fastest truck. The kilometers would fly by, and the fuel would go down at a visible rate.

The date and time

On this dashboard, the current date and time is conveniently displayed. Along with this, the date that the truck was built, and of course the derived age of the truck itself.

To perform this feat, we're using a special object that Flash offers, called the Date object. The Date object contains and returns specific information about a particular date in time.

To create a new Date object, we use the following ActionScript:

```
myDate = new Date();
```

This creates a simple Date object that is set to today's date, and the current time (the time at which the new `Date()` constructor was run). This only happens when we do not pass any data into the `Date()` constructor. If we want, we can also create a new Date object that is any arbitrary date, like so:

```
myDate = new Date (year, month, day,
hour, minute, second, millisecond);
```

So, we could do this:

```
aDate = new Date(1999, 3, 1, 9, 20, 10,
0);
```

This would set 'aDate' to the date value of April 1, 1999 at 9:20:10 am. Note that the month begins at 0, so that 3 is not the third month, March, but is in fact the fourth month, April.

At the beginning of our dashboard application, we create a few Date objects, like so:

```
curDate = new Date();
updatedDate = new Date();
buildDate = new Date(1999, 3, 1, 9, 20,
10, 0);
```

This creates two Date objects called 'curDate' and 'updatedDate', which will both be set to the current date and time. This also creates a third date object, buildDate, which will be set to April 1, 1999 at 9:20:10.

Once a Date object has been created, there are several functions that we have access to. They are:

★ myDate.getHours() – This returns the hour associated with the Date object (0 to 23)

★ myDate.getMinutes() – This returns the minute associated with the Date object (0 to 59)

★ myDate.getSeconds() - Returns the second associated with a Date object (0 to 59)

★ myDate.getMilliseconds() – Returns the millisecond associated with a Date object (0 to 999)

★ myDate.getDate() – Returns the day of the month (1 to 28, 29, 30 or 31)

★ myDate.getDay() – Returns the day of the week from 0 to 7.

★ myDate.getFullYear() – Returns the full, 4-digit year (e.g., 2002)

★ myDate.getMonth() – Returns the month of the year (0 to 11)

★ myDate.getYear() – Returns a 2-digit year (02, 03, 99)

Also, we have access to the similar, but opposite functions, the 'setters':

★ myDate.setHours() – Sets the hour associated with the Date object (0 to 23).

★ myDate.setMinutes() – Sets the minute associated with the Date object (0 to 59)

★ myDate.setSeconds() - Sets second associated with a Date object (0 to 59)

★ myDate.setMilliseconds() – Sets the millisecond associated with a Date object (0 to 999)

★ myDate.setDate() – Sets the day of the month (1 to 28, 29, 30 or 31)

★ myDate.setDay() – Sets the day of the week from 0 to 7.

★ myDate.setFullYear() – Sets the full, 4-digit year (e.g., 2002)

★ myDate.setMonth() – Sets the month of the year (0 to 11)

myDate.setYear() – Sets a 2-digit year (02, 03, 99)

To display the value of a particular Date object neatly in a text field, we would do something like this:

```
currentDateText.text =
updatedDate.getHours() + ":" +
updatedDate.getMinutes() + ":" +
updatedDate.getSeconds() + " " +
(updatedDate.getMonth() + 1) + "/" +
updatedDate.getDate() + "/" +
updatedDate.getFullYear();
```

This would display a date that looked something like this:

4:59:51 9/1/2002

And this is how it's done in our dashboard application, along with the build date:

```
buildDateText.text =
buildDate.getHours() + ":" +
buildDate.getMinutes() + ":" +
buildDate.getSeconds() + " " +
(buildDate.getMonth() + 1) + "/" +
buildDate.getDate() + "/" +
buildDate.getFullYear();
```

getTime and setTime

Each Date object also has another important function: `getTime` and `setTime`. Internally, the computer thinks of all Date objects as really just a single, large number that is measured in milliseconds. This number is measured against a specific, fixed date / time: Midnight, January 1, 1970. Any negative number is before that date, and any positive number is after that date.

If we say:

```
myDate = new Date();
currentms = myDate.getTime();
trace (currentms);
```

Then, at the time of writing this, we will see 1030871230594 traced in the output window. That is the number of milliseconds since Midnight, January 1, 1970. Alternatively, if we say:

```
myDate = new Date();
myDate.setTime(0);
trace (myDate.toString());
```

then we're setting 'myDate' to be the date at Midnight, January 1, 1970. We will see this traced in the output window:

Wed Dec 31 19:00:00 GMT-0500 1969

Since this author's time zone is Eastern Standard Time (EST), then this moment, which is Midnight, January 1, 1970 in GMT, will be displayed as 5 hours previous, Dec 31 at 19:00, or 7:00 pm – five hours before midnight.

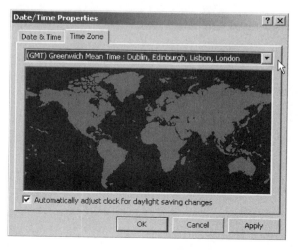

If you were lucky enough to be in Birmingham, UK, like friends of ED, then you'd get this:

Thu Jan 1 00:00:00 GMT+0000 1970

So, if we want to figure out the amount of time that has elapsed between two dates, we simply subtract the computer time of one, from the other, like so:

```
time1 = myDate1.getTime();
time2 = myDate2.getTime();

elapsedTime = time2 - time1;
```

As we saw a moment ago, at the very beginning of our dashboard application we're creating three Date objects. Once these are created, we grab the universal millisecond time of the build date with this code:

```
buildDatems = buildDate.getTime();
```

Now we have the date/time that the vehicle was built in milliseconds. Also, in every frame we're running the new Date command with:

```
updatedDate = new Date();
```

This will ensure that we always have an up-to-the-millisecond accurate current date stored within 'updatedDate'. We're placing the new time and date in the `updatedDate` Date object, and that's what we're using to display the current time and date in the dashboard (as we saw a few pages back).

With the following ActionScript, we can determine exactly how old the truck is in milliseconds:

```
ageNum = (updatedDate.getTime()) -
    buildDatems;
```

The current age of the truck is the 'current millisecond time' minus the 'millisecond date the truck was built'. The result is a number that represents the exact age of the truck.

We can then take that number, and break it into variables for seconds, minutes, hours, days and years:

```
secAge = Math.floor(ageNum / 1000) % 60;
minAge = Math.floor(ageNum / 60000) % 60;
hourAge = Math.floor(ageNum / 3600000) % 24;
dayAge = Math.floor(ageNum / 86400000) % 365;
yearAge = Math.floor(ageNum /
31536000000);
```

The technicalities of these functions are too specific to get into here, but we're basically converting everything from a large millisecond value, into clean and clear component time values of seconds, minutes, hours, days and years. Once we have these values, we can display them in our final text field, 'ageDateText':

```
ageDateText.text = yearAge + " years" +
newline + dayAge + " days " + newline +
hourAge + " hours" + newline + minAge +
" minutes" + newline + secAge + "
seconds";
```

Now, we'll have a display that looks like this:

In the text field, notice that we're using the word 'newline'. This causes the subsequent text to be displayed on the next line beneath. The effect is that each of our time breakdowns is on a clean, new line of its own.

Because 'g' is constantly changing, our truck will be getting constantly older. The last thing we do at the end of our main loop, is:

```
last = g;
```

This is where we store the value of g, in the variable last, for use when we next determine the time interval passed between updates.

Vehicle Exact Age

3 years
153 days
19 hours
2 minutes
30 seconds

The end result

All of this code is running in one simple object called 'updateDisplay', and to see it all together, it looks like this:

```
updateDisplay = function()
{
    g = getTimer();

    /* Move the road dots */
    roadDot._y = 120 + (myDist * 10000) % 250;
    roadDot2._y = 120 + ((myDist * 10000) + 125) % 250;

    /* How much time has passed since last update */
    tPassed = (g - last) / 3600000;

    /* change the things that need to be changed */
    myDist += (mySpeed * tPassed);
    myFuel -= mySpeed / 900000;
    myOil -= mySpeed / 500000000;
    fuelNeedle._rotation = myFuel;
    oilNeedle._rotation = myOil * 20;

    /* Display the dynamic text */
    elapsedText.text = g add "ms";
    speedText.text = mySpeed + " kph";
    distText.text = (Math.floor(myDist * 100) / 100) + " km";
    fuelText.text = (Math.floor(myFuel * 10) / 10) + "L";
    oilText.text = (Math.floor(myOil * 100) / 100) + "L";

    updatedDate = new Date();
    currentDateText.text = updatedDate.getHours() + ":" + updatedDate.getMinutes() +
    ":" + updatedDate.getSeconds() + " " + (updatedDate.getMonth() + 1) + "/" +
    updatedDate.getDate() + "/" + updatedDate.getFullYear();

    buildDateText.text = buildDate.getHours() + ":" + buildDate.getMinutes() + ":"
    + buildDate.getSeconds() + " " + (buildDate.getMonth() + 1) + "/" +
    buildDate.getDate() + "/" + buildDate.getFullYear();

    ageNum = (updatedDate.getTime()) - buildDatems;
    secAge = Math.floor(ageNum / 1000) % 60;
    minAge = Math.floor(ageNum / 60000) % 60;
    hourAge = Math.floor(ageNum / 3600000) % 24;
    dayAge = Math.floor(ageNum / 86400000) % 365;
    yearAge = Math.floor(ageNum / 31536000000);
    ageDateText.text = yearAge + " years" + newline + dayAge + " days " + newline +
    hourAge + " hours" + newline + minAge + " minutes" + newline + secAge + "
    seconds";

    last = g;

}
```

We're also telling this to run, every frame, with this code, which comes at the very end of the ActionScript in frame 1 of the code layer:

```
_root.onEnterFrame = updateDisplay;
```

We're telling Flash to run the `updateDisplay` function, every single frame. In the `dashboard.fla` movie, this would be 31 times per second.

Changing the frame rate

If we want, we can change the frame rate of this movie.

Let's try this. Make sure that nothing is selected, and look at the Properties panel. It should look something like this:

The Frame Rate is listed there as 31fps (frames per second). This is how many times per second the screen is being redrawn.

We can change that to any value between 0.01 and 120. Now, because our truck's movement, speed and distance is timed with a clock, and not the frame rate, we could slow down the movie's frame rate to 1 fps, but still the truck would keep up to a truck with a dashboard running at 31 fps.

This is because we're not slowing down or speeding up the truck itself, but only the rate at which its internal computer is updating the display on the dashboard. Ideally, we would want the rate to be fast enough so that things like speed, distance and time appear to smoothly change on screen, but the main point to remember is that it's not necessary in order for the truck, and the dashboard to operate properly. This is an example of frame-rate independent operation.

Summary

What we've learned here is that Flash has a powerful set of interactive ActionScript tools for both displaying text on screen and for working with the date and time. Using interactive text, we can greatly enhance the functionality and look of our web sites, and as we'll see shortly, we can add interactive components to those text fields to make them even more functional. Also, a computer keeps accurate time because its clock is based on an internal system clock that is very, very accurate. As a result, Flash also has a highly accurate set of time measuring tools that are all derived from the one system clock.

The Road: Driving Conditions and Logic

What's in this chapter:

★ Logical Thinking in Driving

★ How it relates to ActionScript

★ Interactive Simulation

★ Real-World Physics

★ X axis

★ Y axis

★ Both X and Y

★ Rotational Motion

★ Overhead Driving Simulator

The logic of life

When on the road in our brand-new truck, the way that we operate is much like a computer program. We have to follow the rules, pay attention to conditions of the road and gently apply our own tweaks as we see necessary. For example, on a particularly long and empty stretch of road, we may find it acceptable to go 10% above the posted speed limit. Or, if the road is slippery, we may want to adjust our driving to accommodate for the required stopping distance.

Rules of the road

Let's look at some simple rules, as we might apply them to our own driving experience.

```
I'm driving along.
Check the speed limit.
If I'm driving less than the speed
limit, speed up.
What's my mood?
If I'm feeling daring, then I'll set
my personal limit to something high-
er than the posted speed limit.
If I'm feeling timid, on the other
hand, I'll drive slower than the
posted speed limit.
What are the road conditions?
If the road is slippery, then I have
to adjust my stopping distance.
Is that a stop sign? Then Stop.
```

This approximates the thoughts we may encounter on the road. These can be easily translated into computer code, and more specifically, into a Flash MX movie.

To begin with, let's open up `interactiveroad.fla`, and take a look at what we have.

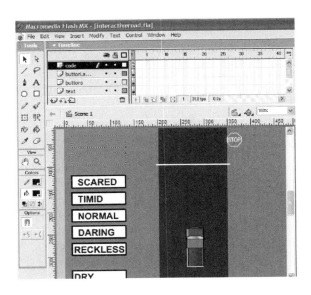

We see a truck, a road, some grass, a stop sign, and a few buttons. Stationary, this doesn't seem like much, but when we run this movie with CTRL/⌘ + ENTER, we'll see something slightly different.

We're looking at an interactive simulation of driving. The simulated diver behind the wheel of the truck is following specific rules, based upon the driving conditions. Our driver tends to be rather emotional and, at the press of a button, we can swing him from scared to reckless.

In the simulation, we can see the current mood of the driver, and the current speed of the truck in the upper left hand corner of the screen. In the top image, the driver is timid, so he's going 70kph in a 100kph speed zone. In the bottom image, however, we can see that he's in a daring mood, and that the road is slippery. The combined effect is that he has gone through the stop sign, and is having trouble slowing down so the truck is starting to fishtail.

In effect, we're "playing God", while our moody truck driver struggles to cope with our actions.

A note to remember: All of our ActionScript code for this movie is found on frame 1 of the layer named 'code'. So, when we talk about looking at and changing code, this is where it's done.

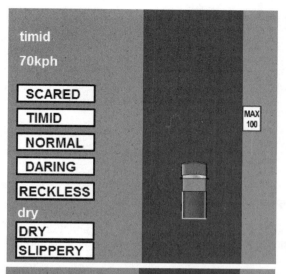

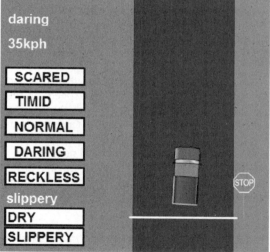

8

Road signs

The first thing to understand is that the road signs are all contained in one movie clip called 'signs'. Each frame of that movie clip represents a different road sign, and there are three frames, and therefore three different types of road signs:

Stop Sign, on frame 1:

Speed limit "50", on frame 2:

Speed limit "100", on frame 3:

See how we only have one movie clip, and it contains all three signs, rather than having three different movie clips? This is a very simple way of organizing our objects, especially since they all fall under the same 'category'; they're all road signs. Also, this way we only really need to have one 'road sign' movie clip on stage at once, and all we have to do is change its 'face'.

Now, the road sign zooms in from the top, and downwards along the screen at the speed of the truck. As it moves, the 'driver' reacts to the sign, by following the rules of his virtual world. Once the road sign is off the bottom of the screen, then we bring it back to the top, and change it to a new, random frame (from 1 to 3), and then the cycle repeats. To set the signs up, the very first two lines of ActionScript are like this:

```
signs._y = -10;
signs.gotoAndStop(Math.floor(Math.rando
m() * 3) + 1);
```

The _y position (vertical position) of the signs movie clip is set to -10, which is off the top of the screen. This is important in order to make sure that no sign is visible when the simulation begins. The next thing we're doing is setting the frame of the sign to a random frame from 1, 2 or 3.

Some math

Briefly, `Math.floor` is a function that simply removes the fractional part from any number. So, `Math.floor(6.5)` returns 6, `Math.floor(22.9)` returns 22, etc.

`Math.random()` is a function that returns a completely random number between 0 and 0.99999. This is very useful when we want the computer to behave in a way that is not always the same, as in the choosing of the road sign. If we multiply the results of `Math.random` by another number, say 'x', then the result will then be between 0 and *almost* x. For example, if x was 10, then the number chosen would be anything between 0 and 9.99999.

So, in the second statement above, we say `Math.random() * 3`. This will return a number from 0 to 2.99999. When we wrap a `Math.floor` around that, we're simply going to be left with 0, 1 or 2, depending upon the results of the random function. Now, since we're putting all this in a `gotoAndStop`, then we know that we're trying to come up with a random frame number. Being a frame, the lowest number can be 1, because in Flash MX, there is no Frame 0. So, in the end, we add 1 (+ 1) to ultimately come up with a number from 1, 2 or 3.

Alternatively, we could use the `Math.ceil` function, which rounds a decimal number up, no matter what the fractional part. So, `Math.ceil(2.2)` is 3, and `Math.ceil(11.8223)` is 12. So, we could do this:

```
signs.gotoAndStop(Math.ceil(Math.random
    () * 3));
```

The main difference? We don't have to add the 1 at the end, because the number will already have been rounded up. There is no preferred method, but we're looking at both here because the `Math.ceil` method is useful when we want a random number between 1 and 3. We would need to use the `Math.floor` method if we wanted to compute a number between 0 and 2.

On our stage, we also have a movie clip called 'truck', with the instance name 'truck'.

This serves mainly as a graphic, and it's used as a reference point for the 'look distance' factor. This is the distance at which the driver spots upcoming signs, and it's measured relative to the truck's on-screen position.

There are also several buttons on the stage. They're all instances of the same Button object, but each has a different instance name. They are, appropriately:

★ slipperyButton

★ dryButton

★ recklessButton

★ daringButton

★ normalButton

★ timidButton

★ scaredButton

The first two are responsible for setting the road conditions, and the remaining five are how we set the emotions of the driver.

There are also three text fields on the stage:

★ roadCondDisp

★ speedDisp

★ moodDisp

The first one displays the road conditions (dry, slippery), the second one displays the truck's current speed, and the third one displays the driver's mood, as a text string ('daring', 'timid', etc.)

World settings

Getting back to the code, the next few lines of ActionScript are:

```
mood = "normal";
doStop = 0;
maxSpeed = 10;
speed = 0;
lookDistance = 250;
roadFriction = .9;
```

The first line is responsible for setting the current mood of the driver to 'normal', the default mood. In this mood, the driver aims to drive at exactly the posted speed limit. 'doStop' is a variable used to determine whether or not the driver is in 'stop mode' or not (when he has spotted a stop sign). More on this in a moment.

Then we have two speed variables, 'maxSpeed' and 'speed'. 'maxSpeed' corresponds to the speed limit, and 'speed' is the actual speed at which the truck is moving. We want the truck to begin stopped, so speed begins at 0. 'maxSpeed', on the other hand, is set to 10, by default, which is about 50kph (multiplying maxSpeed by 5 tells us the real-world kph speed).

'lookDistance' is a value which determines how far ahead along the road the driver is scanning for upcoming road signs, whether they be speed limit signs, or the stop sign. Adjusting this value will give our driver more, or less time to react. 'roadFriction' is a value which indicates how slippery the road is. The default value of .9 is equivalent to a dry road. This value must always be less than 1, but to make the road more slippery, we must set 'roadFriction' to a larger number, like .95 or .97. If we were to set the number to something greater than one, then the road would have the strange effect of *speeding up* the truck! That's right, rather than slow down over time, the truck would start to speed up over time. To make a perfectly frictionless road, the 'roadFriction' would be set to 1. This would, however, ensure that our driver could never stop at any stop sign!

Here is an image that shows the effect that roadFriction has on the truck's position each frame. In this example, because it's stopping over so few frames, this would have a very high amount of friction (roadFriction would be a lower number, below 0.5, because the closer the number is to 1, the more slippery the road will be).

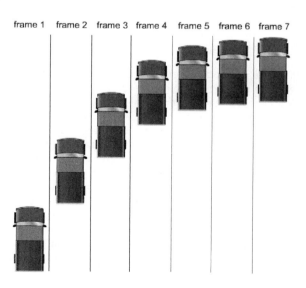

frame 1 frame 2 frame 3 frame 4 frame 5 frame 6 frame 7

Next, we begin our main loop:

```
_root.onEnterFrame = function()
{
```

We're running everything in an `onEnterFrame` event of the `_root` timeline. This is totally acceptable, and it means that the subsequent ActionScript will be run once per frame. Our next line of code:

```
signs._y += speed;
```

moves the sign down the screen, at the truck's speed. Since the truck itself is not moving on screen, we instead move the objects around it to simulate movement.

The next line of code:

```
if (signs._y > (truck._y -
lookDistance))
    {
```

This `if` statement checks to see if the sign has come into the driver's view. It's comparing to determine if the _y position of the sign is closer than the driver's furthest viewable point, which is determined by the _y position of the truck minus the value of 'lookDistance'. Take a look at the bottom image.

We can see that the _y value of signs is between 'truck._y' and 'truck._y' minus 'lookDistance', so the above `if` statement would evaluate as 'true'. When this is the case, then we issue the following code:

```
var c = signs._currentframe;
```

Into the temporary variable 'c', we're assigning the value of the current frame of the 'signs' movie clip. Since the frame number determines what type of sign we're viewing, then we can use this to determine our driver's reaction. We use the 'var' operator to let Flash MX know that once this iteration of the `onEnterFrame` function is complete, we no longer need 'c' to exist; it's purely temporary. Using this method, we can make sure that there are no 'collisions' between variables (say, a variable elsewhere, also called c is erased when we neglect to use the word 'var', thereby making 'c' become a _root variable). We also allow Flash MX to run faster because the processor handles temporary variables more efficiently.

Some more math

We're using the `+=` operator here. As mentioned earlier in the book, this increases a variable by a value. In this case, we're increasing `signs._y` by the value contained in 'speed'. This is called an assignment operator. Often, new programmers express this in the following way:

```
signs._y = signs._y + speed;
```

Assignment operators are quicker, simpler and more optimized to the computer. We have a few more:

★ `+=` increases a variable by a value. "myAge += 2" (look, I'm getting older!)

★ `-=` decreases a variable by a value. "myAge -= 2" (look, I'm getting younger!)

★ `*=` multiplies a variable by a value. "price *= 1.20" (adding 20% tax on price)

★ `/=` divides a variable by a value. "price /= 2" (half price!)

★ `++` A quick way of saying `+= 1`

★ `—` A quick way of saying `-= 1`

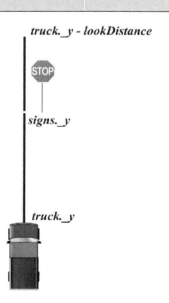

truck._y - lookDistance

signs._y

truck._y

Looking down the road

Next, we have:

```
if (c == 1)
{
    if (doStop == 0) doStop = 1;
}
else if (c == 2)
{
    maxspeed = 10;
}
else if (c == 3)
{
    maxspeed = 20;
}
```

This is responding to the value of 'c'; the type of sign currently zooming towards us. The first type is a stop sign, at which point we set the value of the 'doStop' variable to '1'. We only do this, however, if we haven't already just stopped; we don't want the driver to stop more than once at the same stop sign, no matter how diligent and law-abiding he is. 'doStop' will only be set back to 0 once the stop sign has left the screen, and is no longer in his view range.

The next two types are the 50kph and 100kph speed limits respectively. By setting maxSpeed to 10 or 20, we're telling our driver that the speed limit is 50 or 100kph. Now, going back to the if statement in which we checked to see if the driver has spotted the sign, we have this 'else':

```
else
{
    doStop = 0;
}
```

So, the full structure looks like this:

```
if (signs._y > (truck._y - lookDistance))
{
    .. the sign handling code ..
}
else
{
    doStop = 0;
}
```

Remember, when 'doStop' is 0, then our driver has "permission" to stop at the next stop sign, and what we're doing here is giving him that permission, because there are no stop signs in sight.

Stopping

The next piece of code is:

```
if (doStop == 1)
{
    speed*=roadFriction;
    if (speed < .1)
    {
        doStop = 2;
        truck._rotation = -90;
    }
    truck._rotation+=0.1;
}
```

If the driver is currently in stop mode (has spotted a stop sign) then he applies the brake, and the speed is multiplied by the value of 'roadFriction'. Depending upon the surface of the road, this may see him stopping quickly, or not so quickly. This code will repeat each frame until the driver has come to a *near* complete stop (until his speed is less than .1). At that point, 'doStop' is set to 2, so that he will no longer stop, nor will he spot the same sign again, and try to stop all over again.

Once he has stopped, we set the truck's _rotation to –90, which is pointing straight up. The reason we do this, is to 'right' the trucks orientation should it have fishtailed a lot. Fishtailing occurs as the driver stops, and the longer the stop takes the more the vehicle will fishtail. This is achieved with 'truck._rotation += 0.1'. We're adding 0.1 to the _rotation property of the truck movie clip each frame, as long as it's stopping.

In this image, we can see the effect of the fishtail over a few frames of 'stopping' by the truck. Remember, in a fishtail situation, the vehicle still moves forward even though its orientation does not face the same direction. This is why fishtailing is so dangerous – when the vehicle finally does 'catch' the road, it's pointing in a completely different direction from its momentum. Fortunately, in our demo there will be no vehicle rollovers – unless we're talking about a 'mouse rollover', but that's another chapter.

frame 1   frame 2   frame 3   frame 4   frame 5   frame 6   frame 7

Mood swings

In the event that there's no stop sign in sight, then the driver will obey this set of rules:

```
else
{
    if (mood == "scared") adjustor = .3;
    if (mood == "timid") adjustor = .7;
    if (mood == "normal") adjustor = 1;
    if (mood == "daring") adjustor = 1.3;
    if (mood == "reckless") adjustor = 2;

    if (speed < (maxSpeed * adjustor))
    ➥ speed+=.5;
    if (speed > (maxSpeed * adjustor))
    ➥ speed-=.5;
}
```

Very simply, he's looking at his current mood, as contained in the 'mood' variable, and depending upon what it is, he's setting a variable called 'adjustor' to a number. This is the percentage by which his 'speed limit' will be adjusted. So, when his mood is 'scared', his adjustor will be .3. This means that he will only feel comfortable going at 30% of the speed limit. On the other hand, if he's feeling 'reckless', then look out; he's going to be adjusting his speed limit by a factor of 2, or, he's going to be going twice the speed limit.

A setting of 'reckless', with a roadFriction value of 0.98 (slippery road, as we'll soon see) is a recipe for disaster! He'll most likely skid a kilometer past any stop sign, and spin in a complete circle before coming to a stop.

The next bit of code does some display adjusting and house cleaning:

```
if (signs._y > 1600)
{
    signs._y = -300;
    signs.gotoAndStop(Math.floor
    ➥ (Math.random() * 3) + 1);
}

moodDisp.text = mood;
speedDisp.text = (Math.round(speed) *
➥ 5) + "kph";

}
```

We check to see if the signs movie clip has moved down past _y position 1600, which is long enough for it to be off screen for a few seconds. If so, we move it to _y position −300, which is well above the top of the screen, and then we set its frame to a new, random value; a new road sign is born.

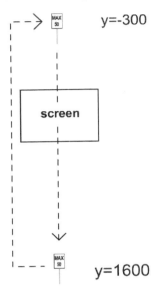

Finally, we're displaying the driver's current mood in the 'moodDisp' text field, as well as displaying his speed, converted to Kph. We're using the Math.round() function to round the value of speed to the nearest whole number (Math.round(4.4) rounds to 4, but Math.round(7.7) rounds to 8). Then we multiply that number by 5 to convert 'speed' into something that resembles kilometers per hour. Then, that's the end of our onEnterFrame function.

The buttons

The remaining code focuses on button presses (or, releases, actually):

```
scaredButton.onRelease = function()
{
    mood = "scared";
}

timidButton.onRelease = function()
{
    mood = "timid";
}
```

```
normalButton.onRelease = function()
{
  mood = "normal";
}

daringButton.onRelease = function()
{
  mood = "daring";
}

recklessButton.onRelease = function()
{
  mood = "reckless";
}

dryButton.onRelease = function()
{
  roadFriction = .9;
  roadCondDisp.text = "dry";
}

slipperyButton.onRelease = function()
{
  roadFriction = .98;
  roadCondDisp.text = "slippery";
}
```

The physics of the world

In the real world, we've all come to understand and intuitively expect objects to behave certain ways when we, or other forces act upon them. For example, when we throw something into the air, we expect it to come back down again, eventually. Or, if something is made of rubber, and it happens to be a ball, then we expect it to bounce when it hits the ground, or the wall.

Well, it turns out that most of these things can be easily re-created by computers, and in fact things like this are what computers excel at. The arc of flight, the path, the gravity, the reflection, are all concepts that we unthinkingly expect to see fulfilled, and they're remarkably easy to simulate.

Part 1: X-axis of motion

Consider this: Imagine a truck tire that is upright on its side, stationary on the spot:

These are all very straightforward. We're setting the value of the 'mood' variable to the appropriate text string when any of the mood buttons are released. The 'dry' button and the 'slippery' button simply change the value of the 'roadFriction' variable, and display the appropriate road condition in the 'roadCondDisp' text field.

And there we have a fully functioning Flash MX driving simulation, showing how the rules of the road and the simple mind of a very moody driver can be easily broken down into logic and code. Next, we're going to look at some basic physics and a little more math.

Now let's imagine that we walk up to this tire, and give it a little nudge. As soon as we push that tire, it will begin to roll at a speed which is relative to how hard we pushed it. Let's say we push the tire so that it rolls away at 1 meter every 2 seconds, or .5 meters per second, along an imaginary axis, x.

elapsed time: 1 second

0.5 meters

We could say that the tire has changed its x position by 0.5 meters. Another, and common way of referring to a 'change' in something is to call it a 'delta'. For example, when the temperature drops 20 degrees overnight, we can say that the delta temperature was −20. When the tire moves, its 'changed x position', or delta x position is 0.5. Or, simply put, its dx (delta x) is 0.5. We will refer to all changes in position in this manner, dx and dy.

Now, imagine Flash MX, where we don't measure things in meters, but pixels, and our distinct unit of time is not a second, but a frame. Now also imagine that this tire is actually a movie clip with the instance name 'tire'. We could run this code every frame:

```
tire._x += 0.5;
```

...to move the tire half a pixel per frame. Or, we could, at the beginning of our program, say this:

```
dx = 0.5;
```

...and then later, in a frame loop, say:

```
tire._x += dx;
```

And suddenly our tire will be rolling at a fixed speed, towards the right. To see this truly in action, take a look at `tireroll.fla`.

We have a movie clip on the stage with the instance name 'tire'. Attached to frame 1 of the code layer is the following ActionScript:

```
moveRoll = function()
{
  this._x += this.dx;
  this.spokes._rotation = this._x;
}

tire.dx = 1;
tire.onEnterFrame = moveRoll;
```

We have created a function called `moveRoll`, and this function works upon itself (`this`), and moves the `_x` position of whatever movie clip is using this code, by the amount contained in 'dx', which is also attached to the movie clip itself.

Then, we're creating the variable `dx` in the tire movie clip with `tire.dx = 1`. Finally, we're telling the tire that its `onEnterFrame` function should be the `moveRoll` function. The effect, when run, is a tire that rolls slowly across the screen at exactly 1 pixel per frame.

Now, there's a unique effect in the tire itself. As it moves, it will appear to rotate (as tires do). The tire movie clip itself, however, is not actually rotating. Instead, there is a movie clip *within* the tire movie clip called 'spokes', and that is what is being rotated.

In this image of the tire movie clip, the spokes are the black areas contained within the box. When those rotate, the chrome beneath and lighting effects on the tire itself do not rotate, and the effect is cool, and realistic. After all, we don't want the light shine to be turning around the tire as if it were painted on; we want it to remain in one spot on the surface of the tire, though the tire itself is rotating. We accomplish this by simply rotating the spokes.

By setting the `_rotation` of the spokes to the `_x` position of the tire (`this.spokes._rotation = this._x;`) the tire will appear to rotate clockwise as the tire moves right, and counterclockwise as the tire moves left. This is a very realistic effect.

Our reason for using 'dx' is simple. If we wanted to stop the tire completely, we would set 'dx' to 0. If we wanted to slow down the tire gradually, all we would need to do is multiply 'dx' by a certain amount, say 0.9, and the tire would slow down as 'dx' was gradually reduced to 0. So,

```
dx *= 0.9;
```

...will slow down the tire by 90% each frame, since 'dx' is its speed. This is known as deceleration. On the other hand, if we multiplied 'dx' by a number greater than 1, then the tire would appear to accelerate.

```
dx *= 2;
```

This would double the speed of the tire every frame. That's a very fast acceleration, and the tire would quickly be gone from site. If we didn't want to accelerate so fast, we could simply use addition, rather than multiplication:

```
dx += .5;
```

This would gradually speed up the tire by 0.5 "pixels per frame", per frame. We could also subtract from the tire's 'dx', like so:

```
dx -= 0.5;
```

But keep in mind, when 'dx' reaches 0 (stationary) and continues to subtract by −0.5, then the tire will effectively change direction.

On the other hand, we could multiply dx by −1, and the effect would be to simply (and instantly) reverse the direction of the tire.

If 'dx' was 8 (moving right 8 pixels per frame) and we did this:

```
dx *= -1;
```

...then 'dx' would become −8, which would mean move left 8 pixels per frame. The moment when we might want to use this? Well, let's think – when *does* a tire instantly change direction? When it hits a wall, or perhaps hits the ground. That brings us to the next part.

Part 2: Y-axis of motion

We just looked at moving along the X-axis; horizontal motion. Now, it's interesting to note that this *always* has nothing to do with vertical motion. In fact, the two operate independently of each other, even though they may be working on the same object at the same time.

The classic (and often surprising) explanation for this is the bullet and the stone. Let's imagine someone standing in an empty field with a gun in one hand, and a stone in the other. Then, they fire the gun perfectly horizontally, and release the stone at the same moment. The bullet will fly quite far horizontally, but it will hit the ground at precisely the same moment as the stone lands by this person's

feet. The gravity pulling down on the stone and the bullet are identical, and are completely independent of the bullet's horizontal (x-axis) motion.

This brings us to `tirebounce.fla`. Open it up, and notice that it's identical to the previous example. However, running it will produce a slightly different result: The tire will not move horizontally, but will instead bounce vertically on the spot. This is its code:

```
gravity = 0.9;
ground = 350;

moveBounce = function()
{

  this._y += this.dy;
  this.dy += gravity;

  if (this._y > (ground - (this._height
/ 2)))
  {
    this._y = ground - this._height /
2;
    this.dy *= -.5;
  }

  this.spokes._rotation = this._x;

}

tire.onEnterFrame = moveBounce;
```

We have a variable called "gravity", which can be adjusted and the effects will be to make the tire appear heavier or lighter. The variable 'ground' is to indicate where the ground is so that the tire doesn't just fall into oblivion.

We're creating a function called `moveBounce`, which begins with us moving the tire's _y position by 'dy'. We're using 'dy', in the same manner as we used 'dx'; as a rate-of-change-in-y value. Notice next that we're increasing 'dy' by gravity. This will have the effect of making the tire's 'dy' get bigger each frame, meaning that the tire will move down more each frame. What does this look like? Falling, of course. Since gravity has the effect of speeding up the descent of something that is in freefall, this will cause the tire to fall faster and faster.

We stop things there, however, when we do this:

```
if (this._y > (ground - (this._height /
2)))
```

We're checking to see if the tire has passed the ground. Remember, the center point of our tire is in the middle of the tire. However, we don't want that position to hit the ground, we want that position plus the _height of the tire, divided by 2 to be the point at which the tire has hit the ground. If we didn't do this, the tire would appear to sink into the ground up to its midpoint.

Now, if a collision is detected with the ground, then we move the tire back up to ground level (just in case its new position is technically below ground (don't worry, it wouldn't appear in its new position until next frame, so if we fix it now, it will never appear below ground). Remember, we're moving 'dy' pixels each frame. If the tire's position is above the ground by 2 pixels, but 'dy' was 10, then the next position would place the tire below the ground by 8 pixels. So, we fix that here.

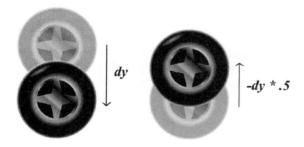

dy   *-dy * .5*

The next thing we do is multiply the tire's 'dy' by -.5, that is, negative 0.5. Why? To bounce, of course. We want the tire's 'dy' to reverse, so that what was a downwards motion turns into an upwards motion; when we move a tire (or any movie clip) on the _y axis by a *negative* number, it will move *up*, not down. Notice though that when we multiply by -.5, and not -1, that some of the momentum is lost. In the above

image, the upward bounce is not equal to the same downward speed. This is to simulate the effect of some energy being lost with each bounce. No object bounces so perfectly as to maintain all of its momentum, and eventually, all bouncing objects will come to rest.

If we want the tire to eventually come to a complete stop (because, in this example it will bounce smaller and smaller forever, but never stop) then we must change the bounce code to this:

```
if (this._y > (ground - (this._height /
2)))
{
    this._y = ground - this._height / 2;
    this.dy *= -.5;
    if (this.dy < 1.4 && this.dy > -1.4)
this.dy = 0;
}
```

The new line checks to see if, on bounce, the tire's vertical speed has dropped to between -1.4 and 1.4, then we know it's as good as stationary, so we set its 'dy' to 0, to be sure that it's stopped completely. This code is found in `tirebouncestop.fla`.

Part 3: Putting them together

Now that we've seen both X and Y axis motion, and how they're similar and how they differ, let's see how we can go about putting them together in the same movie. Seeing as they're independent of each other, it should really be no big deal to act both on the _x and _y positions of the tire with 'dx' and 'dy' at once.

Take a look at `tirebouncewall.fla`. When we run this movie, we'll see the following on screen:

That tire is bouncing both off the ground and off the walls. It is behaving in a way that combines vertical and horizontal motion, and here is the code:

```
gravity = 0.9;
ground = 350;
leftwall = 0;
rightwall = 549;

tire.swapDepths(1000);

moveBounce = function()
{

  this._x += this.dx;
  this._y += this.dy;
  this.dy += gravity;

  if (this._y > (ground - (this._height
➥ / 2)))
  {
    this._y = ground - this._height / 2;
    this.dy *= -.7;
  }

  // hit the right wall
  if (this._x > (rightwall -
➥ (this._width / 2)))
  {
    this._x = rightwall - this._width / 2;
    this.dx *= -.9;
  }


// hit the left wall
  if (this._x < (leftwall +
(this._width / 2)))
    {
    this._x = leftwall + this._width / 2;
    this.dx *= -.9;
  }

  this.spokes._rotation = this._x;

  makeTrail();

}
```

Everything is very similar, except we've added both 'dx' and 'dy' to this. Also, we've defined two new variables, 'leftwall' and 'rightwall', as values for us to use when determining the bounce off the wall. The bounce off the wall works very much like the bounce off the floor; we check to see if the tire has surpassed the left or the right wall, and if it has, move it back into the screen, and then reverse its 'dx' value by -.9.

```
// hit the right wall
if (this._x > (rightwall - (this._width /
➥ 2)))
{
  this._x = rightwall - this._width / 2;
  this.dx *= -.9;
}

// hit the left wall
if (this._x < (leftwall + (this._width
➥ / 2)))
{
  this._x = leftwall + this._width / 2;
  this.dx *= -.9;
}
```

We offset our check by this._width / 2, for the same reason that we subtracted the _height / 2 in the previous floor bounce: To account for the shape of the tire, and the fact that the tire's _x and _y are actually located at its dead center.

We also call a function called makeTrail, which leaves fading copies of the tire on the stage as it bounces around. It's just a cool effect, really, to make the movement look more obvious. We'll look at that function in a moment.

After the moveBounce function is defined, we have this code:

```
tire.dx = 22;
tire.dy = -22;
tire.onEnterFrame = moveBounce;
```

We're giving our tire a bit of momentum to start with (22 pixels per frame to the right, and an upwards speed of 22 pixels per frame), and then setting its onEnterFrame function to moveBounce.

Now, we have this `makeTrail` function:

```
makeTrail = function()
{
    nm = "tr" + cnt;
    _root.attachMovie("tire", nm, cnt);
    cnt++;
    _root[nm]._x = tire._x;
    _root[nm]._y = tire._y;
    _root[nm]._alpha = 50;
    _root[nm].onEnterFrame = function()
    {
        this._alpha -= 2;
        if (this._alpha <= 0)
      ➡ removeMovieClip(this);
    }
    cnt%=50;
}
```

It simply keeps creating instances of the tire movie clip from the library with the `attachMovie` function. The new instances are called 'tr0', 'tr1', 'tr2', 'tr3', etc., and they're positioned on the stage at the exact current location of the tire. Their '_alpha' property is set to 50 by default (which is 50% transparent or see-through), and then each copy is given its own little function. This function causes the copy to fade itself out by 2 percent every frame, until it is invisible, at which point it removes itself from existence with `removeMovieClip(this)`.

We must be sure to remove the movie clips, and not just 'hide' them by setting their `_visible` to `false`, or `_alpha` to `0`. This is because even though they would be invisible, the computer would still be keeping track of them, mathematically speaking, so we `removeMovieClip` them, and then we know that Flash will essentially forget they ever existed.

Eventually, 'cnt' (the instance counter) will loop around from 49 back to 0, with the "modulus assignment operator" of `cnt%=50`. Using this, it's possible to make any number fall within a given range of our design.

Let's imagine that h = 53 and then we perform this:

```
h%=50;
```

...h will be set to 3 because the 50 will have been factored out. So, 53%50 will be 3, then 54%50 will be 4, and it continues. 60%50 will be, you guessed it, 10. What about 99%50? That'll be 49. And how about 101%50? That'll be 1 because everything is a division of 50, and then we simply take the remainder.

By doing this every frame, when `cnt` surpasses 49 it will become 0 again, and our next instance will be `tr0`. This way we don't create potentially millions of movie clips, and instead create a maximum of 50.

> Note: If you don't want the trails, simply remove the line "makeTrail();" in the moveBounce function, and all that will remain is the bouncing tire.

These are the basics of simple physics movement. Though the code is simple, the motions created on screen are elaborate and impressive.

8

Rotational motion

We just saw how to move an object using 'dx' and 'dy'. This is also known as 'rectangular motion', because `_x` and `_y` are being moved by a fixed amount on 'dx' and 'dy', so as to create a 'rectangle' of motion from `_x`, `_y` to `_x + dx`, `_y + dy`.

There's another type of motion, and one that we're familiar with because it's how we move. It's called 'rotational motion', and it involves moving not in squares, but along a fixed path at a particular angle and speed. In order to change the motion, we must turn, or rotate, to a new angle, and then continue along that path.

This is also how vehicles move. We accelerate forward, and turn the steering wheel to change direction. To convey the motion in terms of variables, we must think in terms of two values:

★ ang

★ speed

'ang' is the orientation around a circle (the *ang*le), and 'speed' is how far along that particular orientation we're moving, each frame.

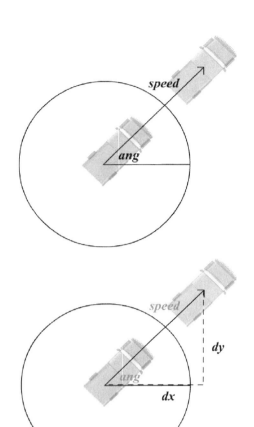

Now, having said that, it's important to realize that when the time comes to actually move an object rotationally, or radially on the screen, we must convert the angle/speed motion into a 'dx' and a 'dy' value because the stage coordinates can only be expressed in the angular (x, y) form. Looking at the next image, we can see how 'ang' and 'speed' can also be interpreted as 'dx' and 'dy':

So, we can move around in a radial, angular way, but when it comes time to placing and moving the truck on screen, we must convert from radial coordinates to rectangular coordinates. We do that, like so:

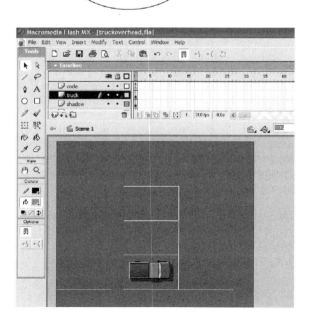

```
dx = cos(ang) x speed
dy = sin(ang) x speed
```

That's it. Both `ang` and `speed` are used in the computation of 'dx' and 'dy', but the difference is the use of the trigonometric function cos versus sin. In ActionScript, we would accomplish this feat, like so:

```
this.dx = Math.cos(this.ang) *
this.speed;
this.dy = Math.sin(this.ang) *
this.speed;
```

We use the `Math.cos` and the `Math.sin` methods of the Math object to perform our conversion.

So, how can we see this all in action? Take a look at `truckoverhead.fla`.

We have a really nice parking lot, with a few painted parking spots and road lines. In the middle of the screen, we have a truck movie clip (instance name: 'truck'), and beneath it is a movie clip called 'shadow'. When we run this, we can drive around the parking lot using the arrow keys. Up is forward, Down is backward and Left and Right are for steering.

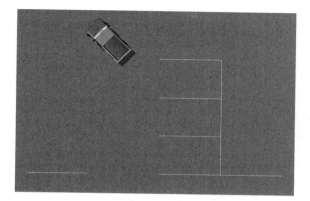

Driving the truck is smooth and clean. There are a few extra goodies as well. The tires, for example, rotate when the truck is turned. The shadow also moves around the truck in correct proportion to create the illusion that the shadow is being cast. The code for this is contained on frame 1 of the code layer, and it goes like this:

```
accel = .3;
decay = .98;
maxTurnRate = 0.01;

truck.onEnterFrame = function()
{

  if (key.isDown(Key.UP))
  {
    this.speed+=accel;
  }
  else if (key.isDown(Key.DOWN))
  {
    this.speed-=accel;
  }

  if (key.isDown(Key.RIGHT))
  {
    this.turnRate += maxTurnRate;
  }
  else if (key.isDown(Key.LEFT))
  {
```

```
    this.turnRate -= maxTurnRate;
  }

  this.leftWheel._rotation =
➥ this.turnRate * 300;
  this.rightWheel._rotation =
➥ this.turnRate * 300;

  this.speed *= decay;
  if (Math.abs(this.speed) < 0.1)
➥ this.speed = 0;

  this.ang+=(this.turnRate * this.speed
➥ * .1);
  this.turnRate *= 0.86;

  this.dx = Math.cos(this.ang) *
➥ this.speed;
  this.dy = Math.sin(this.ang) *
➥ this.speed;

  this._x += this.dx;
  this._y += this.dy;
  this._rotation = this.ang / (Math.PI
➥ / 180);

  shadow._x = this._x + 7;
  shadow._y = this._y + 7;
  shadow._rotation = this._rotation;

}
```

There's a value called 'accel', which is used to define how quickly 'speed' is increased, or, how fast the truck speeds up in a forward direction. We have a value called 'decay', which determines how the truck will slow down over time. This way, when the key is released, the truck will roll to a stop. 'maxTurnRate' determines how quickly the truck can turn – its turning radius. This value should be kept relatively small otherwise it will not turn in a realistic manner.

Then, in the onEnterFrame function of the truck, we're using the Key.isDown function to determine if certain keys are currently being held down, specifically 'Key.UP', 'Key.DOWN', 'Key.LEFT' and 'Key.RIGHT'. If the user is pressing Up, then speed is increased by 'accel'. If the user is pressing Down, then speed is decreased by 'accel'. This will cause the truck to move forward and backward.

If the Left or Right arrows are pressed, then we increase or decrease a value called 'turnRate'. It is 'turnRate' that we use to modify and ultimately determine 'ang'.

We have a cool two little lines of code that set the _rotation of the two front tires within the truck movie clip. This creates the realistic impression that the tires really are turning, and that the truck really is driving.

```
this.leftWheel._rotation =
➡ this.turnRate * 300;
this.rightWheel._rotation =
➡ this.turnRate * 300;
```

As the truck drives, we reduce its speed, and if speed is less than 0.1, then the truck is considered stopped, and speed is set to 0. Next, we increase 'ang' by 'turnRate', and then decrease 'turnRate' by 0.86. This means that the truck will slowly 'accelerate' into and out of a turn. This is simply so that turns are smooth, rather than jarring from one angle to another.

```
this.ang+=(this.turnRate * this.speed * .1);
this.turnRate *= 0.86;
```

Next, we calculate 'dx' and 'dy' from speed and ang, and then we add 'dx' and 'dy' to the truck's '_x' and '_y' position, and the truck will move along at the proper speed and direction, in 'dx' and 'dy'. We also have to set the _rotation of the truck movie clip, using this:

```
this._rotation = this.ang / (Math.PI / 180);
```

In Flash, a movie clip's '_rotation' properties are measured in degrees (of which there are 360 in a circle, as we all know), yet the Math.sin and Math.cos functions require a measurement in *radians* (of which there are 6.28 in a circle, which we may not all know).

Here is the circle as the _rotation property sees it:

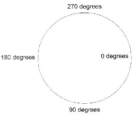

Here is the circle as Math.sin and Math.cos see it:

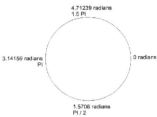

So, this means that ang is actually an angle in radians, not degrees. In order to convert from radians to degrees, we must divide the radian ang by "Math.PI / 180", and the result will be a nice angle in degrees. Note, the Math.PI property returns the mathematical constant, PI, which is approximately 3.14159. Sorry if this is confusing folks, but people go to school for years to learn this stuff. If you're interested in the basics of radian trigonometry, check out a nearby 11th grade math textbook.

The last thing we do is set the '_x' and '_y' position of the shadow movie clip to be the truck's _x and _y, offset by 7 pixels on each axis. Then, we set the _rotation of the shadow to match that of the truck. The end result is that the shadow follows the truck perfectly, yet maintains an offset so that it looks like it's being cast by the truck.

Summary

Phew! That was a lot of math at the end there, and that's only skimming the surface. If interested, readers should look up physics and math of motion on the Internet. There is lots to learn and know, and not enough space in five books to cover it all. What we've looked at here is the basic requirements to get motion graphics working in a square (x, y) and radial (angle, speed) form. Experimenting and playing is the best way to continue from here.

Using logic and physics, we can create incredibly stunning and realistic motion in our Flash movies, and truly 'catapult' them to the next level.

Winch, Lights, Siren, Stereo, Horn

What's in this chapter:

★ Using Sound

  ★ Event sound and streaming sound

  ★ Looking at the sound object

  ★ Attaching and loading sound

  ★ Creating effects with script

  ★ Working with Video

  ★ Video basics

  ★ Compression and optimization

  ★ Manipulating and controlling video

  ★ Understanding Accessibility

  ★ Good practices for accessible movies

  ★ Checking for screen readers

Customizing the car with accessories

There are many different kinds of vehicles, and each model of car and truck has its own features which differentiate one from another. On top of this, you might add your own personal custom add-ons, accessories, or upgrades. These add-ons can make your car unique, and add a lot of value.

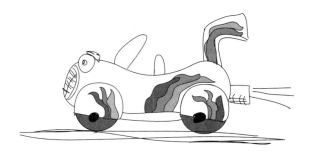

Sometimes the customizations made to the vehicle are performed solely for entertainment value. Other times, they are made for much more substantial reasons: access. A person might not physically be able to drive a standard car, so he or she needs the vehicle to be modified in order to use it. Sporting hobbyists may need a special roof-rack, or an animal shelter worker may need a built in dog-crate and CB radio installed. Purposes and reasons aside, all modifications are easily made after a little knowledge is acquired.

In this chapter, we are going to look at how sound and video can be added to your movie. These special additions can then be manipulated after the fact, all by using ActionScript. Also, you can use code to add special functionality to make your movie more accessible to visitors who are using screen readers to access content. By the end of this chapter, you will be comfortable making these additions and modifications and manipulating them using ActionScript.

Using sound

Adding sound to an interface can make a huge difference in a movie. Although not essential to make a movie run, sound can add intrigue, dimension and act as a different mode of communication. Sometimes sound will be the primary purpose of a movie, and other times it will be a minor effect. You should note that with sound usually comes additional (and sometimes significant) file size, but some planning and organization will definitely help you avoid problems.

Audio and your movie

Audio has always been a challenge in Flash, although Flash MX has some added script which helps make life much easier. Syncing is much easier now with the `Sound.onSoundComplete` handler, which fires a function once a sound has finished playing. Also, the `Sound.position` property has been added which enables you to pause your audio. We will look at each of these later in the chapter.

A common technique for working with audio is to *layer sounds*. Layering can help reduce gaps between loops and other such idiosyncrasies. You should be aware that Flash has eight sound channels for you to work with. This will be particularly important when layering sounds, but also if you have a lot of effects active in the production.

But you don't have to manually edit or manipulate sound right in Flash - you can also dynamically load sounds into your movie and then affect these sounds! Dynamically loading MP3 files is new to Flash MX, and is great for managing user content. Your users can choose when to download particular sounds or content, rather than all at once when they initially load your site. ActionScript can be used to a certain extent to create effects – one of which we will examine later in this section.

Event and streaming sound

You have two options for music in your car: you can turn on the radio, or you can play a CD. Each has their advantages and disadvantages. The radio can continue playing new content for the entire trip, but it might break up or be affected by static. You know the CD sounds great, and you can skip ahead to any track you want. However, the CD only lasts an hour, and repeating it over and over might get boring.

There are two ways you can have audio play in your movies, the first is an **event sound**, which needs to be completely loaded before you play it – a bit like the car's CD. The second is **streaming sound**, which plays more or less as it arrives, like the radio. In reality, streaming is a little different to the radio because it uses a **buffer**.

This works a bit like pouring water through a funnel. If you poured water carelessly into a narrow funnel, the water would still come out at the same speed. The jug is like the server, the erratic flow the result of the way information is sent on the Internet, and the funnel is acting as a buffer.

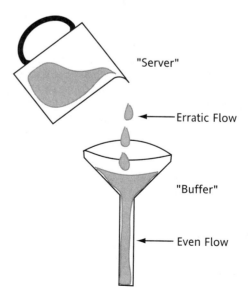

"Server"

Erratic Flow

"Buffer"

Even Flow

Once it has finished playing, it will begin streaming over itself, or a new layer: the piece continues downloading, instead of using the data that was already downloaded.

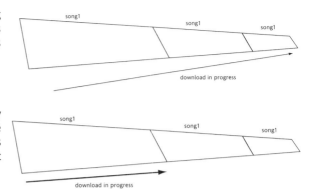

Event sounds, on the other hand, must be completely downloaded before they play. Then, this data can be reused without re-downloading it. You may think this doesn't sound as desirable as a streamed sound, but rest assured each have definite advantages.

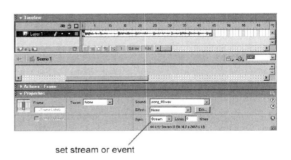

When you load a sound, you can specify whether or not you want it to be a streaming sound or an event sound. This is a parameter you set using the `loadSound()` method, which we will use shortly.

Sounds within your movie can also be designated as an event or streamed sound. If you select the waveform on the timeline, and open the Property inspector (F11), a drop-down box is used to set the sound as one or the other.

set stream or event

You should use streaming for longer pieces of music: ones where waiting for the entire piece to download first would be a pain. Shorter pieces of music, such as loops or sound effects for buttons and so on, will most benefit from using event based sound. This way the sound is in an object, and can be reused without additional downloading.

One of the main issues when using streamed sound is that it affects the timeline. Flash rushes to keep up with the sound if the timeline starts to lag due to heavy graphics or processing. In order to do so, it begins to drop frames. If you have any code on these frames, it will be lost - which could cause some major problems! It is not a good idea to use streaming sound if you might lose important information due to lost frames. However, you can actually use this technique for maintaining a frame rate in your movie. If you load an extremely short 'blank' sound, you can load the sound as streaming so you can keep a particular frame rate (for an animation).

Or, you might want to restructure your movie so it will not be a problem if streaming is the best way to go. You should also remember that streaming sounds do not save what was downloaded for reuse, but instead must be streamed all over again.

You may experience difficulty when importing certain audio files. Some MP3 files have been created or compressed in certain ways that Flash does not support. If you have problems importing a particular MP3 file, try to import it as a WAV. If you are trying to import MP3 files over 160kbps, then you will need Quicktime installed to handle the import.

Working with the Sound object

Now that we know what a sound object is, we can learn how to manipulate it to serve our own purposes. Since we are loading a movie from the Library, we are dealing with event-based sounds in this example.

1. Create a new file called `control_sound.fla`. Import a sound into the Library by selecting File > Import... (or CTRL/⌘+R). You can find two sound files in the **Chapter 9** folder, and either one can be used for this example. They are called `song_09.wav` and `song_09.mp3`.

   After you import a sound, it can be found in the Library (F11).

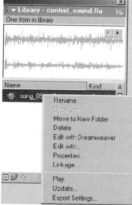

2. The next step is to set up the Linkage properties for the sound. This means that you can attach the sound to an object. If you don't attach the sound to your movie and have the properties set up, then it will not be exported when you publish your movie (remember that all unused elements are not published).

   Right-click on the sound, and select Linkage... In the Identifier text field, enter 'song'. Select Export for ActionScript (which automatically selects Export in first frame), then click 'OK'.

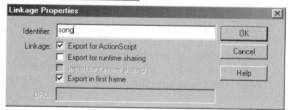

It is very important to make sure that you have both of these check boxes selected before continuing to the next step. Without having these boxes selected or an Identifier set, then you will not be able to use the sound.

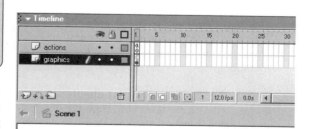

3. We will need two layers: one for actions and another for graphics. On the graphics layer, create two buttons. One button will be for pausing the sound, and the other for playing it.

   The graphics are up to you. We have created very simple buttons to play and pause the sound.

4. In the Property inspector, give each instance an instance name. The pause button has been called pauseMe and the play button has been called playMe.

5. Now for the ActionScript. Open the Actions panel (F9). We are going to create a new sound object called 'my_sound'.

```
my_sound = new Sound();
```

Here we are storing our sound in the 'my_sound' variable. The reason we are using an underscore before sound is because this way we can take advantage of code hinting. We could also use 'the_sound', 'loud_sound', 'jazz_sound': all of these would enable code hints. Refer to **Chapter 2** for more information about code hinting.

6. Now for an important step: attaching the sound. But let's first look at what we want to do here, as if we were dealing with a CD player in a car:

```
Install a new CD player,
Put the CD into the player,
Play the CD.
```

Putting the CD into the CD player is an important step: otherwise, you won't hear any sound! This is where setting our Linkage properties comes into play. Enter the following code into the script pane:

```
my_sound.attachSound("song");
my_sound.start();
```

This code attaches the sound, with the linkage Identifier "*song*" to our new object 'my_sound'. Then, we start playing 'song' using the start() method.

7. Finally, the button code. In **Chapter 6** we learned how to write ActionScript for buttons using inline function. In this step, we simply need to stop and start the sound:

```
_root.pauseMe.onRelease = function(){
    _root.my_sound.stop();
}
_root.playMe.onRelease = function(){
```

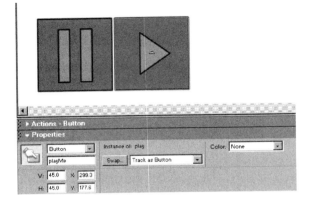

```
    _root.my_sound.start
 ➥ (_root.my_sound.position/1000);
}
```

The first function looks familiar: all we are doing is stopping the sound using the `Sound.stop()` method. Since it stops in place, we can create a new function which will resume the sound: `Sound.play()`. This is our section function for the 'playMe' button.

`Sound.position` is a new property, and is used to resume the Sound object from its current position. You need to divide by 1000 to play from the particular location because `position` is measured in milliseconds instead of seconds (like the Sound object).

Test your movie! When you press CTRL/⌘+ENTER the song will immediately play, but can be controlled using the buttons you just created on the stage.

Loading sound at run-time

You can think of dynamically loaded content like getting the goods on the road, and not having to stop and get out of the car at a CD shop. Maybe a little like a Flash drive-thru! It is not likely you'll find a more efficient way of working with your content. There are a few advantages to this.

Usually people have limited resources, and have to budget for the necessities. When you take your car into the garage to get it looked at, you usually have something specific in mind you want done to the car. If you are in because you know your muffler is about to drop off, you don't want to have to pay for the engine to be overhauled, the radio upgraded and the exterior buffed. You just want your old muffler taken care of, because that's all you came in, and budgeted time and money, for. This is probably a lot like a visitor to your web site.

Loading in MP3s at run-time will benefit your site a great deal because your users won't have to download content that they don't want to see. You can load sound as an event, or as streaming sound. Both of these are accomplished using `loadSound()` method. The `loadSound()` method can load an MP3 file either as an event or as a streaming sound.

If you are working with ID3 tags in an MP3 file, you will need to load the entire sound before the tags can be read. This feature is available in the Flash Player 6 r40 and later.
For more information, refer to:
http://www.macromedia.com/support/flash/ts/documents/mp3_id3_tags.htm

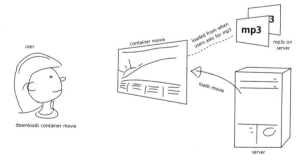

You need to provide a Boolean (true or false) for the isStreaming parameter. True will load the audio file as streaming sound, and false will load the sound as an event. As you know, an *event* sound will need to be completely loaded before it plays, although you can use the sound as an object. *Streaming* sounds will start to play before they are downloaded completely.

If you are using streaming sounds, you can use the _soundbuftime property. This property concerns the buffer time (the time given to allow sound to partially load before starting to play) allotted to streamed sounds. The default value is 5 seconds, but you can change this to a different value (such as 10) by using the property in this way:

```
_soundbuftime = 10;
my_sound = new Sound();
_root.loadIt.onRelease = function() {
    my_sound.loadSound("song_09.mp3",
    ➡ true);
    my_sound.start();
};
```

The sounds loaded into the movie will be buffered for about 10 seconds before they play. The file in this example is an MP3 that is sitting on the server, in the same folder as the SWF. It is being loaded after a button called 'loadIt' is pressed on the stage.

You will want to make sure that you don't set the _soundbuftime too low, or you will get very "choppy" results. On the other hand, set too high and users will have to wait a long time for the music to start! After you have loaded a streamed or event sound, you can start, stop or pause what you have loaded, which we will look at next.

How:
First let's look at how to load an MP3 dynamically as an event.

1. Create a new file called load_sound.fla, and save it in the same directory as you saved song_09.mp3 from the Chapter 9 directory. Either use a button from the Library (Window>Common Libraries>Buttons), or make a simple button. Give it an instance name 'loadIt' after dragging it to the Stage. Create a new layer, and call it 'actions'.

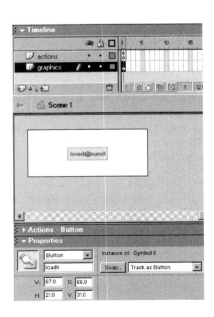

2. On frame 1 of the actions layer, enter the following code onto the Script pane:

```
my_sound = new Sound();
_root.loadIt.onRelease = function() {
    my_sound.loadSound("song_09.mp3",
    ➥ false);
    my_sound.start();
};
```

This code creates a new Sound object, called 'my_sound'. The function following this is for the 'loadIt' button on the stage. When pressed and released, it will load song_09.mp3 (an MP3 file sitting on the server) as an event sound into our movie. Then that sound is started using the start() method.

For more information on functions and callback functions, refer to **Chapters 6** and **10**. In the next section, we will explore the Sound object in greater detail.

Sound events and more

You are able to manipulate sounds in your movie, and probably have a good grasp on loading and controlling sound by now. There are many different things you can do, but in this section we'll take it a bit further and look at onSoundComplete and setPan, two things you can do after your sound has been loaded as an event into your movie.

We are going to turn it up a notch for the last example on using sound, and give you a sample of how useful certain actions can be for manipulation. In this example, we are going to combine some of the things you have already learned, together with one new set of actions (setInterval and clearInterval). You will learn more about these two actions in **Chapter 10**. All you need to realize at this point is that setInterval will repeatedly call a function at specified intervals until it is cleared using clearInterval.

1. Open a new movie, and call it panning.fla. Import song_09.wav or song_09.mp3 into the movie using File > Import. Open the Library (F11) and then right click on the imported sound. From the contextual pop-up, select Linkage..., Select the Export for ActionScript

check box, and enter 'song' into the Identifier field. This will ensure that Flash exports our sound at the beginning of the movie. We do not need any graphics on the stage for this example.

2. Together, setInterval and clearInterval are going to be used to call functions that pan the attached sound 'song' in the my_sound object from the left speaker to the right speaker, and back. Let's first take a look at the functions we will use to perform this:

```
function panR() {
    RightInterval =
    ➥ setInterval(panRight, 200);
}
```

We call panR after we create the sound object (below). The above function starts calling the panRight function using setInterval. The function is called every 200 milliseconds. The ID is 'RightInterval', which is used when we need to clear the interval in our last two functions.

```
function panL() {
    LeftInterval =
    ➥ setInterval(panLeft, 200);
}
```

This function is called after 'RightInterval' is cleared, which means that the sound will start panning left after it has finished panning right. The function panLeft is also called after 200 milliseconds.

```
function panRight() {
    if (_root.my_sound.getPan() < 100) {
        _root.my_sound.setPan
        ➥ (_root.my_sound.getPan()+10);
        //trace("R:"+_root.
        ➥ my_sound.getPan());
    } else {
        clearInterval
        ➥ (RightInterval);
        panL();
    }
}
```

The `panRight` function starts by checking the current pan of the Sound object `mySound`. It is performing the following:

If the pan is less than 100
Then pan in increments of 10.
If not, then get rid of the interval
Then call the panL function.

Now let's look at the next function:

```
function panLeft() {
    if (_root.my_sound.getPan() > -
➥ 100) {
        _root.my_sound.setPan
        ➥ (_root.my_sound.getPan() -
        ➥ 10);

//trace("L:"+_root.my_sound.getPan());
    } else {
        clearInterval(LeftInterval);
        panR();
    }
}
```

As you can probably tell, this function essentially performs the opposite:

If the pan is greater than -100
Then decrement the pan by 10.
If not, then get rid of the interval
Then call the panR function.

This means that our pan will continually swap out what it does (that is, panning left or panning right) for the duration of the movie. Once it hits either 100 or -100, which are the maximum and minimum pan amounts, it will clear the interval and call the other function.

Enter all of the code in this step into frame 1 of the main timeline. You can remove/ignore the commented out trace lines of code, or uncomment these lines if you want the Output window to follow along with the panning progression.

3. Following the functions in step 2, enter the following lines of ActionScript:

```
my_sound = new Sound();
my_sound.attachSound("song");
my_sound.onSoundComplete =
➥ function() {
    my_sound.start();
};
my_sound.start();
panR();
```

You should be familiar with the first six lines of code: we create a new object, attach our sound 'song', and run a function based on the `onSoundComplete` event. When the song has finished playing, the function is called. We start `mySound`, and following this we call the `panR` function.

Test the movie (CTRL/⌘+ENTER), and the song starts in the "middle" of each speaker before it starts panning because we don't set the pan when we start the sound.

There are many ways you can control sound when it is in an object. This is simply one way you can create an affect only using ActionScript. Something like this is useful if you are loading sounds dynamically, and cannot edit them directly in Flash (where you could manually fade sounds from left to right without using scripts).

Using video

"On board" video is the new addition to our truck in many ways. All a driver has to do now is bring along the tapes and the entertainment is available to everyone in the car. On board video is available in every make and model of vehicle without any extra features added or costly workarounds.

As you may already know, Flash MX now supports video, inasmuch as you can import your movies into the authoring environment using the *Sorenson Spark* compressor. This was possible in the past using third party applications such as *Wildform Flix*, *Turbine Video Encoder*, *After Effects 5* to output video as a SWF, or by manually bringing in a series of images and playing them in sequence. But is our on-board video enough?

Compression and optimization

Before we get to the code, we should take a second to consider file size and bandwidth - probably the single most important factor in video for the Web. More bells and whistles in a car mean you can more fully control the way you want your car to operate. A very important aspect of compression is control. The more control you have over compression means you can customize it to hopefully match what your video needs. Every video is different though - if you compress one 10-second video to 80K, another 10-second video will probably not be the same size. Noise, pixels, movement and effects all play a factor in how small you can compress your movie.

Try to remember the following points when editing your video for the Web:

★ **Make your video as short and compact as possible.** This seems pretty straightforward, but also keep in mind that you should trim any empty space at the beginning and end of your video, and crop it as much as you can. It all adds up. And so does your audio track: make sure you disable audio if it's not needed.

★ **Limit those cross-fades!** Lengthy transitions or fade-outs are difficult to compress. Anything with a lot of movement or changes of pixels will be difficult for compressors to handle. The fewer of these effects you have, the better the compression (and file size).

★ **Try many different settings.** If you are happy with your compression, try lowering the data rate even further! Try to find the setting where it offers the lowest possible file size while still having an acceptable quality level for your project.

★ **Don't re-compress compressed video.** If you try to compress something that has already been compressed, you will probably lose detail and quality in your footage. Make every effort to compress from a master copy (uncompressed), or if not, something that has only been very slightly compressed from the original.

★ **Reduce noise.** If you have access to digital video software like After Effects, try reducing your noise and/or altering your color levels or balance. This can make a significant (and beneficial) impact on the final file size of your movie. Sometimes, merely correcting your color levels can cut file size in half. Higher end compressors (like Discreet's *Cleaner 5*, *Sorenson Squeeze* and *Flix*) have controls to handle noise level reduction and "smoothing" which definitely seem to help.

> *Check out a few books on video and the web from friends of ED. A great title to start with is Flash MX Video (ISBN: 1-903450-85-3).*

Flash MX offers several controls to help you to compress a movie (some of which we will look at in the next section), but not as many as third party applications offer. *Wildform Flix* and *Sorenson Squeeze* (containing the Spark Pro compressor) both offer alternative ways of making SWF and FLV files you can use with your movies. Both of these programs offer many more settings you can use when compressing your movies, but check out each program because they offer slightly different (and exciting!) features from one another. As we mentioned, these "bells and whistles" ultimately lead to smaller file sizes, because you can customize the compression more for the particular video you are working with. To find out more information on these products or download demos, visit:
`http://www.wildform.com` and
`http://www.sorenson.com`.

Before we start importing video, let's look at some points to remember:

★ **Frame rate**: Try to keep frame rates a multiple of the original. This means that if your original movie is 29.97 or 30 frames per section (fps), then ideally you would want your frame rate to be set at 15. If you load a movie with a different frame rate into a SWF, the frame rate of the Flash movie will speed up or slow down to match that of the imported video.

★ **Data rate**: Data rate refers to the amount of data which is played each second in your movie. Therefore, data rate is also affected by the frame rate of your movie. If you have the ability to work with data rates, you will find this will make a lot of difference when compressing video. You can control data rate in *Flix* and *Squeeze*.

★ **Keyframes**: Similar to keyframes in Flash, the more 'change' in your video means the more keyframes required to handle them. More keyframes also means higher file size (since more calculations about the changes in your frames are required).

★ **VBR and CBR**: VBR and CBR are used in both audio and video, which stands for variable bit rate (VBR) and constant bit rate (CBR) compression. *Flix* and *Squeeze* both have VBR and 2 pass VBR options. VBR varies compression frame by frame, whereas CBR maintains the same compression rate for all frames.

★ **Quality settings**: In some compressors, quality settings seem to make little or no difference in the output. However, when importing directly into Flash using *Sorenson Spark*, it makes a large difference in the quality of your video. Low quality can sometimes lead to a significantly "blocky" video output.

Compressors like *Squeeze*, *Flix* and *Sorenson Spark* can handle video only up to an upper limit. If the compressor cannot handle your file size, then the player probably can't handle the compressed video either. Videos longer than 4 or 5 minutes usually cannot be handled by Flash because the video has to be loaded into memory.

For longer videos, you will probably want to use other options like *Quicktime* or *Windows Media Player*. Alternatively, you could try loading smaller videos in sequence into the Flash player, or use Sorenson Squeeze 2.02 or greater which features new video stitching capabilities. We will discuss how to load video later in this chapter.

Importing video files

It is very easy to import video files directly into Flash MX. Sorenson Spark is used to compress the video while importing, and decompression is taken care of by the Flash Player 6. Flash MX can handle a wide range of video formats: AVI, ASF, DV, FLV, MPG, MOV, and WMV. You could work with *QuickTime* files within Flash even in earlier versions of Flash. However, you had to export the project as a MOV file instead of as a Flash movie. Now, you have the option of embedding the movie so it can be exported into a SWF.

In this example, we will import a MOV (*QuickTime*) file, using the new ability Flash has to embed video in your movie.

When you are importing movies, you will need to have the codecs used to compress the files on your hard drive installed on your system. Codecs are the software used to compress (reduce the file size of) your movie. This can potentially be a problem if you are using a file supplied by a client who uses different codecs.

1. Start a new movie. The first step is to go to File > Import... (CTRL/⌘+R). After selecting any video file, you will then be given the option whether you want to Link or Embed your video file. Try importing the accompanying video_09.mov (9 MB) file provided for you. You might want to create a new movie clip first, and then import the video onto that timeline.

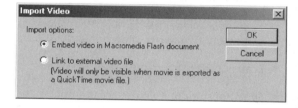

   Or, you can import the file to the Library (File > Import to Library...) and then insert the video on a movie clip timeline. Since you can control the movie clip using ActionScript, this in turn enables you to control the video itself! Choosing where to put your movie entirely depends on how you need to organize your FLA file. In the next section, we will look at some of the differences in where you place your video content and what this means to your file.

2. Another window opens after you press 'OK', which offers numerous import settings for your video file. Because our MOV does not have audio, you should notice an alert in the bottom left corner saying the audio cannot be imported.

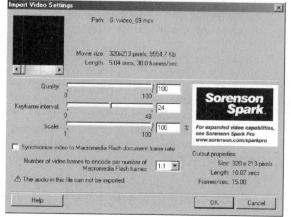

In the 'Import Video Settings' dialog box, you can adjust the *Quality*, *Keyframe*, *Scale*, *Synchronization* and *FPS ratio* for the video.

★ **Quality**: Ranges from 0 to 100, and controls the amount of compression (0 being high compression, 100 being the lowest level of compression). You will notice a large difference in different quality settings. Anything below 50 will usually be quite blocky. It is quite likely you will need a higher setting (in the 70 and greater range) to have acceptable quality levels for your video.

★ **Keyframe interval**: Sets an interval where keyframes are set in the movie. A value of 48 will insert fewer keyframes than a setting of 1. A setting of 0 does not insert keyframes, so it is more similar to a setting of 48 than a setting of 1. If your video has a lot of changes or movement, try a lower interval (but not 0!).

★ **Scale**: Changes the frame size of the movie.

★ **Synchronization**: If you select this option, the imported video will be adjusted (dropping frames) to match the frame rate of your Flash document. The movie will drop frames in order to stay in sync with Flash. If you leave the option unselected, each frame of the video will play in sync with Flash. Remember that dropping frames can lead to lost content (including any code within those dropped frames).

★ **FPS**: Note that this setting creates a ratio between the frame rate of the Flash movie and the imported movie. The original movie in this case is 30 fps, and with a ratio of 1:1 the FPS is 15 (the Flash movie's frame rate).

★ **Audio**: If the audio cannot be imported, such as above (our video clip does not have audio), then you will be notified as such. You might not be able to import audio if you do not have the proper codecs installed on your machine. If your clip has audio, then you will normally see a check box. This gives you the option of importing or not importing sound with your video.

Note:

Audio compression settings for the video are not affected during video import. They are controlled by the settings in the Publish Settings dialogue box.

3. After you have made your setting choices and pressed the 'OK' button, the window will appear if you are importing onto a timeline (or when you drag an instance of a video onto a timeline):

This simply means the timeline will need to resize to fit the duration of your video clip. After pressing 'Yes', the video will appear on the stage. If you are working with larger video files, this step might take a while!

Video playback

When your video is playing back, it can be handled in a few different ways similar to the differences we saw in event and streaming audio. If the video is on the `_root`, the data will stream in. However, if you want the video to play another time then the stream will overwrite itself (unless you load it into a different level). If you have loaded your movie into a movie clip, as we illustrated earlier, the movie clip will need to complete loading before anything is played back.

This is a lot like our event sounds in the Audio section. This does offer you the ability to use your movie clip like an Audio object though - which means you can manipulate and reuse instances like those of any movie clip object.

A video does not have a timeline like Flash does. You can control the video by referencing the frames of the timeline it is placed on.

So when should you use each one? If you have a long video, you will probably want to stream it. A good way of doing this is by first creating a SWF file, and then loading it onto a level of a container movie using a simple `loadMovie` action. This is discussed in the next section.

Loading video files during run-time

Just like we illustrated in the Audio section of this chapter, most people cannot afford needless repairs to their car: just fix what needs to be fixed. Visitors to your site only want to download the content they are actually going to use or want to see. Loading videos that have been requested by the user at run-time help you achieve this and it is done in much the same way as loading sound at run-time.

★ Nine

In the last exercise, we loaded a video into a Flash movie. This can be useful if you want to load SWF files into a different layer of a running Flash movie. If you are manipulating a movie clip which is playing a video file, this can be useful. This is accomplished by using `loadMovie` or `loadMoveNum`.

1. Locate `video_09.swf` and `import_video.fla`. These files have been prepared for you, and the SWF file contains the `video_09.mov` which has been published from a Flash movie. Save both files to a new folder on your hard drive.

2. On the stage you will see a button which says 'loadMovie'. We need to write a function which will load the movie when we press it. Select frame 1 of the actions layer, and open the Actions panel. Type in the following code:

```
root.loadIt.onRelease = function() {
    loadMovieNum("video_09.swf", 66);
    _root.loadIt.enabled = false;
};
```

This ActionScript loads the file with the name `video_09.swf` into layer 66 of the current movie. Then, it will set the button to disabled - which means that it cannot be pressed thereby reloading the movie.

3. Now, this won't do a thing until we have given our button an instance name. Select the button, open the Property inspector and call the button 'loadIt'.

Test your movie. When you press the 'loadIt' button, the movie is loaded into level 66. Now that was pretty easy!

> *Remember that you can also load SWF files into a placeholder movie clip. This is useful if you have plans to manipulate the video after they have loaded into the clip. Remember that the video will load with the top left corner of the frame at the center point of your movie clip. Make sure you take this into consideration when placing your movie clip on the stage.*

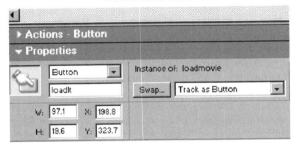

The square outline above is the same size as the video (320x213) and the upper left hand corner is placed at the $0, 0$ X and Y coordinates since the movie's upper left hand corner will be at this location.

Whenever possible, it is a good idea to load large amounts of content only when it is requested by the end user. If you only have short video clips, and perhaps several instances of one of them, you will probably end up loading the video into a movie clip. But what about loading other video files at run-time? You can stream and load FLV files from a server, but you will need the *Flash Communication Server* to do this.

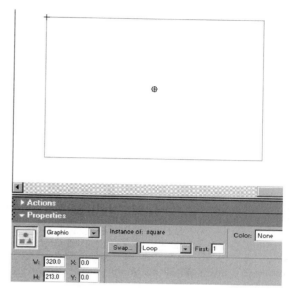

Controlling videos

You can control your movie clips with video within them just as you can control your CD player with a CD inside. You can skip ahead to frames, because the entire movie clip is loaded before you can control it (unlike streaming video). This is similar to a Radio/CD player in your car; you can skip tracks on the CD but you cannot skip ahead 30 minutes in a current radio broadcast.

Most of the methods and properties associated with the Video object only work with streamed video. The Flash Communication Server MX (www.macromedia.com) is used to stream live video content online, so without it these methods and properties are of little use. We will primarily look at how you can control a video while it is inside a movie clip object.

You can create many interesting effects using the MovieClip object. These kinds of effects can be transferred to the video, as long as your video is within a movie clip. Create a new movie, and import video_09.mov into the Library. Drag an instance onto the stage, and call it 'myvideo'. Then by adding the following script to frame 1 you can make it fade out when the mouse moves:

```
myEffect = new Object();
myEffect.onMouseMove = function(){
    _root.myvideo._alpha -= 1;
    updateAfterEvent();
};
Mouse.addListener(myEffect);
```

As you know from **Chapter 6**, this is accomplished by using 'Listeners'. Let's quickly look at a second example, which uses the `startDrag` method of the `MovieClip` object. Drag another instance to the stage, and change it into a movie clip instance by pressing F8. Call the instance 'vidDrag'. You can drag a video around after adding the following code to frame 1:

```
_root.vidDrag.onPress = function() {
    this.startDrag(false);
};
_root. vidDrag.onRelease = function() {
    this.stopDrag();
};
```

In this code we are using event handlers to make our movie act like a button. The `false` parameter locks the movie clip to where the mouse clicks the movie (a `true` parameter locks it to the center of the movie). We stop the dragging action when the mouse is released.

Since there are so many things you can do with movie clips, there are many different effects you can accomplish using video. In the following example, we are going to construct a movie that has buttons which can control a video clip.

1. Open the file called `control_video.fla`. This file contains a video within a movie clip, and several buttons for you to work with. The buttons can be found in the Library (F11) for your use.

   Drag the buttons onto the stage, and give them instance names of 'myPlay' (play button), 'myStop' (stop button), and 'myPause' (pause button). Also, drag the 'myvideo' movie clip onto the stage and give it the instance name 'myvideo'.

   Finally, create a second layer and call it 'actions'. Name the layer with your buttons and video on it 'graphics'.

2. The next step is very simple: add some code onto frame 1 of the actions layer.

```
_root.myPlay.onRelease = function() {
    _root.myvideo.play();
};
```

This function is added for the play button, as was discussed in **Chapter 6**. This button plays the movie clip, which contains our video.

3. Now we need to add more buttons for the pause and stop buttons.

```
_root.myStop.onRelease = function() {
    _root.myvideo.gotoAndStop(1);
};
```

```
_root.myPause.onRelease = function()
{
    _root.myvideo.stop();
};
```

The stop button returns to the first frame of the clip when it is pressed. The pause (using the stop action) pauses the movie. If the play button is pressed, the movie will resume from that location on the timeline.

4. Now let's add a very simple indicator of the length and where our movie is. There is an example within the Library of our sample movie if you run into problems along the way.

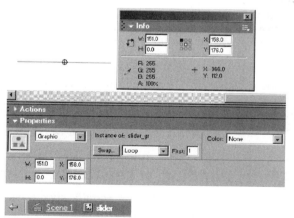

Create a new movie clip called 'slider', with a line graphic **151** pixels long - which is the number of frames in our movie. Therefore, each pixel can represent a frame. You can set the length using either the Property inspector or the Info panel.

Open the slider movie clip.

Use the Property inspector again to place the line graphic's left-most point at the center of the movie clip (**X=0** and **Y=0**).

Now, create a small square graphic inside this. While it is selected, press F8 and turn it into another movie clip instance, called 'playhead'. Return to the Property inspector, and place the playhead at X=1.

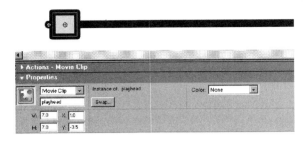

Make sure each of your two movie clips have also been given instance names: 'slider', and 'playhead'. Return to the main movie, and enter the following code.

```
this.createEmptyMovieClip("checkme",
1224);
_root.checkme.onEnterFrame = function()
{
    _root.slider.playhead._x =
_root.myvideo._currentframe;
};
```

What we are doing here is creating a new movie clip called checkme on depth 1224. It contains a function that moves the slider's playhead. It is placed on an onEnterFrame handler, because the new position can be checked at the frame rate of the movie (for example, 12 times per second on a move running at 12fps) because of the looping action. The _x position of the playhead (which starts on 1) is set to the current frame of the movie. Now when you test your movie, the playhead will follow along with the movie, indicating how far it is along in playback.

Since the video object is quite limited when only working with Flash MX and not the Communication Server, you will probably find yourself primarily working with video within movie clips, and controlling them that way.

Understanding accessibility

While many people have little or no difficulty driving just about any model of car, there are still many individuals who need special modifications before getting behind the wheel. Some cars are outfitted with special hand controls which enable those who cannot use their legs to press the pedals to operate the gas and brakes. Such modifications are not difficult, and make the difference between driving and taking a completely different mode of transport - like a bus or taxi. In this section we will explore how to outfit our Flash vehicle with special features to help suit all drivers.

Another way you can add additional functionality to your Flash movie is by making it accessible to those who are hard of sight. An accessible movie is important in that it adds another demographic of end users to those who can access the content of your production.

What is accessibility?

Accessible web sites are similar to a specially-modified car: virtually the same in every way, other than a few added tools to provide different functionality. So in this way, you can think of it as a special (and somewhat necessary) addition to your movie. You can take a few simple steps that will make quite a bit of difference to those "hearing" your websites via **screen readers**.

Until Flash MX, those using screen readers have had to 'take the bus' in most cases (by going to HTML sites), because Flash was not accessible to such utilities. Screen readers are software packages that primarily read the text on the monitor or descriptions of graphics out loud to the user. They are meant to assist those who are blind, visually impaired, or have difficulty reading their computer screens.

Certain modifications could be made to a Flash movie to simulate this (text that could be zoomed in to, a voice narrative and the like); however, **Microsoft Active Accessibility** (MSAA) compatibility was not built into the player. However, at the time of writing, Flash movies can be read by two different screen readers on Internet Explorer for the PC:

★ **JAWS for Windows 4.5** from Freedom Scientific (http://www.freedomscientific.com)

★ **Window Eyes 4.2** from GWMicro (http://www.gwmicro.com).

Both offer screen readers that are compatible with Flash Player 6. This means that the screen reader can read most of the text and buttons within the movie and enable those with sight difficulties to navigate it.

A specific set of circumstances must be in place before a screen reader can access your content:

★ The computer must be running on Windows.

★ The movie must be viewed using Internet Explorer 5 or greater.

★ Your movie cannot be published using either windowless or transparent modes.

★ The visitor must be using either Window Eyes or JAWS for Windows. This is because MSAA relies on *ActiveX* technology, which doesn't exist in Netscape or MAC environments.

> *If you are building a movie specifically for accessibility reasons, it is strongly recommended you test all of your content using both screen readers. Screen readers are very particular about content, and it is very common for unexpected results to occur during testing. Get your hands on a demo, and make sure that what your end user "hears" actually makes sense! It is very difficult to predict how your movie will "sound" unless you actually test the content.*

Why make accessible content?

It is a good idea to always be conscious of who might view your site. Assuming that your site will not be visited by anyone using a screen reader is not a great assumption to make. You simply do not know who will visit, and how! Essentially, there is a movement to make web content meaningful to all who use it. This means taking a few simple steps to allow your site to be read by screen readers.

Secondly, in the US **Section 508** is in place to make sure that certain web sites are accessible. For a long time, regulatory agencies have been pushing for rules to be set regarding this. Section 508 sets this, stating that web sites made for the US government or its agencies must have all content made as accessible as possible.

Note: For more information on Section 508 regulations, check out: http://www.section508.gov.

As mentioned above, the Flash Player 6 has been built to MSAA specifications. MSAA is technology that creates a bridge between the Windows operating system (and programs in this environment) and assistive technologies such as screen and Braille readers. What is beneficial about MSAA is that it sets a standard to which everyone can adhere.

Making a movie accessible: code and process

We will be concentrating on the ActionScript in this section, instead of how to set up each box. Mostly, you need to be aware of the **Accessibility panel** (ALT+F2). When you have different instances, or your movie itself, selected it has different options. When the stage is selected, the entire movie can be made accessible, and given a name and description.

Movie clips, text field and button instances each have their own properties which can be made accessible in various ways. You can add names, descriptions and shortcuts which will be read aloud by a screen reader. These are entered into the Accessibility panel for each instance when it is selected on the stage.

Things to remember:

★ Keep names and descriptions short and descriptive. Try to use short, common words if possible.

★ Turn off Auto Label in the Accessibility panel for the stage if you intend to manually enter descriptions. Otherwise, any text near a button or within it will be used as a description - which may or may not be correct and could interfere with your names and descriptions.

★ Hide content if you have a lot of duplicated or repeated content. For example, you might have a number of instances within a movie clip. In this case you will probably want to turn off Make Child Objects Accessible in the Accessibility panel for that instance. Instead, provide an overall description of the entire clip in the 'Description' field.

> Any rasterized text or graphics in your movie cannot be made accessible. In order to do so, you must change these images into a movie clip.
>
> The **Shortcut** option does **not** actually create a short cut, but instead reads out what the short cut is to the user. You will have to manually create the shortcut using Key listeners.

When creating a movie intended to be used with screen readers, you have to carefully consider how a person who is visually challenged uses your site, and/or a computer. Tabbing and using the keyboard are very important as navigation to those with limited vision. These steps will be covered soon.

Making the movie focused in a browser page

Before your user can use a key press or tab through your content, the movie within the browser window must be in focus. This means that he or she would have to click on the movie itself before tabbing or key presses can be registered by the movie. That might be fine for those who are sighted, but if the user cannot see the browser window to begin with, this is pretty redundant.

Luckily, we can use some JavaScript in the HTML page to give focus to the Flash movie. All you need to do is add the following code between the `<head>` tags:

```
<script language="JavaScript">
<!—
function createFocus(){
    movie_name.focus();
}
//—>
</script>
```

...where `movie_name` is the name of your Flash movie. The name of your movie appears as the ID parameter of the `<object>` tag, and `NAME` parameter of the `<embed>` tag.

And then, within the `<body>` tag, enter the following:

```
<body onLoad="createFocus();">
```

This will put the movie in focus, so tabbing can occur without having to click within the movie area first.

The Key object

Use key listeners when possible for navigation. You can enter a description in the shortcut area of the Accessibility panel.

How:
Let's look at some code that you could use:

```
myKey = new Object();
myKey.onKeyDown = function() {
  if (Key.getCode() == Key.UP) {
      _root.gotoAndStop("home_page");
  }
};
Key.addListener(myKey);
```

If you entered this code onto a frame action in the main timeline, the movie would jump to the `home_page` label when the Up arrow is pressed. The key listener is listening for the Up arrow to be pressed. Whenever it is, the movie will proceed to the home page. Therefore, in the shortcut area, you might signify the UP ARROW as the shortcut for the home page. Refer back to **Chapter 6** for more information on listeners and the key listener, and to **Chapter 8** for a review of the `if` statement.

Tabbing content

Those who have sight impairment use tabbing to navigate through series of buttons and text fields. These elements, and also movie clip instances, can be tabbed when the movie is running within a Web page. It is extremely important that you name and provide descriptions for buttons and text fields within your movie.

`_focusrect` refers to the yellow indicator box that surrounds each instance when it is focused. The `_focusrect` color cannot be changed.

> *In order to tab through instance, you must test your movie using a browser window, not the built-in test feature of Flash MX.*

So how do we control tabbing in our movies? We use the `tabIndex`. The number starts with a positive number, from 1 upwards, providing a different number for each instance. Therefore, if you have three buttons on the stage, you would provide an index for them as follows:

```
button_one.tabIndex = 1;
button_two.tabIndex = 2;
button_three.tabIndex = 3;
```

...where 'button_one' is the name of the instance, and it is first in the tab order. Try adding this code to a frame action, and test your movie in a browser. A yellow `_focusrect` box will appear around your buttons if you press the TAB key. If you keep pressing it, the box will cycle through each button.

You can also put instances nested within movie clips into this order by using the following line of code:

```
myClip.tabChildren = true;
```

This means that the instances within the 'myClip' instance are entered into the tab order. Then, to add them to the index, you would do as follows:

```
myClip.instance_one.tabIndex = 4;
myClip.instance_two.tabIndex = 5;
myClip.instance_three.tabIndex = 6;
```

... and so on! If you want to set focus on one instance in particular, you can use the `Selection` object. Try entering the following line of code to your frame actions for the first three buttons:

```
Selection.setFocus(button_one);
```

When this line is executed, focus is set to 'button_one' as soon as the browser window is opened. If you do not want to include a particular instance in the tab order, you would use the following code:

```
button_one.tabEnabled = false;
```

Try adding this line of ActionScript to the code you have above, and test the movie in a browser window again. Now 'button_one' is no longer in the tab order and cannot be tabbed by your end users.

Checking for screen readers

So now that you have a grasp of what to do to optimize your movie for screen readers - how do we know if one is there? Checking if a screen reader is running is useful if you want to make two versions of your movie, and send different users to a version based on their system requirements. You might initially think that you would use `System.capabilities.hasAccessibility` but you would be fooled. All this does is check if a browser has MSAA technology: and will return 'true' if the movie is playing in Internet Explorer. It does not check for whether or not a screen reader is active, or even installed for that matter.

> Tab indexes do not need to cover all numbers, so you could call them 10, 20, 30, giving you scope to add more in later without renumbering all the others.

In order to check whether a screen reader is active, you need to use:

```
Acessibility.isActive();
```

All you need to do is put this at the beginning of your movie:

```
acc = Acessibility.isActive();
```

Then, you can customize your movie using the following code:

```
if (acc){
    //run accessible modifications
};
```

However, there is an extremely detrimental bit of information you need to know before you use this. **Acessibility.isActive(); must be placed 2 seconds into your movie**. If you do not do this, `Accessibility.isActive` will *always* return 'false'. This is a "feature" (bug) of Flash which may change in future releases of the software - but for now, we just have to remember that the movie will not be able to tell if a screen reader is present until your movie has been playing for two seconds. The most basic, and easiest way of doing so would simply be to put 24 extra frames at the beginning of a movie (when set to play at 12fps, of course). You could also opt to use `setInterval` to wait two seconds before checking as well.

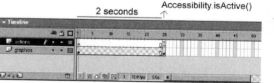

Now you should be ready to start making movies optimized for those using a screen reader to access your content. Keeping some of these simple ideas in mind should help your user greatly in understanding your web site. Simply remember to test your movie against both screen readers!

Summary

In this chapter we learned how to add special features to our movies. During this discussion, we:

★ Learned about different ways to work with sound: either by streaming sound within a movie, or using object-based event sounds.

★ Had hands-on work with manipulating sound within an object, where we panned a song from one speaker to another only using ActionScript.

★ Used video in our movies as a streaming clip, or within a movie clip object instance.

★ Used movie clips as containers which we could manipulate, thereby creating neat effects for our imported video.

★ Two seconds into our movie, we used `Accessibility.isActive` to check for screen readers, and then manipulated our content based on these findings.

Specialized Modules and Functions

What's in this chapter:

- ★ Specialized modules – functions
- ★ Enhancing base functionality
- ★ The scope
- ★ Functions in ActionScript
- ★ Writing functions
- ★ Parameters and returns
- ★ Self-contained functions
- ★ Components
    - ★ Scrollbar
    - ★ PushButton
    - ★ ListBox

Specialized modules – functions

Now comes the time when we call the auto manufacturer directly, and ask them to design some customized functioning parts for our vehicle. We're not just talking cool spoilers, or neat decals – we're talking full-fledged components that enhance the functionality of the vehicle.

Enhancing base functionality

For example, let's say we want our truck to have hydraulic wheels that raise and lower the vehicle on command. This requires some serious rigging, and rewiring of the vehicle. Essentially, the current wheel system must be completely replaced and enhanced with our own customizations.

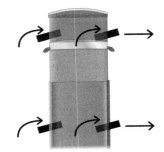

Or, let's say that we want our truck to be able to move sideways. Yes, that's right, we want all the wheels to be able to turn 90 degrees, and allow the vehicle to move left and right without turning. This would make parallel parking a breeze! That would mean adding to the current functionality of the steering mechanism. We're not *replacing* the steering system; we're merely enhancing it.

In Flash MX ActionScript, we're able to do these sorts of things with ease. First, we can add our own functionality to ActionScript completely, by creating functions. Second, we can add functions to the current ActionScript objects, like the Math and String objects, allowing them to accomplish more, if they do not currently suit our needs.

So, what is a function? A function is a named block of ActionScript that we call at any time, and anything within that block of code will be executed. By 'named', we mean that we call it by name rather than replicating the code itself. Think of it as a fancy way of grouping 100 lines of code into 1 line only, and then taking those 100 lines and putting them elsewhere, nicely tucked out of the way.

We've already seen *calling* functions. Anything in Flash that ends with () is a function. In this book, whenever we've shown something like Math.sin(4), trace(), etc., we've been calling functions.

So, when we *call* the `Math.sin` function, it's important to realize that we're not just calling some magical '`Math.sin`', and that's it. No, we must think deeper, and realize that `Math.sin` *contains* code that is responsible for calculating the value of a sine. We won't actually look at that code here, because the computation of sine is a very complex formula, which is why it's all done for us!

However, let's imagine that there's a function called '`traceTheWordTruck()`'. By its name, we can guess what it does. It outputs, in the trace window, the word 'Truck'. So, the contents of this function would look like:

```
trace("Truck");
```

Makes sense, right? So how do we go about packaging that single line of code into a nice little function? There are two ways, both of which will work. First, we can write:

```
function traceTheWordTruck()
```

Secondly, we can write:

```
traceTheWordTruck = function()
```

In the first case, we're creating a new function called `traceTheWordTruck`. In the second case we're creating an anonymous function, and assigning that to the keyword '`traceTheWordTruck`'. That's a bit of a strange concept and there there's noare only a few real differences. The main thing to remember is that the second method must be used if we want to create functions *within* other movie clips. Like so:

```
myMovieClip.traceTheWordMovieClip =
function()
```

Then later on, elsewhere, that function could be 'called' using the following code:

```
myMovieClip.traceTheWordMovieClip();
```

It's important to note that in Flash MX, when we place a function within a movie clip or an object, like the above example, that we would normally say that the function is a method of the movie clip. A method is any function that is contained within an object or movie clip, and is called using the dot syntax above.

That's how we declare the function name. As for assigning the actual *code* of the function, let's look at that:

```
function traceTheWordTruck()
{
    trace("Truck");
}
```

And that's it. It may seem a bit strange to have a function name that is longer than the actual code within it ('`traceTheWordTruck`' is longer than simply, '`trace("Truck")`') but this is simply an example, and most often, functions contain more than one line of ActionScript. For example:

```
function traceALottaWords()
 {
 trace("Truck");
 trace("Car");
 trace("Transmission");
 trace("Steering");
 trace("Wheel");
 trace("Door");
 trace("Paint");
}
```

This function, `traceALottaWords` will cause something like this to happen, when called:

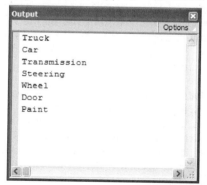

Now, we've replaced seven lines of ActionScript, with one very simple line of code.

So, how exactly do we "call" the function? Well, in a way that's similar to calling any other function in Flash: We simply write its name followed by `()`. So, to call this function we would say:

```
traceALottaWords();
```

Note the semicolon, which is standard to end off any line of ActionScript.

Now, we've seen how to define and call a simple function, but we must first understand a few things about their scope.

The scope

Think of the garage: Rufus, the manager, wants to think of a good way of instructing his staff how to perform their duties, and where to find what hardware.

Let's say that we have an air wrench hanging on the wall of the main garage. The air wrench's main function is 'rotate', so Rufus can instruct his employees to use the air wrench by simply saying "rotateWrench". That would be its 'function'.

Now, any time he wants to instruct his employees on what to do, he must first refer to the location of the hardware. Let's imagine that the main garage is called the 'root'. In this case, he could say "root.rotateWrench", and the employees would know which wrench was to be used.

However, because his instructions are posted on the wall, in the main garage, he does not need to say "root" before "rotateWrench" because when no location is specified, it is assumed to be the wrench that is at the instruction's location. If he really wants to be explicit, he can say, "use THIS wrench", or simply, "this.rotateWrench".

However, let's not assume that this garage has only one air wrench. No, to make matters more complicated the truck sitting in the service bay also has an air wrench sitting inside it for anyone working on the truck. If Rufus wants to instruct his employees to use *that* wrench, then he must say "truck.rotateWrench".

But, that depends upon where the employee is at the time of reading the instructions, right? If the employee is in the root (main garage), then "truck.rotateWrench" will make it clear that he or she is to go to the truck, and use the air wrench from within it. However, let's say that the employee has decided to step *into* the truck, and is now reading the instructions posted next to *its* air wrench.

For Rufus to say "truck.rotateWrench" would, following this logic, imply to the employee that there was some sort of truck, *within* this truck, and that they were to find the contained wrench, and rotate it.

Well, that's all wrong, because we know that Rufus is telling his employees to use the wrench sitting at their feet in the truck. How does he do it? Simple: The instructions posted inside the truck must say "this.rotateWrench". Then, the employee will know that they're to use this wrench, instead of some imagined wrench contained within an imaginary truck-within-a-truck. The word 'this' in this case is actually sort of redundant and Rufus would generally say simply "rotateWrench" and his employees would know that it meant the one at their feet. Look at this:

Truck within a truck, with an air wrench in each truck:

If Rufus wanted to, he could tell the truck-bound employee to reach out into the main garage and use that air wrench, simply by saying "root.rotateWrench", because the main garage is called 'root'. Dutifully, the employee would know which air wrench this means.

Or, if he wanted to, he could say "parent.rotateWrench" because *parent* means 'whatever contains me', and in this case, "root" contains the truck. If for example, there was a tiny truck within the main truck, and within that, a tiny employee was using a tiny air wrench, then to instruct that tiny employee to "parent.rotateWrench" would be telling him to reach out into the big truck, and use its wrench. However, to instruct the tiny employee to "root.rotateWrench" would be explicitly telling him to reach up into the main garage and use that wrench. Quite a reach.

Let's add one more twist. Let's say that there are two trucks in the garage now; blueTruck and redTruck. For an employee within blueTruck, or redTruck, we know that 'this.rotateWrench' means 'reach down, grab the air wrench at your feet, and use it'. We also know that 'root.rotateWrench' means 'reach outside, grab the air wrench in the main garage, and use it'.

The advantage of this is that each truck can come equipped with one air wrench, and one standard set of instructions. Knowing that 'this.rotateWrench' refers to the wrench in the truck, then we can create

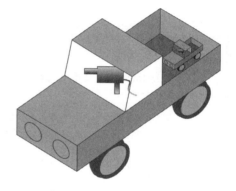

In Flash MX, we could think of this as nested timelines, where the main truck is a movie clip, and the smaller truck is a movie clip within the main truck. Inside of each of those, we have a `rotateWrench()` method.

400 'instances' of the master truck, and any operator inside any one of those instances will know what to do.

What if we wanted the employee in the blueTruck to use the air wrench from the redTruck? Say there's a note at the bottom of the instructions that says, "If THIS air wrench does not work, use the air wrench from redTruck". Nice, okay, but there's a serious problem here. What is the employee going to do? Well, they're going to look around their feet, on the seats, down the crack between the seats for 'redTruck'. They need to know that the redTruck is *outside*, in the main garage.

Rufus' instructions should read:

> "If THIS air wrench does not work,
> then use the air wrench within the
> redTruck sitting out on the root".

Or, put in a way that follows with Rufus's previously established naming conventions:

> "If THIS.rotateWrench does not work,
> then do root.redTruck. rotateWrench"

That's right; Rufus is clearly showing his employees the path to the correctly functioning air wrench. Of course, any instructions out in the main garage could refer directly to both blueTruck and redTruck, because they're both sitting in the root. In Rufus's eyes, the garage looks like this:

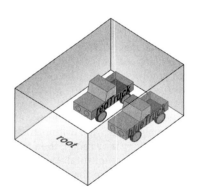

And Rufus would paste his three sets of instructions in their various locations:

These instructions are meant to be posted next to the redTruck air wrench. this.rotateWrench root.rotateWrench root.blueTruck.rotateWrench	These instructions are meant to be posted next to the root air wrench. this.rotateWrench blueTruck.rotateWrench redTruck.rotateWrench	These instructions are meant to be posted next to the blueTruck air wrench. this.rotateWrench root.rotateWrench root.redTruck.rotateWrench

Yes, it's an innovative and clear way of telling his employees how to sit around and rotate wrenches all day. Nobody ever said that Rufus's garage ever actually got anything done.

To ActionScript

If you understood all that, then you definitely understand the scope of ActionScript. Let's take stock of what we have. We talked earlier about the function, `traceALottaWords`. We saw how it was written and how it was called. Let's look at its scope.

A frame on the main timeline would be like the main garage; root. In fact, it's affectionately called '_root' in Flash MX. So, if we defined the function `traceALottaWords` on frame 1, of any layer (most usually a graphic-free layer with an intuitive name like 'code' or 'actions'), like so:

...then we could call it at any time, from any timeline with simply:

```
_root.traceALottaWords();
```

Note that the root has an underscore at the beginning of it, and in the image, notice that the location of that code is shown in the bar above the code itself, where it says 'Actions for Frame 1 of Layer Name Actions'.

In fact, this bar is a drop-down menu, and from within it, we can select any code from within our current timeline.

Let's say that we have a movie clip that contains the function definition for `traceALottaWords` on frame 1 of its timeline. So, we might see something like this:

Everything looks the same, including the code location bar. However, looking closely, we can see that we're looking at the timeline of the movie clip called 'aTruck':

If we wanted to, we could add some code here after the function definition, which says:

```
this.traceALottaWords();
```

and Flash would run that function once the movie loads up, or once an instance of the movie clip is attached to the stage at run-time.

If we go to the main timeline, we can pull an instance of 'aTruck' to the stage and then give it the instance name 'myTruck' from the properties panel, like so:

then, in our main timeline we can call its function like this:

```
myTruck.traceALottaWords();
```

For this reason, the instance name is very important; unless we give it an instance name, we have no way of referring to it. Naturally, a movie clip that has no instance name is able to call its own functions using the 'this' keyword in the code on its own timeline, but we need an instance name in order to call its functions from outside itself (for example, from the _root timeline, or from another movie clip via the _root).

Because this function is placed inside a movie clip, traceALottaWords is technically referred to as a 'method' of the myTruck object. It's the word used to describe a function within an object. We'll call it a function for now, for consistency's sake.

Now that's all established, and we know how to understand the scope of a function, let's look at the details of how they're written.

One thing we must be careful of: Don't call a function attached to a movie clip in the first frame of your main movie. Why? Because the line 'myTruck.traceALottaWords()' will be executed before the function itself has been defined. This is due to the order in which Flash executes code. It will execute the code on the _root timeline first, and then it will execute any code attached to movie clips. The function may easily be called in the next frame. In frame 1, do not have any references to the traceALottaWords() function, but when the timeline has moved along to frame 2, feel free to do: myTruck.traceALottaWords()

Writing functions

Rufus told his employees to "rotateWrench". Let's break that down a bit, and see what the employee manual says this entails:

```
how to rotateWrench:
  squeeze this trigger
wait until wrench stops rotating
release trigger
end of how to rotateWrench
```

Now, let's say that there's another set of instructions called 'putBoltOnWheel'. It could go something like this:

```
how to putBoltOnWheel
  Place root.Wheel on axle
  Pick up root.airWrench
  For all four bolts
  Place root.bolt in wheel
  Place root.airWrench on bolt
  root.rotateWrench
Return root.airWrench to holder
end of how to putBoltOnWheel
```

Notice that from within this set of instructions, Rufus made a reference to 'root.rotateWrench'. That's because the wrench we're talking about is in the root. All the instructions entailed within rotateWrench are executed when that one piece of instruction is read in putBoltOnWheel.

Looking back at ActionScript, we see that when functions are placed within movie clips we can call those functions using the 'movieClip.functionName()' syntax. Well, we're not simply limited to placing functions within movie clips. We can place functions within objects of any type. As we mentioned before, the Math.sin function is really the sin function, contained within the Math object.

This means that we can create functions that operate in context to the object that contains them. For example, rather than calling the context-insensitive 'rotateWrench', we could create a 'Wrench' object, and attach to it a 'rotate' function. So, just like Math.sin, we could say 'Wrench.rotate', or 'Wrench.pickUp', or 'Wrench.adjustSize'. The advantage being that the wrench could refer to itself using 'this.rotate', or 'this.pickUp'.

Doing this is as simple as creating an object using the generic Object object, and assigning functions to it.

```
Wrench = new Object();
Wrench.rotationAngle = 0;

Wrench.rotate = function()
{
   this.rotationAngle++;
}
```

We've now got an instance of Object called 'Wrench', which has one property, 'rotationAngle', set to 0, and one function called rotate. When we call this function with:

```
Wrench.rotate();
```

...then the 'rotationAngle' property attached to the Wrench object will increment. Notice that 'this' is used before 'rotationAngle' in the rotate function. That's because the word 'this' preceding any property means that it's a property of the object containing the function, in this case, Wrench. In other words, saying 'Wrench.rotate()' is the same as saying 'Wrench.rotationAngle++', because in the case of 'this', Flash conceptually substitutes 'this' for the name of the object.

In fact, if we didn't put 'this' in front of 'rotationAngle' then Flash would assume that we meant the 'rotationAngle' that's sitting on the timeline holding the Wrench object. So, if this is sitting on the _root timeline:

```
Wrench.rotate = function()
{
   rotationAngle++;
}
```

then it is not going to increment the 'rotationAngle' attached to the Wrench object. Instead, it will increment a variable called 'rotationAngle' that is sitting on the _root. This is, of course, wrong. If we want the 'rotationAngle' to be held in context to the Wrench; we need to refer to rotationAngle with 'this.' before it..

Parameters and returns

So far, the functions that we've seen have been functions that simply perform a task and then end. In fact, we could say that these are more procedural instructions than functions. That's because, by classical definition, a function normally takes a parameter, and returns a result.

As we discussed, we can attach functions to objects, and we can attach functions to the already existent ActionScript objects, like String and Math. This is much like our new 90-degree-turning functionality was added to our truck's steering system at the beginning of this chapter.

This way, functions can be held in context to their container object. Let's take a look at the classic example: Computing the circumference of a circle. Logically, we will attach this to the Math object.

The formula used to compute the area of a circle (or perhaps a wheel?) is PI x Radius^2. That is, the constant PI, times the radius times the radius. The radius of a circle is the length of the line from its center point out to the edge. Our function would be written as so:

```
Math.computeArea = function(rad)
{
  var theArea = this.PI * rad * rad;
  return (theArea);
}
```

Attaching it to the Math object is as simple as creating it with Math.computeArea = function().

We're seeing parameters and returns for the first time now. Notice that in the brackets after the word 'function', we have the word 'rad'. Passing a parameter is as simple as calling the function like any other Math function:

```
Math.computeArea(3);
```

We've placed the number '3' in the brackets. What this means is that in our function, rad will be set to 3; whatever we place in the brackets is being *passed* into the function, and that value will be stored in the appropriate variable as defined in the function header.

Also, we're saying this.PI because 'this' is really just a substitution for the word 'Math', because of the fact that computeArea is being attached to the Math object. The Math object has a constant called Math.PI that corresponds to the mathematical number pi (which is about 3.14159).

So, our function begins and it creates a temporary variable 'theArea' using the var keyword. That is, a variable that will only exist in the invocation of this function, and then will be eliminated upon completion. Into 'theArea', the result of 'this.PI * rad * rad' will be placed. This is going to be the area of a circle with radius of 'rad'.

Finally, the value within 'theArea' is returned back to the caller. This means that:

```
Math.computeArea(3);
```

is somewhat pointless, because there is nothing ready to receive the return value once it is computed. This is like dialing directory assistance, asking for a phone number and then, just before the operator begins to speak the number, hanging up. We need to do something with the result, like store it in a variable:

```
myArea = Math.computeArea(3);
```

Then, if we were to trace out the value of 'myArea', with this code:

```
trace (myArea);
```

then we would see this:

Or, we could, if we wanted to simply test the function, skip the variable altogether, like so:

```
trace (Math.computeArea(3));
```

Though presumably we would want to actually *do something mathematical* with the result of the `computeArea` function, so assigning it to a variable would be prudent, if not required.

If we want to, we can pass more than one parameter at a time into a function by separating parameters with commas. For example:

```
Math.computeRectArea = function(wid, hei)
{
    return (wid * hei);
}

myArea = Math.computeRectArea (10, 20);
trace ("The Area of the rectangle is: "
+ myArea);
```

This will create a new function, `computeRectArea`, attached to the `Math` object. This will return the area of a rectangle of 'wid' by 'hei' in size. The parameters 'wid' and 'hei' are passed into the function, and the result of the two multiplied together is returned. Above, we're calculating the area of a 10 x 20 rectangle, and tracing it out, like so:

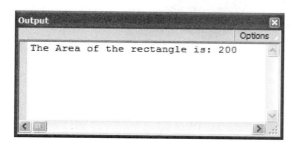

Why would we make such a simple formula into a function? Well, the point of any function is to simplify an operation so that the core functionality of it is hidden and removed from the programmer making use of our functions. It's often called the 'black box' approach. We don't really need to care how it works, just "as long as I pass the correct values in, then pass me the correct results back"; the operation is as if it's contained in a black box.

This ultimately means that a programmer who simply does not understand how to compute the area of a rectangle (maybe they seriously flunked math in school) can still use our `computeRectArea` function and walk away happy with the area of any rectangle.

The uses and applications of functions are far-reaching, much farther than can be covered in this chapter. Function creation is an entire field of computer science study unto itself. Just as long as we remember scope then everything will be fine. Using 'this', versus '_root', versus the movie clip name itself; now we've mastered these concepts, function writing in ActionScript will be a breeze.

Self-contained functions

It's a good idea to write as many of our functions as we can on the `_root` timeline. However, if we want to create movie clips that are portable or "self-contained", then it's best to place their functions within their own timeline.

Much like the air wrench instructions being within the truck itself, we want to create intelligent movie clips that can behave on their own with their own code. For example, we could drag hundreds of tires from the Library to the stage, and they would all come to life on their own.

In **Chapter 8**, the code for the bouncing tire was placed on the `_root` main timeline, and simply attached to the tire via its instance name. Let's instead look at how we could remove all code from the `_root` and make the tire 'self-sufficient'.

Remember the function `onEnterFrame`? Well, this function has a special property in that it is called once per frame, automatically – we do not have to manually call it like we do other functions.

★ Ten

Let's look at the file `newtirebouncewall.fla`:

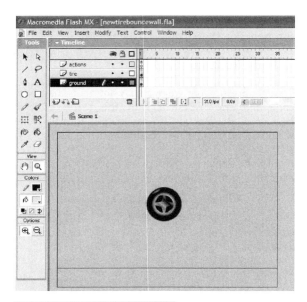

It looks exactly like `tirebouncewall.fla` from **Chapter 8**. However, let's look at the code attached to frame 1 of the actions layer:

```
gravity = 0.9;
ground = 350;
leftwall = 0;
rightwall = 549;
```

That's it. We're creating the variables 'gravity', 'ground', 'leftwall' and 'rightwall'. Because of their location, these variables are going to be sitting on the `_root`, and therefore when we refer to them we'll refer to them as `_root.gravity`, `_root.ground`, etc.

Before looking any deeper, let's run this movie with CTRL/⌘+ENTER. Notice what happens? The tire bounces around the screen just as it did in **Chapter 8**. What we're doing now is attaching the code to the tire movie clip itself. Double-click on the tire to enter its timeline.

Notice that there's an actions layer in the tire's timeline. Let's look at the code attached to this layer:

```
this.onEnterFrame = function()
{

  this._x += this.dx;
  this._y += this.dy;
  this.dy += _root.gravity;

  if (this._y > (_root.ground -
  ➥ (this._height / 2)))
  {
    this._y = _root.ground -
    ➥ this._height / 2;
    this.dy *= -.7;
  }

  // hit the right wall
  if (this._x > (_root.rightwall -
  ➥ (this._width / 2)))
  {
    this._x = _root.rightwall -
    ➥ this._width / 2;
    this.dx *= -.9;
```

```
}

// hit the left wall
if (this._x < (_root.leftwall +
➥ (this._width / 2)))
{
  this._x = _root.leftwall +
  ➥ this._width / 2;
  this.dx *= -.9;
}

  this.spokes._rotation = this._x;

}

this.dx = Math.random() * 40 - 20;
this.dy = Math.random() * 40 - 20;
```

Incredibly, most of the code is identical to the code in **Chapter 8**. Its location, however, means that it is contained within the tire movie clip, thereby making the tire act under its own power. Also, notice that references to 'gravity', 'ground', 'leftwall' and 'rightwall' are preceded by '_root'. This way, any instances of the tire that are created on the stage will still be bound by the same physics, and changing something, like gravity, will instantly affect *all* instances of the tire movie clip.

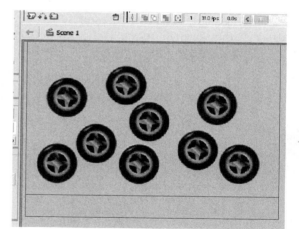

Notice at the very end, we're "initializing" two variables, 'this.dx' and 'this.dy' to be random numbers between –20 and +20. This way, each tire will start out with its own trajectory. Load up newtirebouncewall2.fla, which begins now with 9 tires on screen instead of 1.

If we run this movie with CTRL/⌘+ENTER, we can watch as these tires bounce around the screen on their own power with each one bouncing a different way, but all of them behaving identically. Looking at the properties panel, we can also see that each tire does *not* need to have an instance name.

Instance names are only important if they are going to be referred to from the outside world; from another timeline like the _root. However, these tires are self-sufficient, so they don't need an identity.

Incidentally, if we wanted to, we could attach variables like gravity, ground, leftwall and rightwall to a special object called the _global object. When we place variables inside the `_global` object, they are instantly accessible to all areas of our movie, without the need for any prefix like `_root`, `this`, etc. So,

```
_global.gravity = 0.9;
_global.ground = 350;
_global.leftwall = 0;
_global.rightwall = 549;
```

would mean that anywhere in our code, we would only need to refer to gravity as '`gravity`', and not `_root.gravity`, like so:

```
this.dy += gravity;
```

Components

When we create movie clips that have lots of self-sufficiency (acting on their own accord) as well as providing the overall movie with enhanced functionality, then we have what's often called a 'component'. Much like the modularity of a new truck stereo system, it can simply be plugged in, and then work on its own.

In Flash MX, we're presented with an array of user interface components that can be used to easily add complex user-interface functionality to our movies, very rapidly. The components are located under the Components panel (which is opened by pressing CTRL/⌘+F7). They look like this:

These are the standard elements employed by the user interface in most modern operating systems, like Windows or Mac OS. Up until Flash MX, if you wanted to add something as simple as a scrollbar to a movie, it involved building one yourself, from scratch. Well, now it's as simple as dragging and dropping them onto the stage, and either letting them work on their own, or using their built-in functions to tailor them to our own needs.

Remember, components are simply movie clips that have self-contained code and functionality and data. We're going to look at three components: The **ScrollBar**, the **PushButton** and the **ListBox**.

ScrollBar

In a new movie, create a blank, dynamic, *multiline* textfield about 220 x 125 in size, and give it the instance name 'myTextField'. It must be multiline in order for the scrollbar to work properly. The stage should look something like this:

From the Components panel, click on the scrollbar icon, and drag it so that it is released directly on top of the text field.

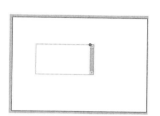

When released, the stage should appear as follows:

That was really easy. Now, as text is added to the text field, the scrollbar will adjust itself so that it can be used to scroll through all the text. As a test, place some code in frame 1 of the _root timeline that fills up the text field, like so:

```
myTextField.text = "This is just a long
test of a very long concept that will
show us how the scrollbar works.  I
must keep adding text until the text
field is filled up, and is more than
full so that the scrollbar will kick
into action.  Apparently, I must keep
going.  Almost there. This is nearly
past the threshold at which point the
scrollbar will spring to life. There we
go!";
```

That's one big-long line of code. This movie can be found in simpleScrollbar.fla. Running this movie will create the following display:

This is just a long test of a very long concept that will show us how the scrollbar works. I must keep adding text until the text field is filled up, and is more than full so that the scrollbar will kick into action. Apparently, I must keep going. Almost there. This is nearly past the threshold at which point the scrollbar will

That's the automatic version of the scrollbar. That's not, however, tapping into its full potential – its ActionScript power. As mentioned, these components have functions attached to them, and the scrollbar is no exception. We can create our own scrollbar and, using code, we can find out the exact position of the scroll thumb (the little box that is moved up and down).

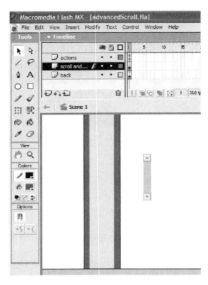

Let's look at `advancedScroll.fla`. In this movie, we have a scrollbar, and a 'fuel level' – a glass tube filled with green fuel of some sort:

When we run this movie with CTRL/⌘+ENTER, we can see that scrolling the scrollbar controls the height of the 'fuelLevel' movie clip, giving the impression that the scrollbar is controlling the fuel level.

Let's look at the code attached to frame 1 of the actions layer:

```
doScroll = function()
{
  fuelLevel._height = 400 -
  ➡ myScrollBar.getScrollPosition();
}

myScrollBar.setChangeHandler("doScroll");
myScrollBar.setScrollProperties(1, 0, 399);
```

Looking at this code, we can pretty much guess that the scrollbar has the instance name 'myScrollBar', and that the 'fuelLevel' movie clip has the instance name 'fuelLevel' as well.

We've got this function called `doScroll`, which sets the '_height' property of the 'fuelLevel' movie clip to be the value 400 minus the value of the current scroll position. That's the first function of the scrollbar right there; `myScrollBar.getScrollPosition()`. This function returns the current position of the thumb in 'myScrollBar', or whatever instance name we want to give to the scrollbar.

In our scrollbar, 0 is at the top, and 399 is at the bottom, so we want to subtract the result of that position from 400 in order to determine the actual height of the 'fuelLevel' movie clip. We want the 'fuelLevel' movie clip to be the *full height* of 400, when the scrollbar is at its lowest value of 0.

We've then got the function:

```
myScrollBar.setChangeHandler("doScroll");
```

This tells the scrollbar what function it is to call whenever the user drags the thumb on the scrollbar. This is how we write code that reacts to the scrollbar actually being used.

The next line of code is what actually tells the scrollbar how to behave; it 'turns on' the scrollbar. This function is `myScrollBar.setScrollProperties`. It takes three parameters; page size, minimum and maximum.

Minimum and maximum are fairly straightforward: They simply define the extent of the scrollbar's possible values where scrolling to absolute top returns 'minimum' and absolute bottom returns 'maximum'. The scrollbar intelligently returns anything in between. The first parameter, 'page size', requires some explanation.

The page size tells Flash what percentage of the scrollbar the thumb must take up. Page size is dependent upon the range from minimum to maximum. So, if a scrollbar is 10 units in length (minimum is 0, maximum is 9) and page size is set to 1, then the thumb will take up 10% of the scrollbar. If the page size were set to 5, on the other hand, then the thumb would take up 50% of the scrollbar.

When the scroll track above and below the thumb is clicked, then that will force the thumb to scroll by 1 page, or, 'pagesize'. In our scrollbar example, we set page size to be 1, so that each 'page' of the scrollbar will equate to one pixel on screen of 400 pixels high.

Remember, this doesn't mean that the scrollbar itself is 400 pixels high; the scrollbar simply returns a value from 0 to 399, but in our example the scrollbar is actually about 100 pixels high on screen. In fact, we can set the height of a scrollbar with ActionScript by calling the `myScrollBar.setSize` function. The function takes one parameter, size in pixels:

```
myScrollBar.setSize(400);
```

...would cause the scrollbar to be 400 pixels high.

It's possible to make a scrollbar into a horizontal scrollbar using the following function:

```
myScrollBar.setHorizontal(true);
```

When we do this, then the scrollbar is simply drawn horizontally, like so:

All functionality, however, remains the same. This can also be changed from the Properties panel at design time, by selecting the scrollbar, and then setting the horizontal parameter to 'true':

There are several other functions available to the scrollbar, but the ones covered here are the most important and commonly used ones. The online help has details of them.

The PushButton

The next component is the 'PushButton' component. To place one of these on the stage, simply drag it from the Components panel, just like the scrollbar. Take a look at pushbutton.fla.

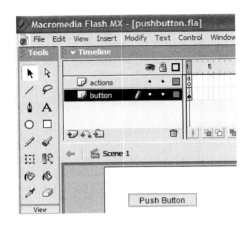

There's a simple generic push button on the stage with the instance name 'myPushButton'. Its label has not been changed from the default 'Push Button', because we want to do it with ActionScript. On frame 1 of the actions layer, we have some code:

```
handleButton = function()
{
  trace ("Disabling Button");
  myPushButton.setEnabled(false);
}

myPushButton.setLabel("Push to Disable");
myPushButton.setClickHandler
➥ ("handleButton");
```

The push button is very simple to use. We're creating a callback function, much like we did for the scrollbar, to be called whenever the button is pressed. This function is called handleButton, and it simply traces out the text 'Disabling Button', and then it does disable the button, by using the setEnabled(false) function. When a button is disabled, it is not clickable, and its label is grayed out.

Before the click:

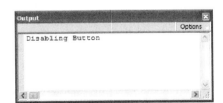

After we've finished defining the handleButton function, there's another call to a push button function; setLabel. setLabel takes one parameter, the label, and it sets the label on the face of the button, and adjusts the width of the button to fit the text. We're setting it to 'Push to Disable'.

After the click:

Finally, like the scrollbar, we're setting the click handler to be the handleButton function. The resulting movie runs like so.

That's the basic functionality required to use the pushbutton component. Again, to dig deeper, refer to the Flash MX guide.

The ListBox

The ListBox is a component that displays a list of values, with a scrollbar down one side. When these values are clicked, they can trigger a function, and we can detect what was clicked. Look at listbox.fla.

There's one listbox on the stage, with the instance name 'myListbox'. Placing a listbox on stage is just as simple as dragging it from the Components panel, and then giving it an instance name. In the Properties panel of the listbox, we can see that there are a number of options:

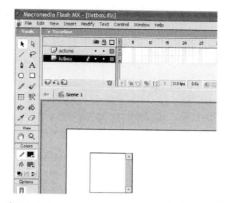

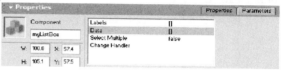

We will not, however, be using any of these. We're going to use ActionScript to bring our listbox to life. Let's look at the code attached to frame 1 of the actions layer:

```
myListBox.addItem("Joe");
myListBox.addItem("Rufus");
myListBox.addItem("Jimmy");
myListBox.addItem("Paint");
myListBox.addItem("Door");
myListBox.addItem("Truck");
myListBox.addItem("Wrench");
myListBox.addItem("Tire");

pressItem = function()
{
   trace (myListBox.getSelectedItem()
   ➥.label);
}

myListBox.setChangeHandler("pressItem");
```

First, we're making several calls to the addItem function of the listbox. This, as you can guess, adds that text into the list.

Next we're creating a callback function called pressItem, and it will be invoked whenever an item in the list is selected by clicking on it. In the function, we're tracing out the label of the item that was selected, using myListBox.getSelectedItem().label. The getSelectedItem returns an object that contains two values: 'label' and 'data'. Label is the text that we originally passed in, and 'data' is another optional value that we could have defined when building the list. Say for example 'ages', like so:

```
myListBox.addItem("Joe", 45);
myListBox.addItem("Rufus", 50);
```

Then, if 'myListBox.getSelectedItem().label' was 'Rufus', then 'myListBox.getSelectedItem().data' would be 50. In our movie, we're only using labels.

Finally, we're setting the change handler to be the pressItem function, so whenever an item in the list is clicked, the pressItem function will be invoked. When we run this movie, we'll see the following:

There are several other functions available to us with the listbox. We can, for one, sort our listbox in alphabetical order, ascending or descending by using the sortItemsBy function, like so:

```
myListBox.sortItemsBy("label", "ASC");
```

This will sort the list according to label, in an ASCending fashion, like so:

We can, if we want, sort by 'data' instead of 'label' (to sort our name/age list by age, for example), and we can sort from highest to lowest, in descending order using "DESC" as the order.

We can also set the width and height of a listbox using the setSize function, which takes as parameters both width and height:

```
myListBox.setSize(200, 100);
```

will produce this:

The text field is 200 pixels wide, and 100 pixels high. If we use the setRowCount function, then our height will be overridden, as setRowCount sets the absolute number of rows visible in a listbox:

```
myListBox.setRowCount(3);
```

shows up like so,

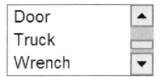

That encompasses the major uses for the listbox. However, the listbox is a very detailed component with many functions, so check out the Flash MX Reference to see what else can be done.

Summary

Those are three of the major components. Most others operate according to the same general scheme, and can be easily and quickly learnt. There are also many other custom components that can be downloaded and used, and they can be found at Macromedia's web site as well as sites like flashcomponents.net.

Now that we fully understand the concept of a function, please use the proper terminology when referring to a function within an object (like a movie clip, or a custom object) as a 'method'. See, methods are functions, and properties are values (variables), so we must be explicit when talking about the 'contents' of an object.

We've attacked functions from many different angles in this chapter, and hopefully we're able to take what we've learned and truly unleash the power of functions in all their uses and applications.

Oh, and one way to get the most out of functions is to pick up the most detailed reference text you can. We tend to think that our *Flash MX Designer's ActionScript Reference* (ISBN: 1-903450-58-6) is the best (and heaviest) book on the market...

The truck of the future

What's in this chapter:

★ Dynamically loaded content

- ★ Loading movies
- ★ Loading images
- ★ Using getURL
- ★ The LoadVars object
- ★ Loading data
- ★ Using HTML text
- ★ Checking data loaded
- ★ Sending data
- ★ Sending and loading data
- ★ Flash and Servers
- ★ Sending mail using ColdFusion

Customizing the car with accessories

It is true that a basic car shell, four wheels and a small motor will get you around. This might even be all you need for the kind of driving you do. However, most of the time a driver will at least want more features to accompany the basics. Adding more functionality to your car makes it more useful to you. It broadens the horizon of what the car itself can do, and usually optimizes the functionality for the user. With a better engine, you will probably get many more miles to the gallon.

Flash can hook up with a server to transfer data back and forth. Flash is growing when it comes to how it can communicate with them, too. Information can be sent and received in many different ways. For example, a car might receive information but not send it back, such as with a radio.

You might have a continuous two-way communication. This might be like a cell phone that is left on speakerphone for constant open communication.

Or, you might have a walkie-talkie style communication that is controlled by you, and can only be answered by your host.

You also might have communication with a warehouse guy who then provides you with the merchandise required to run your garage.

These diagrams are similar to the different kinds of communication that are possible when you use Flash. You can use Flash alone to open another web page or dynamically load images, text, variables, other movies or sound. However, you can also use Flash with other technologies to send data to a server, or grab data from a server (perhaps a database) for higher levels of interactivity. You can even use a socket server to achieve near real-time communication. This would be like a constantly open radio where two users can talk continuously, and data can be pushed to one user who does not need to request it. This is a significant change from the usual method, in which the Flash end must request content to come from the server.

Flash and the server

Flash works with the server in a couple of different ways: by requesting data or by having data pushed to it. Think of a server like a tow truck. The garage is like Flash, which will call out an order to the tow truck to go do something. The tow truck - like a server - answers the request and executes the order. However, the tow truck does not initiate the work. The tow truck relies on the garage to dispatch what work needs to be done. This kind of communication is called HTTP transfer, which is based on such **requests**.

In comparison to this are special servers, like **socket servers**. In a socket server, the communication flows in both directions instead of relying on a central dispatch. It is like the tow truck could push work orders to the garage, and the garage push work orders to the truck as well.

Using socket servers is not nearly as common in Flash movies as HTTP transfer. Socket servers can be used to make cool real-time chats and even multi-user games, but they require a certain degree of understanding about XML and Flash. This is beyond the scope of this chapter and book, but more information on this subject can be found in other friends of ED titles.

Therefore, there are many different kinds of interaction that can exist between Flash and a server other than opening a new browser page. Flash can receive data, send data, and a combination of sending and receiving.

Dynamically loaded movies, images and sound

So let's get down to it. You can load images and other movies using the `loadMovie` action. Similarly, you can load sound dynamically using the `loadSound` action.

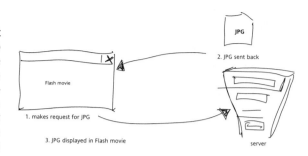

1. makes request for JPG
2. JPG sent back
3. JPG displayed in Flash movie
Flash movie
server
JPG

As you can see in this diagram, a Flash movie will request something which sits on the server. It is good to organize a movie using `loadMovie` or `loadSound` because you can let a user decide what content they want to download, as opposed to making a user download a lot of content they are not interested in seeing or using. As we have already done many times already in this book, you can load content into a target movie clip, or you can load content onto a new level.

Refer to **Chapter 9** for more information on using `loadSound` to dynamically import MP3 files.

Using loadMovie for loading at run-time

By using `loadMovie`, you can load other SWF files or JPG images from a server into your Flash movie.

> *You must take care when saving JPG images for use in Flash. You cannot dynamically import progressive JPG files into your movie. Progressive JPG files mean that the image is **interlaced** instead of saved using normal scan lines, so that it can be partially drawn on screen before it is fully loaded. You cannot dynamically import other kinds of files, such as GIFs or PNGs.*

In the following example, we are going to dynamically import JPG files into movie clip placeholders when the user clicks a button at run-time (i.e. when a movie is run on the Web).

1. Open a new movie, and save it as `loadmovie.fla`. Locate `loadme.jpg` in the

Chapter 11 folder and save it in the same folder as your new FLA file. This JPG has the dimensions of 320x240, and is saved as a non-progressive file. If you cannot import your file, you might have to re-save the image in a photo editor making sure that the *progressive* option is **not** selected.

2. Create an *actions* layer and a *graphics* layer. Select the Rectangle tool, and draw a stroke outline - a rectangle with no fill - that is 320x240. With the rectangle selected, use the Info panel (CTRL/⌘+I) or Property inspector (CTRL/⌘+F3) to specifically set your width and height to these sizes.

3. Select the rectangle, and press F8. Change this graphic into a movie clip, and give it an instance name of 'placeholder'.

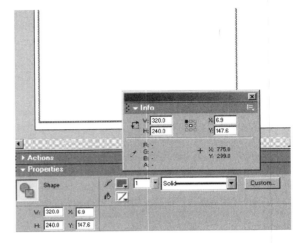

Remember to move the center registration point to the upper left-hand corner of the rectangle graphic. You can do this by selecting the rectangle, opening the Property inspector and setting the X and Y co-ordinates both to 0. Or, you can select the rectangle and manually move the upper left hand corner to the center registration point.

Your graphic will load with its upper left-hand corner at this registration mark. Therefore, if you do not move your rectangle to this point, your image will load and will not be entirely within this area!

4. Place this graphic on the stage where you want the JPG file to load in to. Feel free to add any other graphics or text as you see fit. In the source file, we have an additional layer called 'bg' for this.

Using a placeholder helps if you are creating an image gallery or portfolio site because it allows you to visually place where your image will be at run-time.

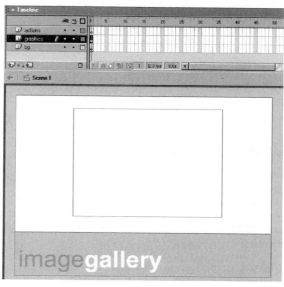

5. Open the Components panel (CTRL/⌘+F7), and drag an instance of the PushButton component onto the stage on the 'graphics' layer. Select the PushButton and then open the Parameters tab in the Property inspector. Set the Click Handler to 'loadIt' and change the Label to 'load JPG', or another descriptive name.

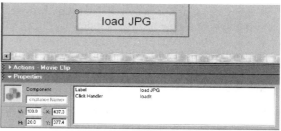

Then, give the PushButton component an instance name of 'loadjpg'.

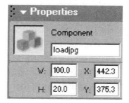

6. Open the Actions panel (F9), and select frame 1 of your *actions* layer. Enter the following code into the script pane:

```
function loadIt() {
  loadMovie("loadme.jpg",
  ➥ "placeholder");
  loadjpg.setEnabled(false);
}
```

Since we set 'loadIt' as the Click Handler, this function is called when the button is pressed. The `loadIt` function will load the image called `loadme.jpg` from the server into the 'placholder' movie clip. Then, it will disable the component instance 'loadjpg' so the image cannot be re-loaded.

7. Test your movie by pressing CTRL/⌘+ENTER. When you press the 'load JPG' button, the image will load into the 'placeholder' movie clip dynamically.

For a finished version of this FLA, refer to `loadmovie.fla` in the **Chapter 11** folder.

Using getURL

You will probably find that the `getURL` action is very commonly used in many of your web sites. You will probably want to have links in your movies to other places on the Web, or even other areas of your web site. Using `getURL` is useful for a few reasons, since you can:

★ create links to any web site

★ open up a new page in the current browser window, or a new browser window.

★ use JavaScript with your Flash movie. This is used for such things as opening a user's default e-mail client.

★ Use POST or GET to send variables

Let's look at a couple of different ways you can use this action. First of all, and probably the simplest is creating a link to a new web page. Open a new movie, and drag a button instance to the stage from Common Libraries (Window > Common Libraries > Buttons). Give the button an instance name of 'myButton'. In frame 1, enter the following code on frame 1 of the main timeline:

```
_root.myButton.onRelease = function() {
     getURL("http://www.google.com",
"_blank");
};
```

If you test the movie and press the button, a new browser window will open and load Google. The URL seems straight forward enough, but what about that `_blank`? This refers to how the browser window will open. Here are your options:

★ `_self:` This will open the new web page in the same browser window as the movie is currently playing in. If you are using an HTML frameset, it will load the new page into the current frame in that HTML page.

★ **_top**: You might use this when you have a movie using frames. If you are using a frameset on the page containing your Flash movie, the new URL will load over the top of the entire browser window.

★ **_blank**: This is a common one to use. The URL will load in a new browser window.

★ **_parent**: Another one to use with framesets. The URL will load into the parent frame of the current browser window frameset.

Finally, you might use a target name if you are using a frameset on your HTML page. You would type in the name, instead of one of the options listed above. This means if you have a frame called "content", it would load the new URL into that particular target window, as in:

```
_root.myButton.onRelease = function() {
    getURL("garage.html", "content");
};
```

Now try changing the code for the button on your Stage URL to the following:

```
_root.myButton.onRelease = function() {
    getURL("mailto:you@yoursite.com?
    ➥ subject=Feedback about yoursite.
    ➥ com&body=my comments are:");
};
```

Test this version in a **browser window** (CTRL/⌘+F12). Now you are using getURL to open the default email client, and insert some information in the *Subject* and *body* sections of the email client. Do remember that not all of your end users will have an email client set up, and a user may not be at his or her own computer.

The difference between GET and POST

You can also use the GET and POST parameters in the getURL action. These are used for sending variables. If you are not sending variables, you do not need to use this parameter. The POST method is used when you are sending a longer string of variables, and is done so in the HTTP header - meaning that it is sent along with the transfer information, and is not visible to the end user. The GET method is used for short variables, and is sent as part of the URL. There will be more about variables in the next section.

The LoadVars object

The LoadVars object is like our tow truck scenario where the garage sends a request out to the tow truck, which answers and processes the request that is made. However, the garage this time uses a complex two-way radio. This time, the two-way radio includes a special tracking device. This two-way radio monitors what is happening between the truck, the towed vehicle and the garage.

> *You can also load pages from within HTML text fields (that is, when you set a text field to contain HTML text in the Property inspector). You simply use the <a href> tag in the same way you use it in an HTML page. When you click on the link, it will open the web page. We will discuss how to load and work with HTML text later in this chapter.*

Once the tow truck enters the garage with its car (the data), a special alarm alerts the dispatcher announcing the arrival of the towed car. The garage workers can now start work on the car. This makes life a lot easier for the garage. No longer does the garage need a minimum-wage clerk to watch down the road for a car, and ring a bell when the tow truck drives in with the car. They laid off Ricky, the bell-ringer boy, because the alert system has this feature built right in. That's technology for you.

With the `LoadVars` object, you are actually populating the object instance with variables. These variables become properties of the object instance. The `LoadVars` object enables you to check whether or not data is loaded (using a callback function), send, receive and 'sendAndLoad' data as well. Therefore, it has a lot more to offer than the `loadVariables` action we looked at earlier.

The `LoadVars` object is created using a constructor, like any other object in Flash:

```
myVar = new LoadVars();
```

This creates an instance of the `LoadVars` object called 'myVar'. 'myVar' can be populated with variables using the `myVar.load()` method. `myVar.send()` is used to send data to the server. You can very easily check that data has been loaded using the `myVar.onLoad` event handler. You create a callback function using the handler, which is executed once the data has loaded. This is much easier than the method we used to check whether or not our variables were loaded using `loadVariables`. We will do an exercise covering all of this below.

The `LoadVars` object offers you additional features and an elegant way of loading data into Flash. The `loadVariables` action remains useful in that it is a quick and easy way of loading simple information into a movie.

Loading new data into Flash

You can load new data into Flash just like we did earlier using the `loadVariables` action. The end result will look exactly the same; however, we will be able to check that our data has loaded before displaying it on the stage in a much easier way.

Let's try loading a bunch of text like we did in the `loadVariables` example again. This time we will be using `LoadVars` instead. You might want to use the same file you did earlier, but change your code and instance names accordingly.

> *Earlier, we loaded text into a dynamic text field using loadVariables. One thing loadVariables cannot do is work with a ScrollBar component. However, you can use a ScrollBar with the LoadVars object.*

1. Open a new movie, and create an *actions* and *graphics* layer. On the graphics layer, create a dynamic text field with an instance name 'myField'. This time, drag a ScrollBar component from the Component panel (CTRL/⌘+F7) onto the 'myField' text field.

   Save this file as `loadvars.fla` in the same folder as the `content.txt` file we used in the previous example.

2.. Open frame 1 of the 'actions' layer and enter the following code:

```
loadtext = new LoadVars();
loadtext.onLoad = function(success)
{
  if (success) {
    myField.text = this.mytext;
  }
};
loadtext.load("content.txt");
```

   In this code, we create a new instance of the LoadVars object called 'loadtext'. `loadtext.load` loads the content.txt file. We use the `onLoad` callback function to check whether or not the data from `context.txt` has finished loading. After it has finished loading, success evaluates to `true`. When it is `true`, the text is displayed in the 'myField' text field.

3. Test your movie using CTRL/⌘+ENTER. As long as your files are within the same folder, the contents of your TXT file will appear on the stage within your dynamic text field.

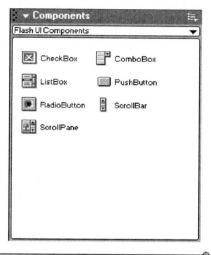

Loading HTML text

HTML text uses a handful of HTML tags to make text you load into dynamic text fields hyperlinked, underlined and so on. It does not support all HTML tags, but it does support the following

`<a href>`	You can use this to create a hyperlink to a web site. For example:`<a href="http://www.yoursite.com">Your site</a>`
`<font>`	Used to manipulate font using the styles listed below. For example `<font face="Arial>This is type</font>`.
`<font face="Arial">`	Used to change the font face.
`<font color="#99CCFF">`	This is used to change the color of a portion of text.
`<font size="2">`	This is used to change the size of a portion of the text.
`<p>`	This is used to create a new paragraph.
`<p align="right">`	Used to align a paragraph to the right.
`<p align="center">`	Used to center a paragraph.
`<p align="left">`	Used to align a paragraph left.
`<u>`	Used to make the type-face underlined.
`<i>`	Used to make the type-face italic.
`&lt;`	Used to show the < character.
`&gt;`	Used to show the > character.
`&apos;`	Used to show the ' character
`&quot;`	Used to show the " character.
`&amp;`	Used to show the & character.

In the following example, we will load a text file that is HTML formatted.

1. Open up the file called `htmltext.txt` from the Chapter 11 folder. Take a look at how we used HTML within the text in this field. Otherwise, it is set up exactly as we did in our previous example (except this time we didn't use an ampersand before the variable). We have started the file out with `myhtml=`

   The URL with `target="_blank"` means that a new window will open.

2. Now create a new file called `htmltext.fla`. Create a dynamic text field on the stage, and give it an instance name 'myField'. Make this text field Multiline, and be sure to select the Render text as HTML button, shown:

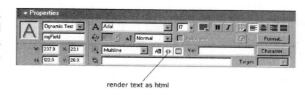

render text as html

3. Optionally, you can drag a ScrollBar component onto this text field and add any graphics onto the stage.

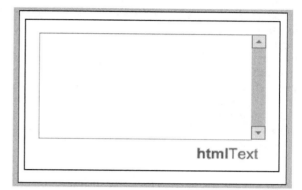

4. Create a new layer, and call it actions. Select frame 1, and enter the following ActionScript:

```
loadtext = new LoadVars();
loadtext.onLoad = function(success) {
    if (success) {
        myField.htmlText = this.myhtml;
    }
};
loadtext.load("htmltext.txt");
```

The only difference here is that we have changed `myField.text` to `myField.htmlText` (which means the text will be rendered as HTML text).

5. Test the movie by pressing CTRL/⌘+ENTER. As you can see, the text has been rendered in HTML format. Note that in order to get a typical hyperlink style, we have manually had to underline and colour the text using HTML tags.

Try clicking on one of the links. As you can see, a new window will open with the designated web site.

Application servers and server-side languages

Our application servers are like the variety that you see in tow truck systems. A tow truck company might only understand a certain kind of data transmission in the language the radio is built to understand. The tow truck companies all work in different ways, although in many ways the functions they perform are very similar. You might have a tow truck that is built to tow huge trucks, others that are flatbed carriers, some that are really fast but only carry light vehicles, a company that is run by felons, or one that works by donation. Each company uses their own dispatch systems that transmit on different frequencies in different languages. However, they all receive requests and information on where to go, and tow vehicles to and from garages or impound lots.

All servers are not created the same. If you have put your Flash SWF files online, the files are sitting on a server. But what if you want to increase the dynamic nature of your web site? Maybe take user information and put it in a database, store the results of a poll, or send mail in a way that doesn't open the end user's e-mail client? You will need the help of an application server, and server side scripts.

Application servers are software that sits on a server machine. The software is built to understand a particular language like ColdFusion, ASP, PHP or Perl. For example, the ColdFusion Server understands the CFML language.

Some languages are easier to use than other languages because each language is constructed using a different form of syntax. Each language has its benefits though. PHP is well liked in the community because it is free to use. ColdFusion is known to be a relatively easy language to learn. ASP is popular because it is included with the servers most people have readily available - IIS. Luckily, all of these particular languages can be used in Flash with `LoadVars`.

> *A new language involved with Flash is Server-Side ActionScript (SSAS), which you save as ASR files. We will look a bit more at these files, which are used for Flash Remoting, in* **Chapter 12**.

Security and working with servers

When you are connecting your Flash movie to external content, security becomes an issue. As soon as you connect to anything, there is usually a risk to the computer who is watching your movie. A two-way radio between our tow truck server and the Flash garage is set to limit conversations between two individuals only. Like this, Flash has set up security measure to limit who you can load information from: your own domain, or domains which specifically allow you to have access.

When using Flash in this chapter, you will "talk" with the server your Flash movies are hosted on. However, all other SWF, JPG or server side-scripts must be within the same domain as the movie calling for dynamic content.

Sending and receiving data

So far we have used one-way communication in our Flash files. This is very useful for loading dynamic content from a server. But really dynamic sites usually involve two-way communications. Therefore, we are going to use the ColdFusion Server to send email from a web site, without using the end user's e-mail program. When the data has been received, we will send back an alert that the data was sent successfully.

In this section, we are going to send email using Flash and ColdFusion. The server side script is very simple, and is used to direct e-mail from a Flash site to a designated e-mail address. First let's take a look visually at what we are going to do in this example:

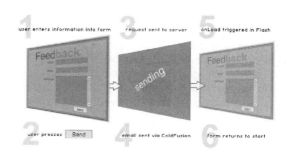

Using this method for sending e-mail or feedback from a site is useful for a couple of reasons. First of all, you do not need to rely on a user's e-mail client. It is very typical for a user to press a button on a site to send e-mail, and it pops up the default e-mail client on the user's computer. This is not desirable if that person is not at his or her own computer, or does not have the e-mail client set up to handle e-mail. Using this method, feedback can be sent back to you only using Flash.

So, let's get started. ColdFusion can be written in any text editor. You simply need to remember to save the file with a .cfm extension, which is what ColdFusion templates (pages) are saved as.

You will need ColdFusion 5 or MX installed on your server or personal computer for this example. ColdFusion MX will run on Macintosh OSX, but at the time of writing, is not officially supported yet.

1. Open up a text editor, and type the following code:

```
<!-- feedback.cfm -->
<cfmail from="#form.myEmail#"
to="you@yourdomain.com"
subject="feedback from
yourdomain.com."
server="mail.yourdomain.com">
name : #form.myName#
email : #form.myEmail#
comments : #form.myMessage#
</cfmail>
```

The first thing to notice about this file is the variables. These are contained within the # signs. Later we will set 'myName', 'myEmail' and 'myMessage' as instance names of input text fields in the FLA file. form is a keyword in ColdFusion, and creates a name/value pair.

In this file we begin by using the <cfmail> tag. We send parameters from our Flash movie to the template. Therefore, it will set the from in the e-mail to what the end user enters for his or her e-mail address. Enter the e-mail you want all of these feedback forms sent into the to parameter. The subject of the e-mail should be descriptive of what your Flash form is all about.

And then server should be set to whatever the incoming mail server is of your domain. For example, this might be as mail, an IP address or `mail.yourdomain.com`. Obviously, you will have to change the domain names in this .cfm to those of your domain. Keeping in mind that not all servers are the same, you might want to try an IP or even 'mail' in place of `mail.yourdomain.com`. Ask your hosting company what is the proper set up. If you have mail sent through this domain, it is probably the same as your Incoming mail setting in your e-mail client (such as Outlook Express).

The body of the sent e-mail will look like what is below the `<cfmail>` tag. For instance, ColdFusion will write name: and then after this will be whatever the end user enters into the `myName` field in the Flash movie.

Save this file as `feedback.cfm`.

> *The CFM file in this section does not require the ColdFusion MX server to work. This script will work just fine with the ColdFusion servers back to version 3.*

2. The next step is going to be in Flash. Open up a new movie and save the movie as `feedback_form.fla`.

   Create four new layers on the stage: 'actions', 'labels', 'text' and 'bg' (background).

3. As we have already seen in step 1, we are going to have three different input text fields called 'myName', 'myEmail' and a 'myMessage'. Create these text fields on the *text* layer. You will probably want to make the 'myMessage' text field slightly larger because more text will probably be entered in this field than others.

   Make sure that the fields for 'myName' and 'myEmail' are **Single line** and the 'myMessage' field is set to **Multiline**. Also make sure that your text color contrasts from the background color that you have selected.

4. After you have finished creating the three input text fields, drag a PushButton component onto the stage. In the Property inspector under the Parameters tab, select Label and type 'Send'. Then select Click Handler and type in 'sendit'. This will serve as our function name later in this exercise.

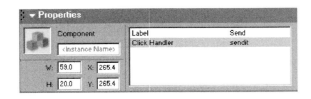

It is also a good idea to add a scrollBar component onto the 'myMessage' text field. You do not necessarily know how much text needs to be input into this area by your users. Therefore, a scrollBar means that the text field will scroll as the user enters more text.

Make sure that you set the 'Target TextField' to the same instance name as the input text field 'myMessage'. If the 'Target Textfield' is not the same name, your scrollBar might still be attached to the right text field, but it will not scroll the content within.

After you are finished, your stage might look as follows:

In this file, we have created a background region graphic to go with our text fields on the stage. We have placed this graphic on the 'bg' layer.

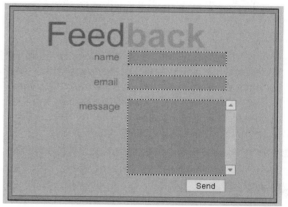

5. Now open up the Actions panel and select frame 1 of the *actions* layer. Enter the following code into the script pane:

```
//cf_loadvars.fla
stop();
function sendit() {
  myVar = new LoadVars();
  myVar.onLoad = function() {
    _root.gotoAndStop("start");
  };
  myVar.myName = _root.myName.text;
  myVar.myEmail = _root.myEmail.text;
  myVar.myMessage = _root.myMessage.text;
  myVar.sendAndLoad("feedback.cfm",
➡ myVar, "POST");
  _root.gotoAndStop("sending");
};
```

Remember that we set the Send button's Click Handler to sendit. This means that the sendit function will be called when a user clicks the button. This function creates a new instance of the LoadVars object called 'myVar'. The values from 'myName', 'myEmail' and 'myMessage' input fields are added as properties of the `LoadVars` object. These properties are posted back to the `feedback.cfm` template, and while doing so, the movie goes to the 'sending' frame. When data is loaded back the `onLoad` callback is triggered and the movie is sent back to the 'start' frame.

6. You probably noticed a couple of frame labels in that code which do not exist yet. Let's add them to our timeline now. On the 'labels' layer, enter 'start' as a frame label for the first frame. But as you can see in our code, we also need a frame for 'sending'. Around frame 5, press F6 to create another keyframe on the 'labels' layer. Enter a frame label name for this frame called 'sending'. You will probably want to add a graphic or some text on the stage which will indicate that the message is being sent. Simply add a keyframe on the 'text' or 'bg' layers at this point and add some new content, as we have below:

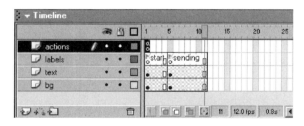

7. Test the movie by pressing CTRL/⌘+ENTER. Nothing happens! What we need to do now is upload our files to the server, into the same folder. Once it is uploaded, try sending a message and watch your Inbox for a message!

The completed versions of `feedback.cfm` and `feedback_form.fla` can both be found in the Chapter 11 directory. If you have problems, try changing the mail server designated in the CFM file and double check that you have both of your files in the same folder.

You do not need to use ColdFusion and CFML to send e-mail using Flash - this same example can be accomplished using other languages such as ASP and PHP. The ActionScript will pretty much be the same, the only difference will be noticed in the server-side

language. You will probably find ColdFusion to be the easiest language to use for this task (and many others too).

Now we have explored a couple of the ways to get you started using a server alongside your Flash projects. However, this chapter is merely a start in the possibilities that are open to you in this area. In the next chapter, we will look at some of the other methods you might want to start exploring in this area. These areas include socket servers, the Flash Communication Server, Flash Remoting and XML. Flash MX has a lot of features to offer developers!

Summary

In this chapter you learned about many different ways to communicate with a server. We have discussed:

★ How to use the GetURL action to open new web pages in the same or different browser windows.

★ How to dynamically load SWF, JPG or MP3 files into your movie.

★ Using `loadVariables` to load data into a Flash movie.

★ How the `LoadVars` object works to load and send data between a server and Flash.

★ How to write a simple server-side script, and have Flash send data to the script.

Tuning and Customizing

What's in this chapter:

★ Programming Flash

    ★ What to do

    ★ Resources

    ★ Dynamic Flash

    ★ Flash Remoting

    ★ Flash Communication Server

    ★ Flash and XML

    ★ Learning XML

    ★ Where is XML used?

    ★ Resources

    ★ Wireless technologies

    ★ Working with Mobile devices

    ★ Custom Components

    ★ Application development

Your next destination

It is true that a basic car shell, four wheels and a small motor will get you around. This might even be enough for your basic needs. Although, your garage clients will probably have more complex vehicles that need work and repairs done to them. Or, eventually you might even get bored of doing the same task over and over.

You probably won't find yourself wanting to stay doing the same few things day in and day out. Learning and expanding your capabilities is usually what makes work fun. Optimizing your vehicles, adding more bells and whistles, building a complex truck from scratch - these are the next steps in your development!

This chapter will look at where you might want to go next in learning about Flash and ActionScript. There are so many exciting areas you can explore! Hopefully you will be raring to go by the end of these pages, and learning new code and practices in no time.

Learning more about programming

You have learned how to build a car, get it on the road, and perform the main tasks in moving it around. From there, you have a wealth of knowledge that you can apply to almost everything you do with your vehicle. You have learned the basics, the foundation that will help you make your truck fly with many new and exciting add-ons and optimizations down the road. Hopefully, you are excited and you want to further your knowledge of ActionScript to create more involved and intricate applications in the future.

You have conquered a lot of script in this book, and hopefully you feel you have a good grasp of ActionScript by now. However, you can certainly go further with your coding skills from the foundation we have provided you with. Now that you have *learned* ActionScript code, practices and concepts, you can now *create* your own interesting, dynamic and entertaining projects using Flash. Learning any programming language is a great tool to have at your disposal, particularly an object-based one such as ActionScript.

As you may know already, ActionScript is a lot like JavaScript. You might want to continue learning ActionScript, and about object-oriented programming in general. Or, at some point you might want to try out some other languages. If you have made earlier attempts and then given up, you will almost certainly find it easier now after learning a lot of ActionScript!

Secondly, learning a bit more about JavaScript means that you will be able to use it in your Flash movies. It can come in handy for opening up browser windows from your movie and manipulating them. You can also use it to interact with movies embedded within a browser page. You might also look into `LocalConnection`, and `Local` and `SharedObject` as alternatives. Learning more about writing HTML, and how you can work with a web page to display your Flash movies effectively will also benefit your projects greatly.

Regardless, your foundation in ActionScript will be a lot of help when you tackle any other programming language. The knowledge in this book can be applied in many other places. If you take a good look at some of the resources online (listed in the next section), you will probably get a good idea of where you want to take your knowledge next.

Resources

The Web is a good place to start, and from the Web you can figure out where you might want to take your programming skills next. Check out some of these web sites:

★ http://chattyfig.figleaf.com
  The *Flashcoders* (e-mail list) and *Flashcoders Wiki* (editable web site) both provide a wealth of information on ActionScript and Flash. There are several e-mail lists available based on your main interests and knowledge base.

★ http://www.debreuil.com/docs/
  This website will provide you will several chapters about object oriented programming. Although written in relation to Flash 5, it is still extremely relevant, helpful, and funny as well!

★ http://www.webmasterbase.com/article/470
This series of tutorials are about programming JavaScript. You will notice the similarities between ActionScript and JavaScript if you check out these pages. These articles will give you a good idea of where you are at with the language.

Books can provide in-depth tutorials and complete reference materials about any programming knowledge that web sites usually cannot provide. Here are a few suggestions of what to check out in the bookstore:

★ *Macromedia Flash MX Designers ActionScript Reference*, published by friends of ED. ISBN: 1-903450-58-6

★ *Beginning JavaScript*, published by Wrox Press. ISBN: 1-861004-06-0

★ *HTML 4.01 Programmer's Reference*, published by WROX. ISBN: 1-861005-33-4

Dynamic Flash

Over the years there have been a lot of new things you can do online, and particularly with Flash. As you continue to learn about the program, you will find new ways to work with your content. One of the many tools available to you is making your movies dynamic. As we saw at in a few of the earlier chapters you can load data, pictures, sound, and movies dynamically.

Learning how to organize your movies in such a way means that your end user does not have to download unnecessary content. While using server-side languages with Flash, it is possible to integrate complex and vast amounts of data into your movies. Even when using a Flash front-end, you can have entire registration processes, e-commerce solutions, or giant searchable databases.

Flash and server-side scripts

It's a good idea to at least be familiar with server-side languages. In many development environments, you might find that you will be working with a developer who is quite experienced in working with the back-end of a web site. This means that you will only have to be concerned with ActionScript and making the movie talk to the server.

That said, you will probably want to learn how to create simple server-side scripts on your own to use with your Flash projects. Many solutions are not difficult to achieve. For instance, you saw in **Chapter 11** how easy it was to create a feedback form that sent e-mail using ColdFusion. There are many things that you can accomplish quite easily without having to hire a developer.

Server-side scripts can be used to integrate your Flash sites with a back-end. For example, you might want to create a login for your web site. You will probably want to have a database you can search for usernames and passwords. Or, you might have a database of JPG images and have your Flash site load in images upon request.

A great server-side language, probably the first one you will want to consider, is Server-side ActionScript (SSAS). This language can be used with Flash Remoting and the Flash Communication Server (Flashcom). The biggest bonus about learning SSAS is that you are already familiar with the language. Another bonus is that it works with technologies specifically designed to integrate a server with Flash. We will discuss these technologies (Flashcom and Flash Remoting) later on in this chapter.

There are many books on the market that teach you the fundamentals of one or many different server-side languages. You might want to check out a few of those listed below.

Resources

There are many great books available on integrating Flash with different server-side languages. Just about any language has an associated book. Here are a couple of titles which are guaranteed to get you started:

- ★ *ASP.NET for Flash*, published by friends of ED. ISBN: 1-904344-08-9

- ★ *Foundation PHP for Flash*, published by friends of ED. ISBN: 1-903450-16-0

Flash Remoting

Remember when we spoke about the tow truck scenario in Chapter 11. In this example, we have a garage that operates a tow truck. The tow truck stays on the road, and receives messages (data) from the garage that the truck uses to get the job done. This is so it knows where to go and what cars to tow. The radio transmission sent back and forth between the garage and the tow truck is much like Flash Remoting.

Flash Remoting is used to transfer the information between a Flash movie, and a server (such as one running ColdFusion or .NET). Why you might consider it so useful is that you can use ActionScript for a great deal of your work, instead of another server-side language.

What it does, and why you would need it

Flash Remoting allows you to harness the power of server-side scripting languages such as ColdFusion, .NET and Java. However, you only have to know very little about any one of these languages, because you will mostly use your ActionScript skills to create the interaction between Flash and the server. Server-Side ActionScript (SSAS) is written in ASR files. SSAS is used in this form of communication so you do not have to learn a server-side scripting language.

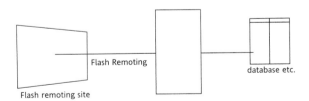

Flash Remoting

Flash remoting site

database etc.

Have you ever thought how it would be pretty cool to interact with web sites and pull the information you need from them? For example, you want to incorporate the local weather reports on your web site. Or perhaps you want to allow a user to track the shipping status of his or her book order on your web site. However, the tracking information needs to be pulled from the web site of the shipping company. These sorts of things, known as **web services**, are possible using Flash Remoting. You can use your Flash movie to go to a web site which has web services set up, and pull certain data from that location and display it in your movie.

Resources

There are many different places on the Web that deal with the new Flash Remoting technology. Be sure to check out the web forums on the topic, some of which are listed at the bottom of the page.

★ http://www.macromedia.com/support/flash /flashremoting/
This site is a great jumping point for a lot of Flash Remoting topics. It includes a download area including Flash Remoting documentation and Flash Remoting components. The Flash Remoting components install the NetServices API.

★ http://www.webmasterbase.com/article/816
This article by Mike Chambers (of Macromedia) gets you started with Flash Remoting, and will answer a lot of the questions you might have. You will need to have the ColdFusion server installed in order to follow this tutorial.

★ http://www.xmethods.com
Check out this web site for more information on web services.

★ macromedia.flash.flash_remoting
Visit this newsgroup forum using the Macromedia news server `forums.macromedia.com`.
They can also be accessed online at:
http://www.macromedia.com/support/forums/

★ http://livedocs.macromedia.com/frdocs /Using_Flash_Remoting_MX/contents.htm
Check out the live docs for Flash Remoting - a series of short documents about getting started with Flash Remoting.

Flash Communication Server

The Flash Communication Server (Flashcom) is a new piece of software released by Macromedia, specifically for integration with Flash MX. The Flashcom server enables you to make your movies that are "merely" dynamic into full, real-time environments. This was possible to some extent using socket servers and XML, but now you can also use video and audio in these environments!

What it does

The Flashcom server is used to stream video, audio and text data between connected users. It is different from what you can achieve using other server-side software because you can send audio and video streams between a server and your users.

For example, you can set up a webcam at your house. Using the Flashcom server means that you can stream your video to those visiting your Flash web site. Your users can also set up a webcam, and stream their video to other people connected to the web site. Actually, it is possible to record video that is streamed through the Flashcom server as well!

You can control what happens on the web site with a second Flash movie. You can watch who is connected, change bandwidth rates, and connect or disconnect users. But it doesn't just have to be video! You can create a radio station, monitor live data feeds, simple text transfer, or instant messengers. There are many possibilities using the Flashcom server.

How you use it

The Flashcom Server uses Server-Side ActionScript alongside the client-side ActionScript you use for communication between a Flash movie and the Server. Luckily, you can also download and install Flashcom components to help you create standard applications such as chat rooms, whiteboards and video conferencing.

Flashcom also works with Flash Remoting and ColdFusion to create truly "rich" applications. The Flash movie communicates first with the Flashcom server using RTMP (Real-Time Messaging Protocol) protocol. Then, the Flashcom server uses Remoting to talk with an application server, such as ColdFusion.

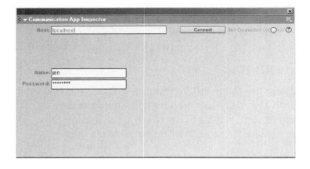

When you install the Flashcom server, use the Communication App Inspector panel to monitor and debug your Flashcom applications. This panel can be found under the Window > Communication App Inspector.

You can also download and install components that can work with the Flashcom server. They radically simplify the coding process. Most of the components can be dragged onto the stage, and all you have to do is set the parameters in the Property inspector.

For large, custom projects things aren't quite as simple. Although the outcome of your efforts is extremely cool, you will probably find the learning curve involved with Flashcom to be relatively steep. Particularly so if you are intending to merge Flashcom, Flash Remoting, an application server like ColdFusion or even a database! That said, if you are looking for an exciting way to explore and learn new scripts, Flashcom might very well be the most exciting way to go.

Resources

Offerings on the Internet are a little slim at the time of writing. However, stay tuned to the Macromedia Desdev for the latest developments and links to the community on this exciting new technology.

★ http://www.macromedia.com/desdev/mx
/flashcom/
The Macromedia Desdev site for Flashcom is a great place to get started. This developing

resource includes whitepapers, tutorials and product overviews.

★ http://www.macromedia.com/software/flashcom/
Download the trial for the Flashcom server and components at this location.

★ http://chattyfig.figleaf.com
You can subscribe to a mailing list called Flashcomm from this location. This new mailing list is devoted to Flash Remoting and Flashcom application development.

★ http://bilbo.macromedia.com/audioblog/
A small example of what you can do using ColdFusion MX with Flash Remoting and the Flashcom server.

There are several upcoming books devoted to this exciting new technology. It is probably a good idea to check out books on the subject, given how involved the Flashcom server can be.

Flash and XML

Flash and XML can help create some very powerful projects. XML is frequently used when you have to use data that needs to be structured and organized in a very particular way. Perhaps you have a bunch of clients with several pieces of information grouped together into addresses and contact methods. Or, you might have a bunch of books you need to categorize and list. You might want to use a newsfeed from a web site, and display the news titles in your Flash movie.

XML is great for, but not limited to, organizing and retrieving data of this kind. Not only this, but socket servers can be used in conjunction with XML to create near real-time applications in your Flash movies.

Learning XML

XML is a highly intuitive way of organizing data. If you are familiar with other tag-based languages, such as HTML or ColdFusion, you have a good start on XML already. The main difference is that you get to name the tags in XML, and this helps sort your data. It makes a lot more sense if you actually see an XML structure, so let's take a very quick look at some XML.

```
<person>
    <name>Jen</name>
    <age>25</age>
    <email>jen@ejepo.com</email>
</person>
```

Just by reading that, you realize these are some things that describe a person. You can even structure data in more complicated ways than this, by nesting some data further:

```
<person>
    <name>Jen</name>
    <age>25</age>
    <email>
        <home>jepo@ejepo.com</home>
        <work>jen@ejepo.com</work>
    </email>
</person>
```

Nesting a piece of information may or may not make sense to your document. However, the good thing about XML is that such formatting is entirely up to you. You can also have information in the form of an attribute.

```
<person age=25>
    <name>Jen</name>
</person>
```

And by now, you probably have a very good start on writing XML! You can order the data how you see fit, and then it can be used in your Flash movie.

Where is XML used?

XML and Flash is brought together all the time, too. Since it is a great way of organizing data, you can probably find many different forms of data where it makes sense to use it.

You can organize lists of MP3s in the form of an XML structure.

You could use the data as the text associated with buttons in your Flash movie.

You can take an XML *newsfeed* and display the data and links within your Flash movie. A commonly used newsfeed is from Macromedia: http://www.macromedia.com/desdev/resources/macromedia_resources.xml

You can use XML for text fields where you want to display some data.

XML data can hold URLs of JPG files, which can be put into your movies. Or, it can hold URLs of links in your movie that might change later on.

You can even take data input into a movie by a user, and send the data to a server formatted as XML. Then you can store or use this data as necessary.

You can use a socket server to create a near real-time environment.

Still not convinced that XML is powerful? Well then, think of how easy it is to update your movie. Instead of having all of your links or button names within a FLA file you would have to open and search through to edit. All you have to do is open a text document, edit, and press 'Save'. For example, this menu of a standard Flash site can be updated at any time. You can edit buttons without having to open the FLA file and change text within buttons or movie clips:

Secondly, XML is not a difficult language to use. Nor is it particularly difficult to use with Flash after you understand a few fundamental aspects of the language. XML files are loaded into Flash, which parses the data. You use ActionScript to extract data from these XML structures.

```
<?xml version="1.0" encoding="iso-8859-1"?>
<menu>
    <projects>
        <flash-mx/>
        <flashcom/>
        <sockets/>
    </projects>
    <portfolio>
        <books/>
        <web/>
        <photos/>
        <video/>
        <other/>
    </portfolio>
    <about>
        <site/>
        <resume/>
        <contact/>
    </about>
    <home/>
</menu>
```

Resources

Web sites with information about using XML with your Flash work include:

★ http://www.tupps.com/flash
This web site includes information and source files about using XML and Flash together.

★ http://www.moock.org/unity
Interested in socket servers? Check out this site for demonstrations, and downloadable socket servers for commercial, or non-profit use.

★ http://www.moreover.com
Check out this web site for more information on newsfeeds.

★ http://www.samuelwan.com/information/archives/000091.html
Check out this web site for more information on RSS parsing and Flash.

Nice examples of web sites using XML and Flash together include:

★ http://www.philterdesign.com
Extensively uses XML and XML feeds to create an interface, and many great example files demonstrating the power of XML when used with Flash.

★ http://www.ngarte.com
This web site uses XML and a socket server to achieve a really interesting real-time environment.

Check out the following books on XML and Flash:

★ *Flash XML StudioLab*, published by friends of ED. ISBN: 1-903450-39-X

★ *Macromedia Flash MX Designers ActionScript Reference*, published by friends of ED. ISBN: 1-903450-58-6 (Yes, ok, the second time we've mentioned it, but it's really good.)

Wireless technology

Handheld devices, such as the many devices that are running on Pocket PC technology, are a relatively new and emerging market for web designers and developers. Making Flash movies or applications specifically for these devices is an art in itself. Developers have to be conscious of the many requirements of creating movies that work on a different OS and player with its own idiosyncrasies. You also have to be aware of the limited bandwidth and memory that wireless users have when downloading and playing your movies.

Since wireless communications are seemingly a growing market for Flash work, you might want to get involved in learning more about making movies for devices. Many new handheld devices are being released with the Flash player already bundled with the device software. This means that you do not need to be quite as concerned about your end user having the Flash plug-in.

> *At the time of writing, the Pocket PC 2002 device operating system has a version of Flash player 5 included.*

Given that there are predictions that wireless technology could be a huge movement in communication, the fact that it involves Flash is very exciting.

Templates in Flash

Within the Flash authoring environment you can use templates provided which are designed to match the size of devices running Pocket PC 2002. You can access this template from File > New From Template. Then, in the New Document dialogue window, choose MobileDevices. As you can see, there are a few choices available: PocketPC 2002, and two templates for the Nokia 9200.

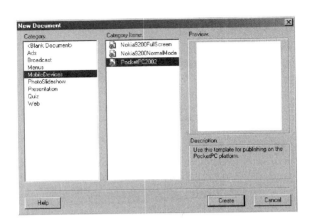

Press "Create" and then you will see the following movie:

The graphics and text you see here are actually a guide, which provides you with some information about the template. You can delete or hide the layer - it won't publish with your movie.

This is simply a start, though. There are actually quite a few design and development tips you can pick up from many different places online and in books. Development for mobile devices is an art in its own right, and there are a lot of very important things to learn about creating Flash for devices. You can find some suggestions in the next section.

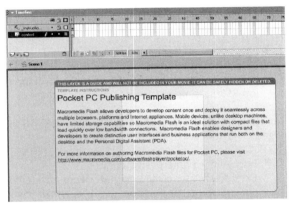

Resources

Since there is a lot of excitement about Flash applications made for wireless devices, you might want to check out the following online resources:

★ http://www.macromedia.com/desdev/mobile/
The Macromedia mobile device Desdev is a great jumping point on this subject. It includes articles, tutorials and links to some great resources on the subject.

★ macromedia.flash.handhelds
This is a newsgroup dedicated to Flash development for handhelds. The Macromedia news server is forums.macromedia.com. The newsgroup is also accessible through macromedias online forums (http://webforums.macromedia.com/flash/). The newsgroup is frequented by some of the

top players in the community who are creating Flash apps for mobile devices.

★ http://forums.devbuzz.com/tt.asp?appid=10
A forum dedicated to creating Flash for wireless devices.

★ http://www.flashenabled.com/mobile
An excellent resource on everything you could need to know about devices and Flash.

★ http://www.pocketpcthoughts.com
A good resource for information, news and thoughts on Pocket PCs.

Custom component development

We discussed components within this book, but you can certainly take this foundation knowledge a lot further in your work. Custom components are an exciting proposition! You can develop small Flash applications as a component, and distribute the component to clients or others who use Flash. There are many places on the Web where you can exchange custom components.

Creating your own components means that you can distribute your ideas or your projects easily. There is also a market for well-built components. So not only do they mean an easy way to pass on your Flash work, but it might also end up being profitable!

Resources

There are many different places where you can find components for download. In most of these places, you can also upload your own components to distribute with other Flash developers and designers. A couple of good places to get started are:

★ http://www.macromedia.com/exchange/flash
The Macromedia exchange is the place to go for the latest components available. You can download components, or upload them for distribution. You can download the free Extension manager, which helps you install and manage your extensions. You can use this manager for your extensions for many different Macromedia products.

★ http://www.flashcomponent.com
This web site has a wealth of components available for you to download. You can also submit components for distribution.

Components are essentially movie clips in FLA files. However, developing a good component takes some careful planning alongside your ActionScript! Many books on Flash MX will include pointers on creating custom components; however, check out the following book that will focus on working with components exclusively:

★ *Flash MX Most Wanted Components*, published by friends of ED. ISBN: 1-904344-10-0

What you can do with all this knowledge?

So you have finished mechanic training - now you have your first job in the garage. You have been given a vehicle to work on, tune up, customize. Now you are ready to go and create your own vehicles. There are many different kinds of machines on the road, so where do you start?

In this section we will look at some of the different kinds of applications you might want to try creating.

Game creation

You have probably all tried playing Flash games at one time or another. There are many excellent games online that are both wonderfully animated and highly interactive. Flash has become an excellent medium to build involved interactive games that are wonderfully suited for the Web.

You will probably find out that there is a lot involved in building a game. They frequently involve mathematical concepts like physics to imitate real-life movement. User interaction is of course another important concept. Nothing replaces well-thought-out planning and imaginative yet intuitive game design.

Good game design and creation takes a lot of forethought and planning. To get started, you might want to check out an excellent book on game design and programming: *Flash Games Studio*, published by friends of ED (ISBN: 1-904340-67-5). You might also want to check out some of the third-party 3D tools, such as Swift 3D at http://www.electric-rain.com/.

Rich Internet Applications

As the power of Flash develops, and the tools that can integrate with Flash become more diverse, your options as a developer continually expand. In order to keep up to date on what they are, it is important to keep an eye on community web sites and www.macromedia.com in particular.

In this chapter we have looked at many of the tools involved in creating what Macromedia calls "*Rich Internet Applications*". These include Remoting, Flashcom and other server-integrated technologies. Video, audio and dynamic features are all possible - but we are sure to see this develop with future products that will likely tie in with Flash MX. There are many more exciting products to tie in with Flash that are currently being developed.

E-commerce and business solutions

Banners, online stores and professional web presences are only a few of the uses of Flash in a commercial light. Many clients are looking for new ways to present their web sites, and Flash is increasingly an answer for these business projects.

Now that the Flash Player is installed by a vast majority of those surfing the Internet, using Flash as a front-end is more of an accepted solution. Check out some of the resources below for inspiration or information. Commerce and business solutions will usually involve some back-end (i.e.: server-side languages) development.

★ http://www.macromedia.com/desdev /mx/blueprint/
The Macromedia Pet Market "Blueprint Application" is intended to be an example of how you can use Flash for a commercial front-end. You can even check out how this solution was built by visiting the web site listed above and downloading the source. This project is targeted at advanced Flash developers.

★ http://reservations.broadmoor.com
This web site is an excellent example of how you can use Flash and ColdFusion together. On one single page, you can enter all of your information in a highly interactive and intuitive interface. We are not used to seeing Flash used in such commercial solutions. However, it is likely we will begin to see a lot more of this in the future.

Flash is taking off in other forms of offline media too. Many television commercials (and motion graphics in general) are using Flash as an animation tool. Therefore, it is quite obviously gaining a lot of ground in areas where it was previously unused. For more information on getting your Flash files ready for television, check out:

★ http://www.macromedia.com/support /flash/how/expert/flashontv/flashontv03.html

★ http://www.ultrashock.com/ff.htm?http: //www.ultrashock.com/tutorials/flash5 /flash4broadcast.html

★ http://www.flickerlab.com/flashtovideo/

Experimentation

ActionScript use in Flash design has had a lengthy history of "art for the sake of art". Many developers have had a lot of fun with what are typically called "experiments". These files usually involve a lot of complex scripts and concepts, and are typically not for the faint of heart! If math doesn't scare you (or perhaps if you want to conquer this fear), you might want to check out:

★ *Flash Math Creativity*, published by friends of ED (ISBN: 1-903450-50-0)

★ Robert Penner's Web site at http://www.robertpenner.com/index2.html.

CD-ROMs and e-learning

Using Flash to develop CD-ROMs is commonly practiced. You can create self-contained EXEs (*projectors*) in your Publish Settings, which can be burnt to CD-ROMs for distribution. There are many practices (such as using FSCommand and ActionScript) that are used for Flash projector projects. Creating these applications might be something you would want to look into, as many clients will want to develop kiosks or information they need to distribute on media.

E-learning is another area that is being seen a lot more frequently nowadays. Universities, colleges and other educational programs have discovered that wide audiences of students can be reached by using the Internet as a classroom. Flash is a great way to join these students together with other students, professors and the curriculum.

The Flash Communication Server is perfect for many kinds of e-learning projects. In fact, its development and product outline has this purpose in mind. The ability to join many users together in the same environment in real-time is a huge educational advantage. Also, the extended forms of communication available, such as video conferencing, whiteboards and other forms of net-meetings can be easily executed using the Flashcom server. E-learning and the Flashcom server are two great areas to explore, since they are so intriguing to many educational entrepreneurs.

Going to the forums

You will certainly find web forums devoted to Flash another valuable resource when furthering your skills in ActionScript. If you have a tight deadline, or perhaps an unusual client request, many problems can be discussed and solved with your Flash peers. Here are a few (busy) forums to check out:

★ http://www.friendsofed.com/forums
The friends of ED forums are the place to go for support regarding any of our books, and other questions you might have about the software we cover. The forums are divided into all of the topics covered by friends of ED publications, and are frequented by helpful moderators, authors and fellow readers alike.

★ http://www.macromedia.com/go/home_forum_fl/
Macromedia offers forums covering their suite of products. The forums on Flash themselves cover many different disciplines, as we have seen earlier in this chapter. They can be accessed online, or via their news server forums.macromedia.com.

★ http://www.ultrashock.com
These forums are frequented by new users to Flash, as well as the experts. Ultrashock is a highly respected and heavily-used forum in the Flash community. Ultrashock also includes discussion on After Effects, which is a great program to integrate with Flash.

★ http://www.were-here.com/forums
Were-here forums are also widely respected in the Flash community. You will also find new and master Flash users on this forum, and even people who work for Macromedia!

★ http://board.flashkit.com
The FlashKit forums are very active, and cover the many different areas of Flash.

Another way to get involved is by attending one of the many conferences which occur annually around the globe. *FlashForward*, *Siggraph*, *FlashKit*, *FlashintheCan* and Macromedia *Devcon* are some of the larger conferences to watch for. Not only can you find out the latest on what developers and designers are working on – but you will probably benefit from the samples, freebies, promotions and prizes these conferences usually offer too.

Keep up to date on the latest news pertaining to Flash by checking out the following resources:

★ http://www.actionscript.com

★ http://www.flashmagazine.com

Also, there are a ton of Flash "blogs" on the scene at the moment. These are excellent resources for finding out the latest in tips, tricks, bugs and development practices. To get started checking out the "ring" of blogs, go to Mike Chambers' blog at http://radio.weblogs.com/0106797/. Not only is it a great blog, it also contains a thorough list of other Macromedia-related blogs online.

Check locally for a Macromedia or Flash user group. Many cities internationally have user groups dedicated to developers and designers using Macromedia software. For more information for a group in your area, check out the following link:

★ http://www.macromedia.com/v1/usergroups/

The Flash community is one of the largest and most active web development communities online and in bookstores. Take advantage of the wealth of information out there when you are moving ahead with your ActionScript development!

Summary

As this chapter makes blatantly obvious, the road doesn't end here! There are many areas to explore while developing your Flash and ActionScript skills. Some of the areas you might want to start learning more about are:

Object-oriented programming, whether it is more ActionScript, Server-side ActionScript or another language altogether.

★ Server-side languages and how you can integrate them with Flash. These languages might include ASP, ColdFusion, PHP or Perl/CGI.

★ Working with Flash Remoting and Server-side ActionScript, and integrate it into your application server (currently supporting ColdFusion, .NET or Java).

★ Developing rich Internet applications using the Flash Communication Server (Flashcom).

★ Using Flash together with XML. Start developing streamlined Flash applications that grab data from XML structures.

★ Optimizing your Flash movies for use with wireless technologies.

★ Developing custom components for distribution online. Learn how to make the most out of your components, effective for use in anyone's own application.

★ All of the different kinds of applications you can build using Flash. From games to business e-commerce web sites, Flash can be useful in a wide range of online or offline software applications.

Index

The index is arranged hierarchically, in alphabetical order, with symbols preceding the letter A. Many second-level entries also occur as first-level entries. This is to ensure that you will find the information you require however you choose to search for it.

friends of ED particularly welcomes feedback on the layout and structure of this index. If you have any comments or criticisms, please contact: feedback@friendsofed.com

★

★

isbn: 1-904344-06-2
price: $29.99
publication date: october 2002

Fireworks MX: Zero To Hero is intended for the majority of readers who don't need to be told when to jump, or ask how high. If you're new to Fireworks MX, this book will provide you with a fast learning curve to get you swiftly up to speed, and progressing towards the **creativity** you want to achieve; and if you already have some familiarity with any version of Fireworks, it'll provide many, many exercises and case studies that will extend your knowledge of techniques, **tips**, and **tricks**. In addition, the book serves as a handy **reference** to a reader of any level.

isbn: 1-904344-23-2
price: $29.99
publication date: december 2002

Heralding the arrival of a new concept in computer books, the **Zero to Hero** series helps you make the same leap that others promise, without treating you like a fool. Divided into two sections, the book starts by guiding you through all of Photoshop Elements's features, in plain English. Every tool is covered in a easy-to-follow way, with full **illustration** at every stage. Other books call themselves **visual** guides, this **book really is**.

isbn: 1-903450-73-X
price: $29.99
publication date: june 2002

One of the biggest compliments paid to a friends of ED book last year was Amazon.com's judgment that ***"Foundation Actionscript is perhaps one of the finest introductory programming books ever written"***.

With the release of Flash MX, scripting in Flash has moved from being a desirable asset to an **essential** skill in the world of web design. It's also become a whole lot more difficult, and the major advances with Flash MX are code based. If you're scared of the idea of code, but even more scared of missing out, this is the book for **you**.

isbn: 1-903450-58-6
price: $49.99
publication date: september 2002

This title provides the **Flash MX designer** with a rich reference for all things ActionScript-related. It features a designer-oriented A-Z reference of the ActionScript language, all appropriately demonstrated in FLAs on the accompanying CD. These examples illustrate **ActionScript** in context - that is, in the combinations that you're likely to encounter them in the real world. The book also has substantial narrative sections that cover global approaches to solving common design problems with ActionScript. This book is designer-focused, and aims to be the richest and most practical ActionScript **reference** ever created.

isbn: 1-903450-50-0
price: $49.99
publication date: january 2002

Forget school math class, **Flash Math** is about fun. It's what you do in your spare time - messing around with little ideas until the design takes over and you end up with something **beautiful**, **bizarre**, or just downright **brilliant**. It's a book of iterative experiments, generative design; a book of inspiration, beautiful enough to leave on the coffee table, but **addictive** enough to keep by your computer and sneak out while no-one's looking so you can go back to that Flash movie that you were tinkering with 'til 3 o'clock this morning.

isbn: 1-903450-99-3
price: $49.99
publication date: september 2002

From the acclaimed team that brought you **Flash Math Creativity** comes this inspiring volume, full of brand new effects and discussion on what Flash MX is going to do for designers -- and where we go from here.

FLASH MX APPLICATION
& INTERFACE DESIGN

Data delivery, navigation, and fun in Flash MX, XML and PHP

Pete Aylward
Ken Jokol
Jamie Macdonald
Paul Prudence
Glen Rhodes
Robbie Shepherd
Todd Yard

friendsof

isbn: 1-904344-07-0
price: $49.99
publication date: october 2002

This book takes the view that Flash MX can be used as the **ideal medium**.

Spotlighting nine inspiring projects, it charts their develpoment **process** through **interface** design and **back-end** application to produce a snapshot of some of the **hottest** Flash techniques around.

ASP.NET for Flash MX

isbn: 1-904344-08-9
price: $49.99
publication date: november 2002

The absolute cutting edge for application development at the moment is using Macromedia's Flash MX (the premier software for designing **fantastic looking interfaces**) with Microsoft's .net framework (tremendously powerful server-side technology). Combining these technologies has been greatly aided by the release of Macromedia's Flash Remoting MX, which is covered fully in this book. Designers and developers involved in the creation of this technology impart their knowledge to you in this book through extensive **case studies**. Flash Remoting is not the only way to **combine** these technologies however, so this book will fully cover **Flash/.net** integration using **ASP.net**.

friendsof

D E S I G N E R   T O   D E S I G N E R™

friends of ED writes books for you. Any suggestions, or ideas about how you want information given in your ideal book will be studied by our team.

Your comments are valued by friends of ED.

For technical support please contact support@friendsofed.com.

Freephone in USA	800.873.9769
Fax	312.893.8001
UK contact: Tel:	0121.258.8858
Fax:	0121.258.8868

Registration Code: 4119T463I1619701

ActionScript: Zero to Hero - Registration Card

Name ....

Address ....

City ....State/Region ....

Country ....Postcode/Zip ....

E-mail ....

Profession: design student ☐   freelance designer ☐

part of an agency ☐   inhouse designer ☐

other (please specify) ....

Age: Under 20 ☐   20-25 ☐   25-30 ☐   30-40 ☐   over 40 ☐

Do you use: mac ☐   pc ☐   both ☐

How did you hear about this book?..

Book review (name)..

Advertisement (name) ....

Recommendation ....

Catalog ....

Other ....

Where did you buy this book? ....

Bookstore (name) ....City..............................

Computer Store (name)...

Mail Order...

Other..

How did you rate the overall content of this book?

Excellent ☐   Good ☐

Average ☐   Poor ☐

What applications/technologies do you intend to learn in the near future?...

....

What did you find most useful about this book? ....

....

What did you find the least useful about this book? ....

....

Please add any additional comments ....

....

What other subjects will you buy a computer book on soon?

....

....

What is the best computer book you have used this year?

....

....

Note: This information will only be used to keep you updated about new friends of ED titles and will not be used for any other purpose or passed to any other third party.

DESIGNER TO DESIGNER™

NB. If you post the bounce back card below in the UK, please send it to:

friends of ED Ltd.,
30 Lincoln Road,
Olton,
Birmingham.
B27 6PA

NO POSTAGE
NECESSARY
IF MAILED
IN THE
UNITED STATES

BUSINESS REPLY MAIL

FIRST CLASS   PERMIT #64   CHICAGO, IL

POSTAGE WILL BE PAID BY ADDRESSEE

friends of ED,
29 S. La Salle St.
Suite 520
Chicago Il 60603-USA